JOURNAL FOR THE STUDY OF THE OLD TESTAMENT
SUPPLEMENT SERIES
307

Sheffield Academic Press

The Shape and Message of Book III

(Psalms 73–89)

Robert L. Cole

Journal for the Study of the Old Testament
Supplement Series 307

Copyright © 2000 Sheffield Academic Press

Published by
Sheffield Academic Press Ltd
Mansion House
19 Kingfield Road
Sheffield S11 9AS
England

Typeset by Sheffield Academic Press
and
Printed on acid-free paper in Great Britain
by Bookcraft Ltd
Midsomer Norton, Bath

British Library Cataloguing in Publication Data

A catalogue record for this book is available
from the British Library

ISBN 1-84127-100-4

CONTENTS

PREFACE

This study is a revised version of my doctoral dissertation completed in 1996 at UCLA under the supervision of Professor Stanislav Segert. The original dissertation included a detailed rhetorical study of each psalm, beginning at the level of individual cola and continuing on through bicola, verse paragraphs and strophes, before examining the role of each Psalm in Book III. In the present monograph I have focused on the latter aspect.

It is with pleasure that I thank Professor Segert who read the entire (lengthy) original dissertation, and whose advice was always expressed in a most gracious manner. He is indeed the epitome of a scholar and a gentleman. Likewise, thanks are due to Professor Yona Sabor who read the entire dissertation and who offered kind words of encouragement throughout the process.

I was first introduced to the canonical approach by Professor John Sailhamer. His stimulating ideas, winsome pedagogical style, and love for the Hebrew Bible stirred a curiosity in me that continues to this day. It was a rare privilege to sit under his teaching.

To my parents thanks and honor are due for teaching me the Bible from an early age, an example to emulate with my two children Rachel and Nathan. Above all I would like to express gratitude and love to my wife Pati, without whose sacrificial support and patience this work would not have been possible: כי אשת חיל את (Ruth 3.11d).

ABBREVIATIONS

AB	Anchor Bible
AUSS	*Andrews University Seminary Studies*
BDB	Francis Brown, S.R. Driver, and Charles A. Briggs, *A Hebrew and English Lexicon of the Old Testament* (Oxford: Clarenden Press, 1907)
BHS	*Biblia hebraica stuttgartensia*
Bib	*Biblica*
BK	*Bibel und Kirche*
BN	*Biblische Notizen*
BTB	*Biblical Theology Bulletin*
BZ	*Biblische Zeitschrift*
CBQ	*Catholic Biblical Quarterly*
EstBíb	*Estudios bíblicos*
GKC	*Gesenius' Hebrew Grammar* (ed. E. Kautzsch, revised and trans. A.E. Cowley; Oxford: Clarendon Press, 1910)
HALAT	L. Koehler and W. Baumgartner, *Hebräisches und aramäisches Lexikon zum Alten Testament*
HAR	*Hebrew Annual Review*
HTR	*Harvard Theological Review*
ICC	International Critical Commentary
Int	*Interpretation*
JANESCU	*Journal of the Ancient Near Eastern Society of Columbia University*
JBL	*Journal of Biblical Literature*
JQR	*Jewish Quarterly Review*
JSOT	*Journal for the Study of the Old Testament*
JSOTSup	*Journal for the Study of the Old Testament,* Supplement Series
NRT	*La nouvelle revue théologique*
SBL	Society of Biblical Literature
SBLDS	SBL Dissertation Series
ScEs	*Science et esprit*
Sem	*Semitica*
SJOT	*Scandinavian Journal of the Old Testament*
TynBul	*Tyndale Bulletin*
UF	*Ugarit-Forschungen*
VT	*Vetus Testamentum*
VTSup	*Vetus Testamentum,* Supplements
WBC	Word Biblical Commentary

INTRODUCTION

The study of Hebrew poetry has evolved in the modern era in a manner that could be described as the extension of parallelism. Two and a half centuries ago Robert Lowth observed parallelism at the level of bicola and categorized it into three basic types.[1] More recently, James Muilenburg challenged biblical scholars to pursue a new type of analysis which he dubbed 'rhetorical criticism',[2] thereby extending the search for parallels and repetition to the entire text. As stated by him, 'repetition serves many and diverse functions in the literary compositions... whether in the construction of parallel cola or parallel bicola, or in the structure of the strophes, or in the fashioning and ordering of the complete literary units'.[3] Adele Berlin in a similar vein notes:

> And if we do not restrict our search for linguistic equivalences to adjacent lines or sentences, but take a global view, finding equivalences anywhere within a text, we raise the incidence of parallelism still more... For instance, the device known as inclusio... is actually a form of parallelism and should be recognized as such.[4]

In an article on Psalm 145 she defends the use of rhetorical criticism as follows:

> The potential success of rhetorical critricism lies in the fact that the devices and symmetries that are present in a poem are not merely decorations—esthetically pleasing ornaments surrounding the meaning—but are pointers or signs which indicate what the meaning is. To understand how a poem is constructed is to begin to understand what it expresses.[5]

1. R. Lowth, *De sacra poesi hebraeorum* (Oxford, 1733).
2. J. Muilenburg, 'Form Criticism and Beyond', *JBL* 88 (1969), pp. 1-18 (8).
3. 'Form Criticism and Beyond', p. 17.
4. A. Berlin, *The Dynamics of Biblical Parallelism* (Bloomington: Indiana University Press, 1985), p. 3.
5. A. Berlin, 'The Rhetoric of Psalm 145', in A. Kort and S. Morschauser (eds.), *Biblical and Related Studies Presented to Samuel Iwry* (Winona Lake, IN: Eisenbrauns, 1985), pp. 17-22 (17-18).

It has become clear in recent years that the phenomenon of parallelism and repetition in the Psalter must be extended beyond that of individual poems to the surrounding psalms and finally the entire collection. The ordering and shaping of the collection casts the individual psalms in a new light, even beyond that discerned through rhetorical criticism. Such a focus moves from what the individual poem expresses to a meaning implied by the final compilation, the latter becoming a single 'text'. Consequently, the study of the final shape of the Psalter is simply a recognition that parallelism is not restricted to the individual poem. Muilenburg's challenge thirty years ago was to supplement form criticism with rhetorical criticism, or in his own words, 'form criticism and beyond'.[6] It is the assertion here that rhetorical criticism in the Psalter must be supplemented with canonical criticism—'rhetorical criticism and beyond'.

The original dissertation from which this work is derived examined parallelism and repetition from the level of individual cola (where abundant phonetic or sound repetition was observed), to bicola (or occasional tricola), verse paragraphs, strophes, complete psalms, and finally the stretch of psalms from 73 to 89 known as Book III.[7] In the work presented here, emphasis is placed on the shape of Book III, utilizing only the final results of a previously detailed rhetorical analysis of each psalm.

Often rhetorical analysis of individual poems contributes to understanding their role in the continuing dialogue that is Book III. For instance, the rhetorical analysis of Psalm 79 leaves vv. 8 and 13 somewhat 'unparalleled', but the latter two resemble the previous Psalm 78 closely in their vocabulary and answer directly to issues raised there. Similarly, the first rhetorically defined strophe of Psalm 73 is the most direct response to the previous Psalm 72, while the last two strophes of 73 clearly anticipate 74. Following Psalm 89 at the other end of Book III, Psalm 90 functions as an answer to questions in the final strophe of

---

6.   'Form Criticism and Beyond', p. 18.

7.   Form criticism is a method of recategorizing the psalms according to genre, and yet it is usually practiced without paying attention to the categorization apparent in the final shape of the Psalter. Psalms 86 and 88 are classified as individual laments, but in the present study an analysis will be made to understand why Ps. 87 (a song of Zion) intervenes between them. A form critic would presumably lump Pss. 88 and 86 together, while the final compiler of the Psalter has deliberately chosen to separate them.

89 and to other similar complaints throughout Book III. The latter evidence from either end of Book III demonstrates that it is impossible to examine Book III in complete isolation from the surrounding Books II and IV, and, in fact, much of Book III is a response to the promises of the preceding Psalm 72.

Study of the canonical shape of the Psalter was greatly advanced more than a decade ago in a study by Gerald Wilson.[8] Brevard Childs had already raised the question in his introduction to the Old Testament, 'In what way does the final editing of the Psalter testify as to how the collectors understood the canonical material to function for the community of faith?'[9] Wilson concluded:

> (1) that the 'book' divisions of the Psalter are real, editorially induced divisions and not accidentally introduced; (2) the 'separating' and 'binding' functions of author and genre groupings; (3) the lack of a s/s as an indication of a tradition of combination; (4) the use of *hllwyh* pss to indicate the conclusion of segments; (5) the use of *hwdw* pss to introduce segments; (6) the existence of thematic correspondences between the beginning and ending pss in some books... Without denying the existence of previous collections, I feel it is possible to show that the *final* form of MT 150 is the result of a purposeful, editorial activity which sought to impart a meaningful arrangement which encompassed the whole.[10]

As can be seen, much of his attention was directed to the superscriptions (numbers 1-3), which are especially relevant to Book III. There the superscriptions contain authorship ascriptions which serve also to bind or separate psalm groups. Psalm 72, the final psalm of Book II refers to Solomon, while Psalm 73, the beginning of Book III, contains no link to the previous psalm either in author designation or genre. This corresponds to the book division indicated by the doxology at the end of Psalm 72. There are, nonetheless, highly instructive verbal parallels between 72 and 73 revealing the contrast between eschatological promises in the former to the present distress of the latter.

A recent work edited by J.C. McCann is another sign of the interest growing in the final shape of the Psalter. As Walter Brueggemann there

8.   G.H. Wilson, *The Editing of the Hebrew Psalter* (SBLDS, 76; Chico, CA: Scholars Press, 1985).

9.   B.S. Childs, *Introduction to the Old Testament as Scripture* (Philadelphia: Fortress Press, 1979), pp. 512-13.

10.   Wilson, *The Editing*, p. 199.

states in response to James Mays, 'The questions he raises are important because it is clear that we are at the threshold of a quite new season
in Psalm studies'.[11] Wilson expresses the same opinion, 'We now stand
on the borders of the promised land'.[12] At the beginning of the last
decade Joseph Reindl recommended a wholistic approach to the book:

> Through the structure given to the book, the redactor of the Psalter has
> therefore quite clearly revealed his interpretation of the Psalms. In this
> regard it is worth noting first of all that the Psalter now no longer appears
> as a more or less ordered collection of individual psalms, but rather has
> been presented as *a book*, a whole.[13]

More recently Erich Zenger and Frank-Lothar Hossfeld have begun a
commentary on the psalms in which the canonical shaping is taken very
seriously:

> The biblical book of Psalms is a compilation of 150 poetic texts of varied
> provenance and time, which are intended to be read and understood on
> the one hand as individual texts and on the other as portions of larger
> 'Psalm groups,' and/or of the entire Psalm book.[14]

This recent interest in the final shape has not been without its
scattered precursors. In the last century Franz Delitzsch addressed the
issue in the introduction of his commentary, under the title 'Arrange-

---

11. W. Brueggemann, 'Response to James L. Mays, "The Question of Context" ', in J.C. McCann (ed.), *The Shape and Shaping of the Psalter* (JSOTSup, 159;
Sheffield: JSOT Press, 1993), pp. 29-41 (29).

12. G.H. Wilson, 'Understanding the Purposeful Arrangement of Psalms in the
Psalter: Pitfalls and Promise', in McCann (ed.), *The Shape and Shaping of the
Psalter*, pp. 42-51 (51).

13. Author's translation of 'Durch die dem Buch gegebene Rahmung läßt der
Redaktor des Psalters also recht deutlich seine Auffassung von den Psalmen erken-
nen. An ihr ist zunächst bemerkenswert, daß der Psalter nun nicht länger als eine
mehr oder weniger geordnete Ansammlung von einzelnen Psalmen erscheint, son-
dern als *ein Buch*, ein Ganzes vorgestellt wird.' J. Reindl, 'Weisheitliche Bearbeitung von Psalmen: Ein Beitrag zum Verständnis der Sammlung des Psalters', in
J.A. Emerton (ed.), *Congress Volume: Vienna 1980* (VTSup, 32; Leiden: E.J. Brill,
1980), pp. 333-56 (339).

14. Author's translation of 'Das biblische Buch der Psalmen ist eine Zusam-
menstellung von 150 poetischen Texten unterschiedlicher Herkunft und Zeit, die
einerseits als Einzeltexte und andererseits als Teiltexte größerer »Psalmengruppen«
bzw. des ganzen Psalmenbuchs gelesen und verstanden sein wollen.' F.-L. Hossfeld
and E. Zenger, *Die Psalmen I: Psalm 1–50* (Die Neue Echter Bibel, 29; Würzburg:
Echter Verlag, 1993), p. 5.

ment and Inscriptions'.[15] Within the commentary itself he notes linking devices between psalms. Emmanuel Cassutto referred to Delitzsch in an address where he explored the arrangement of the psalms, and lamented the fact that Delitzsch's comments were forgotten by most commentators.[16] Christoph Barth, looking at Psalms 1–41 and noting *'concatenatio'* between each successive psalm was an exception to this general trend.[17] Amos Hakham in his (modern Hebrew) commentary, at the conclusion of comments on each psalm, observes some of the more obvious verbal and thematic links to those previous.[18] It is only in the past few years that interest has grown noticeably in study of the canonical shape of the Psalter. A thorough review of recent interest in the final shape of the Psalter and of the history of interpretation in general is given by David Mitchell in the first chapter of his recent study on the Psalter.[19]

The call for a study such as this of Book III and the rest of the Psalter has been made by Wilson, dovetailing with the purposes of this study:

> As must be obvious by now, I am convinced that any progress in understanding the purposeful arrangement of the psalms in the Psalter must begin, as in these last two studies, with a detailed and careful analysis of the linguistic, literary and thematic linkages that can be discerned among the psalms.[20]

The two studies to which he refers are that of David Howard on Psalms 93–100 and another by McCann, both within the same volume.[21] His call is accompanied by a legitimate warning to interpreters against bringing too many hypotheses to the task:

15. F. Delitzsch, *Commentary on the Old Testament*. V. *Psalms* (trans. F. Bolton; Grand Rapids: Eerdmans, repr. 1982), pp. 19-23.

16. U. Cassutto, 'The Sequence and Arrangement of the Biblical Sections', in *idem, Biblical and Oriental Studies*. I. *Bible* (trans. I. Abrahams; Jerusalem: Magnes Press, 1973), pp. 1-6 (2).

17. C. Barth, 'Concatenatio im ersten Buch des Psalters', in B. Benzing, O. Böcher and G. Mayer (eds.), *Wort und Wirklichkeit: Studien zur Afrikanistik und Orientalistik* (Festschrift E.L. Rapp; Meisenheim am Glan: Hain, 1976), pp. 30-40.

18. A. Hakham, *Sefer tehillim: Sefarim gimel–heh* (Jerusalem: Harav Kook, 1979).

19. D.C. Mitchell, *The Message of the Psalter: An Eschatological Programme in the Book of Psalms* (JSOTSup, 252; Sheffield: JSOT Press, 1997), pp. 15-65.

20. Wilson, 'Understanding the Purposeful Arrangement of Psalms', p. 50.

21. J.C. McCann, 'Books I–III and the Editorial Purpose of the Hebrew Psalter', in *The Shape and Shaping of the Psalter*, pp. 93-107.

Such working hypotheses, as we have seen, often distort the interpreter's vision and prevent the true nature of the material from coming into focus. In my opinion, the only valid and cautious hypothesis with which to begin is that the present arrangement is the result of purposeful editorial activity, and that its purpose can be discerned by careful and exhaustive analysis of the linguistic and thematic relationships between individual psalms and groups of psalms.[22]

This hypothesis is amply supported and confirmed as valid in Book III, where a dialogue consisting of lament over the nonfulfillment of the Davidic covenant as enunciated in Psalm 72 and corresponding divine answers dominates the collection. While this dialogue gives a discrete tone and quality to Book III, it will be shown that the preceding Psalm 72 and following 90 play a vital role in understanding the message of Psalms 73–89. Therefore, the following study is only a beginning, and similar analyses of the remaining four books of the Psalter would put the evidence from Book III and its immediate boundaries into a broader perspective.[23]

---

22. Wilson, 'Understanding the Purposeful Arrangement of Psalms', p. 48.

23. A comparable study is that of D.M. Howard, *The Structure of Psalms 93–100* (Winona Lake, IN: Eisenbrauns, 1997). However, as the title indicates, Pss. 90–92 which begin Book IV have not been the focus of his study (nor the final six psalms, 101–106), although they have certainly not been overlooked (see pp. 166-71). His statement that Ps. 90 serves as 'an effective bridge' between Books III and IV (p. 169) coincides generally with conclusions reached here. He also recognizes the 'necessary background' that Book III and Pss. 90–92 provide for Pss. 93–100 (p. 166).

Chapter 1

PSALM 73

Between Psalms 72 and 73 the superscription of the latter announces a new psalm, while the doxology of the former (72.18, 19) and its final note (72.20) confirm the end of Book II.[1] Further confirmation of this division are the different author ascriptions and lack of genre similarity.[2] On the other side of Psalm 73 is the superscription of 74, announcing a new literary unit, but also ascribing authorship to Asaph and thus providing a measure of continuity.

These different author ascriptions and the doxology which create a break between Books II and III, correspond to a new perspective in Psalm 73. Psalm 72 envisions a universal and eternal kingdom of peace and justice free from oppression and violence, while 73 brings the reader back to the hard reality of the present, a situation quite opposite to that just described. Oppression and violence are practiced by the wicked while enjoying continual peace. The terminology is exactly parallel: שלום, 73.3 and 72.3; חמס, 73.6 and 72.14; עושק, 73.8 and 72.4;

---

1.   It should be noted that the doxology and subscript of Ps. 72, while apparently canonical additions, cohere rhetorically with the body of the poem. It begins with a reference to Solomon and the 'son of the king' (72.1), and the subscript of v. 20 speaks of David, 'son of Jesse', so that three generations surround the poem. The blessings on Yahweh of vv. 18-19 follow directly the blessings promised upon the king in vv. 15, 17. Yahweh's glory is to fill all the earth in this final doxology (v. 19), following promises that the king's dominion would extend to the ends of the earth (v. 8, also vv. 6, 16). As in the message of the final psalms of Book III, this ruler and his kingdom become identified closely with Yahweh and his rule. Likewise, the doxology concluding Ps. 89 blends well with the rhetorical and thematic contours of the psalm itself, as will be demonstrated later.

2.   Wilson, *The Editing*, pp. 155-67. Note his comment, 'Basic divisions of the pss are indicated by the disjuncture (in the Pss-headings) of author attributions and genre designations. Such disjuncture is most noticeable at the "seams" of the Psalter: at the book divisions' (p. 167).

עולם, 73.12 and 72.17; all of which occur in the first strophe of Psalm 73 (vv. 1-12) following 72. The canonical editor's intention to create a contrast is explicit. (Likewise, terms and themes parallel to the following Psalm 74 occur predominantly in the second two strophes of 73; vv. 13-17, vv. 18-28.[3]) The righteous and just peace (שלום, 72.3, 7) of Solomon (שלמה, 72.1) has not appeared, instead it is the peace of the wicked (שלום רשעים, 73.3) which the speaker beholds. The violence (חמס) and oppression (עשק) from which the humble were promised rescue in 72.4, 14, are governing in 73.6, 8. Conditions in 73 are the opposite of those promised in 72.

Pride worn as a necklace by the wicked (73.6) is in direct contrast to the promise of justice for the poor and humble of 72.4. While 72.14 declares that the blood of these humble ones would be precious in the eyes (בעיניו) of this righteous ruler, the situation of 73 reveals the opposite. The eye(s?) of these proud and violent ones in 73.6 (עינמו) 'protrude from fat'. Whatever the meaning of this clause, it assuredly contrasts the gaze of the prosperous wicked with that of Psalm 72's king. This just king was to enjoy eternal and universal dominion in 72.17 (לעולם), but all the speaker of 73 can see is that the wicked continue increasing without interruption in their prosperity and power (עולם, 73.12).

The inclusio created around the second verse paragraph (73.3-12) of strophe I (vv. 1-12), by the semantically and phonologically similar שלוי and שלום (73.3, 12),[4] as descriptions of the wicked, contrasts powerfully with the שלום of Ps. 72.3, 7. Such is the state of affairs that instead of continual offerings, worship and blessing being brought to God's king by foreign rulers, as promised in 72.10-19 (ישיבו, v. 10), his very own

---

3.   Consistent with this observation is the fact that כלה of 73.26 in the final strophe, corresponds by root to כלו of 72.20, but the former does not appear to function in any way as a response to the previous Ps. 72. Likewise, the glory (כבוד) of 73.24 repeats the same found in 72.19 (twice), but again, at first glance does not seem to create any canonical dialogue with Ps. 72. Alternatively, it is important to notice that these two paralleled terms are found either in the doxology of 72.18-19 or the subscript of 72.20. The latter appear to have been added by the editor of the canonical Psalter, who, as will be seen, displays a meticulous knowledge of this psalm. Such parallel forms after the juxtaposition of these two psalms would certainly not have been missed. However, their contribution to the dialogue between 72 and 73, if any, is not clear.

4.   Compare Ps. 122.6, 7 for two pairings of these within consecutive bicola. See below for further discussion of Ps. 73.3, 12.

people turn away from him to the wicked (יָשׁוּב, 73.10, *qere*).[5]

Psalm 73.1 does not repeat identical vocabulary from the previous 72, but a link does exist. By declaring that God is good to the pure of heart in Israel (לְיִשְׂרָאֵל אֱלֹהִים), the speaker concedes the promise in Psalm 72 of divine righteousness, peace and justice for the oppressed of the nation through Israel's king (אֱלֹהִים...לַמֶּלֶךְ...עֻמָּךְ, 72.1, 2). Thus, a similar construction at the outset of 73 acknowledges the initial words of 72. Having acknowledged a belief in the words of the previous psalm, v. 2 immediately follows with the disjunctive (וַאֲנִי, 'But as for myself...'), describing the perplexity felt by the speaker. Answers to this dilemma of strophe I (vv. 1-12) finally come in II (vv. 13-17) and III (vv. 18-28), which, as will be seen, anticipate those given by the following Psalm 74.

The initial particle of v. 1 (אַךְ) is repeated at vv. 13 and 18, giving Psalm 73 a tripartite structure which progresses logically and is symmetrical in size.[6] Strophe I (vv. 1-12) details the prosperity of the wicked and the speaker's doubts, strophe II (vv. 13-17) describes the escape from this confusion, and finally strophe III (vv. 19-28) the destruction of the wicked and restored confidence. This aforementioned particle signals a new theme and strophe in each case and no other examples of it are found, although similar forms of rhetorical importance are found in strategic locations (אֵיכָה, v. 11; אֵיךְ, v. 19). Strophes I and III are almost identical in size, the first being twelve bicola in length, and the last eleven bicola plus one tricola. The central strophe is five bicola in length, roughly half the size of the two surrounding it.

The particle אַךְ in v. 1 is followed by three words in the same clause which form an inclusio or envelope figure with members of the psalm's final verse (v. 28). The first colon of v. 1 states that God is good to Israel (טוֹב לְיִשְׂרָאֵל אֱלֹהִים), and the last that he is good to the speaker (אֱלֹהִים לִי טוֹב). The syntax has been neatly reversed with the middle

---

5. It is clear that the editor of Book III reads Ps. 72 as not simply a prayer of David (v. 20) but as a promise. The bitter complaints of Ps. 73 seen also throughout Book III presume an expectation that the ideal reign of Ps. 72 would become a reality. Here prayer becomes prophecy in the canonical arrangement.

6. For a similar structuring of the psalm see J.C. McCann, 'Psalm 73: A Microcosm of Old Testament Theology', in K.G. Hoglund, E.F. Hutwiler, J.T. Glass and R.W. Lee (eds.), *The Listening Heart: Essays in Wisdom and the Psalms in Honor of Roland E. Murphy* (JSOTSup, 58; Sheffield: JSOT Press, 1987), pp. 247-57 (249-50).

member being changed from 'Israel' to 'me', while the preposition is unchanged. This type of 'altered' inclusio has been defined by Grossberg as:

> a type of correspondence wherein the artist repeats the literal stem of a word but in so doing he alters the morphology, phonetics, semantics or syntax of the closing element. The inverted, reversed or somehow opposed relationship of the two parts of the inclusio constitutes a widespread variation of that device in Hebrew poetry, a rhetorical embellishment in the work, and a complement to its theme.[7]

Grossberg's description of inclusio describes precisely the situation of Psalm 73. The speaker apparently feels excluded from the maxim of v. 1 and so begins contrastively in v. 2 by means of the independent first person singular pronoun, 'But I...' (ואני). God was supposed to be good to Israel but personal experience belied that assertion. This separation between vv. 1 and 2 is finally resolved in v. 28, where the speaker's inclusion (no pun intended) in this goodness is affirmed (ואני קרבת אלהים לי טוב). Goodness and the individual psalmist (first person singular pronoun again) are reunited, thereby answering the basic conflict of the psalm. The inclusio not only defines the limits of the psalm, but in its variation resolves the major conflict. Incidentally, the suggestion by the editor of *BHS* and various commentators that לישראל be emended to לישר אל disrupts the precise correspondence of the aforementioned inclusio.[8]

The final term of v. 1 (לבב) is ubiquitous in the psalm (vv. 1, 7, 13, 21, 26 twice), revealing the importance of the interior life to the speaker. Verse 13 (the beginning of strophe II, which also includes the same particle אך as v. 1) expresses the integrity of the speaker and inclusion with the pure in heart of v. 1, in contrast to the proud hearts of v. 7. Finally, in vv. 21-26, where a paragraph is bounded on either end by לבבי, the psalmist progresses from a bitter heart to one that is sus-

---

7. D. Grossberg, 'The Disparate Elements of the Inclusio in Psalms', *HAR* 6 (1982), pp. 97-104 (98).

8. For instance, H. Gunkel, *Die Psalmen* (Göttingen: Vandenhoeck & Ruprecht, 5th edn, 1968), pp. 311-16, who also transforms אלהים into יהוה and moves it to the second colon to give, what is ostensibly, better semantic parallelism and consistent meter (3x3) with the rest of the poem. Similarily, H.-J. Kraus, *Psalms 60–150: A Commentary* (trans. H.C. Oswald; Minneapolis: Augsburg, 1989), p. 83, and A. González, *El libro de los Salmos: Introducción, versión y comentario* (Barcelona: Editorial Herder, 1966), p. 331.

tained by God, in spite of outward weakness. The speaker does experience in v. 26 the good which v. 1 proclaimed was due to the pure of heart, but not without first experiencing grave doubts and troubles in that same heart (vv. 13, 21).

The collocation of divine names is a common mode of structural organization in the psalms.[9] Here in Psalm 73 the full form אלהים begins and closes the psalm in its entirety (vv. 1, 28), while the abbreviated אל is close to the end of strophe I (v. 11) and closes II (v. 17). The God of v. 1 who is good to Israel turns out to be good also to the individual (v. 28). Those wicked who question God's knowledge in v. 11 are shown to be mistaken when understanding comes in v. 17. Consequently, both of these divine names are located so as to respond to each other while addressing main issues of the poem, namely God's goodness and knowledge.

Since Psalm 73 is found in the 'elohistic' stretch of psalms it is not surprising that only one instance of the Tetragrammaton is found. In the final verse of the psalms it appears when the speaker confesses 'Adonay Yahweh' as refuge, after realizing the goodness of Elohim. Here in one single verse then, are found three different divine names. Furthermore, it is a tricolon, breaking with the consistent pattern of bicola since verse one. Not coincidentally then, the immediately following Psalm 74 is filled with references to the name of God (vv. 7, 10, 18, 21).

The second verse paragraph in strophe I stretches from vv. 3 to 12. This unit is strictly confined to describing the wicked, and inclusio is evident between beginning and end, as noted above. Verse 3b is especially relevant in this regard. There the construction שלום רשעים is matched in v. 12 by רשעים ושלוי. Both verses show identical forms describing the 'wicked' (רשעים), and they are phonologically and semantically similar (שלום, ושלוי), the first meaning 'quiet, at ease', and the second 'peace, prosperity'. The final verb form אראה of v. 3 demonstrates how the poet 'contemplated' the wicked, and, by use of the presentative particle הנה, v. 12a then requests that the reader 'behold' their state after an extended description of their prosperity. These parallels between vv. 3 and 12 mark off the boundaries of this verse paragraph and שלום of v. 3 is a fitting title to the life of ease and prosperity described therein.

As just stated, the verb אראה of v. 3 and particle הנה in v. 12 form an

9. R. Youngblood, 'Divine Names in the Book of Psalms: Literary Structures and Number Patterns', *JANESCU* 19 (1989), pp. 171-81.

inclusio of semantic type for verse paragraph two. This extended description of the wicked serves to explain the doubts in v. 2. It also serves to highlight the apparent contradiction between the statement of v. 1 that God is good to the pure in heart and the prosperity of the wicked in vv. 3-12. The final and third use of the presentative particle הנה is found in v. 27, with the result that it occurs once in each strophe (vv. 12, 15, 27). Verse paragraph two (vv. 3-12) of strophe I begins with the particle כי and ends with הנה, a long description of the success of the wicked. These same two particles are united in v. 27 for the last description of the wicked and their destruction. Their long-lived prosperity as described between v. 3 (כי) and v. 12 (הנה), has been reduced in v. 27 to one short statement of destruction (כי־הנה...יאבדו).

Especially noteworthy in verse paragraph two is the archaic suffix מו-, used extensively throughout (vv. 5, 6 twice, 7, 10) and referring to the wicked introduced in v. 3.[10] Referring to the use of this specific suffix, Gesenius remarks, 'that they are consciously and artificially used is shown by the evidently intentional accumulation of them',[11] an observation clearly applicable to the first strophe of Psalm 73. Once again in 73.18 is found למו and the preposition כמו ('like') of v. 15, which with its formal similarity to the previous examples also contributes to the rhetorical purposes of the poet. This latter preposition lacks a formal complement and so *BHS* suggests emendation to כהם. However, since the previous examples of the suffix מו- all refer to the wicked (vv. 5-10), the preposition כמו in v. 15a refers cryptically to the same group. A literal translation of the clause would be, 'If I said I will speak like', but given the previous use of מו- the alert reader understands, 'like them' (i.e. those wicked of vv. 3-12).

The third masculine singular pronominal suffix of עמו in v. 10 of the final sub-section of verse paragraph two has no apparent antecedent, and thus *BHS* suggests a change to first person suffix (עמי) following the LXX and the Syriac. Support for the originality of the MT is the fact that the form עמו resounds with the numerous other examples of the aforementioned plural third person suffix מו- (vv. 5, 6, 7, 10, 18). Here the resonance between the archaic plural suffix in vv. 5, 6, 7 referring to the wicked, and the singular of 'his people' implies their inclusion in that

---

10. Such is the ubiquity of this suffix in these verses that for the prepositional form למותם of v. 4, *BHS* suggests emendation to למו תם.

11. F.W. Gesenius, *Gesenius' Hebrew Grammar* (ed. E. Kautzsch, revised and trans. A.E. Cowley; Oxford: Clarendon Press, 1910), §91*l*.

group. This ubiquitous suffix מו- has thus become a codeword for the wicked, and sound resemblances to it carry the same implication.

The concept of 'his people' has been introduced already in v. 1. There the proper name 'Israel' is used and is followed in 1b by either a restriction or identification of that entity ('the pure of heart'). This ambiguity is resolved somewhat by v. 10, in that 'his nation' is not equivalent to 'the pure' since they have slipped and fallen, even as the poet himself was tempted to do in vv. 13-15a. On a formal level at least, the proper name 'Israel' in v. 1a corresponds to the nation of v. 10a, and the name 'God' in v. 1a likewise serves to identify the pronominal suffix of the same (עמו). At the same time, this suffix could be taken as proleptic, anticipating the reference to God in v. 11 (אל), which creates an inclusio around strophe I with the divine name of v. 1 simultaneously. The inglorious end of the prosperous wicked in strophe I will be described in vv. 18-20, 27 of strophe III, and the following psalm (74) confirms that the nation suffered the identical judgment. Consequently, the form עמו is consistent with the message implied by the rhetorical flourishes of 73 itself and its collocation with 74. The innocent speaker stands out from the nation, not having joined their apostasy (vv. 15-17), a pattern to be seen again in Book III.

Further proof of reference to Israel can be found in the wording of v. 27 where destruction is assured for 'all those who fornicate against you' (כל־זונה ממך). Such a statement can only refer to members of Yahweh's own faithless nation and confirms the above reading of v. 10. Turning to the place of the wicked (v. 10) is another way of describing religious adultery (v. 27). Such destruction promised for unfaithfulness in 73.27 anticipates the havoc wrought on the nation in the following Psalm 74.

Verse 10b, 'abundant waters are drained out by them' (ומי מלא ימצו למו), is difficult to interpret, but undoubtedly plays a role within Book III.[12] Ps. 75.9 reveals similar terminology (מלא...ימצו), the liquid in question being the wine of God's judgment, instead of water as here in

---

12. For two examples of the interpretations given to this verse see Gunkel, *Die Psalmen*, pp. 311, 318, who emends מי מלא to מליהם and thus they 'greedily lap up their words' ('schlürfen ihre Worte gierig'); C.A. Briggs and E.G. Briggs, *A Critical and Exegetical Commentary on the Book of Psalms* (ICC, 38; 2 vols.; Edinburgh: T. & T. Clark, 1906), p. 144, call it 'a marginal note of consolation that subsequently crept into the text', taking colon A as a promise of return (ישׁיב) from exile.

73.10. The parallel verb in 75.9 to יִמְצוּ ('they drain out') is יִשְׁתּוּ ('they drink'). Consequently, 73.10b must refer to some kind of plenty for these wicked, who are identified as 'his people' in 10a. Judgment meted out in Ps. 75.9 to the same wicked (רְשָׁעִים, vv. 5, 9, 11) seen in Ps. 73.3, 12, resembles the original apostasy verbally and in substance.

The questioning of God's knowledge by the wicked in v. 11 (יָדַע־אֵל) is in stark contrast to the attitude of the psalmist who struggles to know in v. 16 (לָדַעַת), admitting ignorance. In v. 22 (לֹא אֵדַע) the same is stated more explicitly. Ignorance is admitted instead of accusing God of the same. The identical verb form (יָדַע) is found in 74.5 and 9, the latter occurrence being ironic in view of Psalm 73. God's people do not know how long (וְלֹא אִתָּנוּ יֹדֵעַ עַד מָה), and there is no prophet (אֵין עוֹד נָבִיא), that is, God is not revealing anything to them. In 73.11 the same nation had questioned God's ability to know (יָדַע אֵל) and now they confess their own ignorance. All they do know or 'perceive' (יוֹדֵעַ, 74.5) is that their land and temple have been decimated. The question of 73.11 is actually answered in the same psalm (73.18-20, 27) and also in the following 74.[13] God does know, as the judgment meted out in vv. 18-20, 27 proves, and the sad fate of the nation in Psalm 74 further answers the sceptical question of 73.11b.

Verse 17 of strophe II refers to the 'dwellings of God' (מִקְדְּשֵׁי־אֵל) and this plural has provoked a variety of opinions among scholars.[14] Here the important point is its relation canonically to the following psalm, as McCann has rightly pointed out.[15] In Psalm 74 from vv. 2-8 there are repeated references to the temple (מוֹעֲדֵי־אֵל, v. 8; מִקְדָּשֶׁךָ, מִשְׁכַּן־שְׁמֶךָ...v. 7; מוֹעֲדֶךָ, v. 4; בְּקֹדֶשׁ, v. 3; הַר־צִיּוֹן, v. 2). Note the plural common to 74.8 and 73.17. The term for 'ruins' in 74.3 is repeated in 73.18, לְמַשּׁוּאוֹת.[16] Clearly this juncture of terms for both temple and ruins in these contiguous psalms is intentional. The temple is destroyed in the judgment upon wicked Israel in 74. The speaker in Psalm 73

---

13. A similar phenomenon occurs between Ps. 88.11-13, a series of rhetorical questions, and the following Ps. 89. The difference is that there are no answers in Ps. 88 to its questions, the answer being delayed until Ps. 89. See later discussion of those two psalms.

14. See J.C. McCann, 'Psalm 73: An Interpretation Emphasizing Rhetorical and Canonical Criticism' (PhD dissertation; Durham, NC: Duke University, 1985), pp. 37-9, 212-13 for samples of opinion.

15. McCann, 'Psalm 73: An Interpretation', p. 38.

16. The form in 74.3 is spelled 'defectively'—לְמַשֻׁאוֹת.

sought to understand (לדעת), but could not until (עד) coming to the 'sanctuaries of God' (73.16-17). Arrival at the sanctuaries brought enlightenment because, as Psalm 74 later explains, they were in ruins.[17] Not only is the sanctuary destroyed, but prophecy has also ceased, with the result that no one knows how long (עד־מתי אלהים יֵדַע עד־מה:, 74.9-10) the enemy will revile. The unanswered question of 74.9-10 is asked of God, now seen as knower of the future. This is in stark and ironic contrast to the question of 73.11, where the nation, after joining the wicked, cast doubt on God's ability to know (איכה ידע־אל ויש דעה בעליון).

The third verse paragraph of strophe III consists of vv. 27-28. Verse 27 introduced by the particle כי presents the fate of the wicked in contrast to that of the faithful in 28 (ואני). The reverse order occurs in vv. 2-3, where the righteous speaker's condition was described in v. 2 (ואני), followed by a description of the wicked (vv. 3-12), introduced also by כי:

A	–	ואני	v. 2	–	individual speaker suffers
B	–	כי	vv. 3-12	–	wicked at ease
B	–	כי	v. 27	–	wicked suffer
A	–	ואני	v. 28	–	individual speaker at ease

As noted above, v. 27 is a clear reference to faithless Israel and so the contrast between the righteous individual and the wicked nation is drawn again.

A further contrast appears between vv. 27 and 28. While God destroys 'all' those unfaithful to him (כל־זונה ממך), the faithful poet declares 'all' his works (כל־מלאכותיך). In v. 28b the finite verb and object (שתי אדני) bring together the same verb root (תשית) of v. 18 and divine name (אדני) of v. 20, creating inclusio around the bulk of strophe III. In v. 28 the speaker has made אדני his refuge, while in v. 18a the Lord has placed the wicked in slippery places. It is in v. 20 that אדני is formally identified as subject of the verb in 18a. This divine name (Lord) is found appropriately only in strophe III, where sovereignty over wicked enemies is assured. The twofold use of the verbal root שית in strophe III is matched rhetorically by similar forms in strophe I (vv. 6, 9).[18] The wicked had usurped God's place (שתו בשמים פיהם, v. 9a) and he has

---

17. I owe insight on this point to Rudy Rusali, a former student.
18. The root in v. 9 is technically שתת, but the formal similarity produces the rhetorical effect. GKC §67ee calls שתו a by-form of שתו (שות).

responded by putting them in slippery places (בַּחֲלָקוֹת תָּשִׁית, v. 18). If
the wicked had put on violence as a garment in the first strophe (שִׁית
חָמָס, v. 6), the righteous speaker had made the Lord a refuge in the third
(שַׁתִּי בַּאדֹנִי...מַחְסִי, v. 28). Identical consonants found in 'violence'
(חָמָס) and 'my refuge' (מַחְסִי) strengthen the contrast through paronomasia.

Verse 27b shows that the wicked are those who have been unfaithful
to Yahweh, and in 27a they are described as those far from him. Their
fate, as stated in this verse, is destruction and annihilation. Another
contrast between unrighteous Israel and the voice uttering the words of
the psalm can be seen by comparing vv. 27 and 28. Israel is far from
God but this individual remains close:

$$כִּי הִנֵּה רְחֵקֶיךָ יֹאבֵדוּ - \text{v. 27a}$$
$$וַאֲנִי קִרֲבַת אֱלֹהִים לִי טוֹב - \text{v. 28a}$$

It appears that paronomasia (repetition of qoph and resh) is utilized here
to highlight the semantic contrast between 'far' and 'near'. Added to
this is the disjunctive waw opening v. 28 ('But as for me ...') and the
obvious difference between destruction awaiting the wicked on the one
hand, and the good experienced by this speaker. If one includes the testimony of v. 26b, the effect of meaning and sound together is striking
across these three verses.

$$חֶלְקִי אֱלֹהִים - \text{v. 26b}$$
$$רְחֵקֶיךָ - \text{v. 27a}$$
$$קִרֲבַת אֱלֹהִים לִי - \text{v. 28a}$$

Two confessions of relationship with God surround a characterization
of those far from him. The first and third consonants of 'my portion'
(heth and qoph) are consecutive in the second term, 'those far from
you'. Then the first and third consonants of the latter (resh and qoph)
are consecutive in the final form, 'closeness to ...' All three of these
phrases are expressions of proximity to God, and the sound parallels
underscore restored confidence and faith.

The infinitive 'to recount' (לְסַפֵּר) of v. 28c repeats a root utilized in
v. 15, where the temptation to 'speak' (אֲסַפְּרָה) like the wicked was
strong, but had been resisted. This individual finally perseveres and
eventually tells *all* (כָּל־, v. 28c) Yahweh's deeds, which certainly
includes the destruction of *all* (כָּל־, v. 27b) the unfaithful. Their
destruction was first related in vv. 18-20, where they are put in slippery
places (בַּחֲלָקוֹת), ruins (לְמַשּׁוּאוֹת) and calamity (בַּלָּהוֹת), creating a sound

sequence which the psalm's final noun echoes (מלאכוֹתיך, v. 28c). These parallels at the extremes of strophe III are those that link most pointedly to the subsequent psalm. The term 'ruins' in v. 18 (למשואות) is repeated in Ps. 74.3,[19] while the declaration of God's works (מלאכותיך) in 73.28 is detailed by the speaker in Ps. 74.12-17. Again, the righteous speaker has been proven innocent when compared with his doubting compatriots. Their fate to be cast into 'slippery places' (בחלקות, v. 18) also resounds phonologically with the speaker's confession that God is 'my portion' (חלקי, v. 26) and further accentuates the contrast.

The clustering of the adjective 'all' (כל) at Psalm 73's end (vv. 27-28) is also an appropriate introduction to Psalm 74. 'All' those who apostasize from God in 73.27, (which in v. 10 is described as the nation) anticipate the destruction of 'all' the sanctuary (74.3) and 'all' the meeting-places (74.8) in the land. Since God has allowed such a totality of destruction in the land and temple of 74.1-11, it can be included among 'all' his works to be recounted in 73.28c. Works of power and creation in 74.13-17 would fall under this totality, as do the works of destruction allowed in 74.1-12.

To summarize, the aforementioned inclusio at Psalm 73's extremes (vv. 1, 28) represents a resolution of the central problem. Whereas God was surely good to Israel, the speaker in v. 2 felt excluded—until v. 28, where confidence in that goodness is again restored. A formal and actual realization of goodness in v. 28 resolves the separation from it in vv. 1 and 2. God's faithless people who apparently enjoyed endless prosperity will suffer destruction in the end, and this righteous speaker has refrained from following their example. In fact, the subsequent Psalm 74 describes explicitly the results of their disobedience and faith-lessness. The ideal conditions portrayed in 72 have not been fulfilled, but the speaker has regained confidence in God's word and ultimate justice. Judgment described in the third strophe of 73 (vv.18-28) has answered the doubts, while Psalm 74 provides further details. The latter describes in its very first strophe how the wicked within Israel have been judged, and so functions canonically as a further answer to and confirmation of 73. The question raised in 74 becomes not why the wicked are prospering, but how long their judgment will endure.

Before proceeding to Psalm 74, it is worth pondering from a canoni-cal standpoint the identity of this righteous individual speaking in

19. An example of *dis legomena*, where a form appears only twice in the whole of the Hebrew Bible.

Psalm 73, who stands out from the wayward nation. In a recent article, Brueggemann and Miller have suggested that the speaker of Psalm 73 is the king, or 'Davidic torah keeper', and also recognized 73's position in relation to 72 as intentional.[20] Indeed, it would be most appropriate for a Davidic figure to lament the seemingly broken promises of Psalm 72, as does the speaker of 73. As will be argued for Psalm 75, the dominant voice in that psalm appears to be of the same individual heard in 73, but now taking part in the destruction of those same wicked and arrogant ones. When Psalm 89 complains again over the apparent nonfulfillment of the Davidic covenant, the speaker is undoubtedly 'your anointed' (89.39, 52). The previous three Psalms 86–88 leading up to 89 are also arranged so that the righteous Davidide is portrayed lamenting (again) the present sad state of affairs. In fact, his voice is heard throughout Book III, as will be shown in subsequent chapters.

Brueggemann and Miller in the same article have noted how Psalm 73 recalls themes introduced in Psalms 1 and 2.[21] Both Psalms 1 and 73 begin with a look at the wicked (רשעים, 1.1; 73.3) and end with assurance of their destruction (אבד, 1.6; 73.27). The trust (מחסי) shown by the speaker of 73.28 in Adonay matches the trust (חוסי) of those in 2.12. Further comparisons can be made as well. If Psalm 73 is a complaint based on the nonfulfillment of Psalm 72's promises, Psalm 2 begins asking why the judgment of the wicked promised in 1.5, 6 has not taken place. The stand of the nations against God and his anointed (2.1-2) seems to contradict the assertion that they would not stand in the judgment (1.5). However, the destruction of the wicked is reaffirmed explicitly in the latter half of Psalm 2 by use of the same verbal root אבד and noun דרך (2.12). Likewise, Psalm 73 concludes by reaffirming the destruction (יאבדו) of the wicked. Furthermore, the anointed Davidide of Psalm 2 is the instrument for divine judgment upon the wicked nations (vv. 8-9). As will be seen in Psalm 75, this same individual of 73 judges in tandem with the deity, hewing down the arrogant wicked (רשעים, 73.3, 12 and 75.5, 11). It is noteworthy that the divine judgment of 75.3, 8 (compare also 76.10) is described by the same root שפט also seen in Ps. 1.5.

---

20. W. Brueggemann and P.D. Miller, 'Psalm 73 as a Canonical Marker', *JSOT* 72 (1996), pp. 45-56 (48, 50, 52). In an earlier work, J.H. Eaton, *Kingship and the Psalms* (Naperville, IL: Allenson, n.d.), pp. 75-78, has also argued for the royal nature of Ps. 73.

21. 'Psalm 73 as a Canonical Marker', pp. 52-53.

In spite of the fact that Psalm 73's speaker is mollified by assurance that the wicked will be destroyed eventually according to the promise of 72, the complaints and laments erupt again and again (Psalms 77, 79, 80, 83, 85, 86, 88) and Book III concludes (Psalm 89) on the same note.

The specific pattern of promise, complaint at the opposite conditions to those promised, reassurance, and then further complaints is not new, since the Psalter opens in the same manner. If Psalm 2 reaffirms the promises of judgment for the wicked and blessedness for the righteous in Psalm 1, Psalm 3 opens with further protests by a righteous individual. The speaker of Psalm 3 protests twice that enemies have multiplied against him (עלי, 3.2, 7). Those enemies are the nations (3.7) seen in 2.1, that were supposed to have been destroyed (2.8-9). They rose up against (על) Yahweh and (על) his anointed but their destruction was assured by the end of Psalm 2. Consequently, the complaint of Psalm 3 is uttered by Yahweh's anointed Davidide mentioned in 2.2. Then, true to the form seen in Psalm 73, Psalm 3 concludes with assurance that those wicked ones (רשעים, 3.8) seen before in 1.1, 5, 6, and now including the nations of 2.1 and Psalm 3, will be subdued.[22] The common references to the 'holy mountain' of God in 2.6 (הר־קדש) and 3.5 (מהר קדשו), whence victory over the enemies derives, confirms that Psalm 3 serves as a furthering of the dialogue begun in Psalms 1–2.[23] Undoubtedly, the song of David in Psalm 3 has been interpreted by the postexilic canonical editor(s) as the prayer of God's righteous anointed king who awaits the final destruction of his enemies.[24] Psalms ascribed to Asaph, the sons of Qorah and the Ezrahites in Book III (along with Psalm 86, also ascribed to David), are likewise read as words of that royal figure. This Davidic prince awaits not only the coming of the universal kingdom of Psalm 2, but now also its form in the expanded description of 72.

22. Psalm 4 will continue in the same mood of assurance that ends Psalm 3 and at the same time will warn against the 'emptiness' (ריק, 4.3) imagined by the nations in 2.1.

23. In the subsequent discussion of Ps. 74, its opening interrogative particle למה will be shown to perform a role similar to that of the identical particle opening Ps. 2.

24. What then is the purpose of Ps. 3's superscription? One wonders if the rebellion against David by his own son may not be a preparation for descriptions of the chosen nation's disobedience in later psalms. It is not only the nations which conspire against the anointed but the king's own family joins in the uprising. In Ps. 73, as seen above, the nation has joined the wicked, the רשעים seen in Ps. 1. They suffer the same destruction in 73.27 (אבד) promised in Pss. 1.6 and 2.12.

Chapter 2

PSALM 74

The superscription of Psalm 74, like the preceding 73, ascribes the poem to Asaph, while the type of composition is different in each case, מזמור (73) versus משכיל (74). The latter term is found again in Psalms 78, 88 and 89 within Book III. Numerous parallels exist between 74 and 89 that envelope the larger part of Book III, but the role played by this enigmatic noun in the final editing is unclear.

Continuity between the content of 73 and 74 is quite obvious. The promise to declare 'all your works' in 73.28c is kept in 74.12-17, while the 'work' of destruction in 74.1-11 is that wrought by God upon the wicked, as already described in 73.18-19, 27. Further continuity can be seen by the distinction made between the righteous speaker and unrighteous nation within Psalm 73, the same contrast created by juxtaposition of 73 and 74. Across the entire Psalm 73 the individual speaker retained his integrity and did not join the wicked as had the nation. Wicked Israel's voice is heard once in 73.11 when accusing God of ignorance. After this faithlessness the nation then complains in the first strophe of 74 ('our signs', אותתינו; 'among us', אתנו; 74.9),[1] that God's hand is continually withheld (ידך ימינך, 74.11), while in 73.23 the individual affirms that throughout his ordeal that same hand had sustained his own (ביד־ימיני).

The national complaint of 74.11 included the verb תשיב ('withhold'), in reference to God's hand allowing the evil enemy to revile. Such a complaint was ironic since they had 'turned' (ישוב, qere, 73.10) to the wicked. Apparently the answer to the question by the nation of 74.11 (למה תשיב ידך, 'Why do you withhold your hand?') can be found in the previous description of their own apostasy of 73.10. Because the speaker kept faith in 73, God's presence and revelation sustained him,

---

1.   Note the alliteration at work here between the preposition and feminine plural noun.

in contrast to the nation which was without revelation and support of his hand.

Within the nation of 74.9 no one who 'knew how long' (עד ידע...ולא מתי עד :מה) the enemy would continue reproaching. Ironically, the same faithless people had questioned in 73.11 God's ability to know (ידע...דעה), since the wicked were continually prospering. Doubts on the part of the individual speaker himself (לדעת) in 73.16 were finally resolved when coming to the sanctuaries of v. 17 (destroyed, as Psalm 74 explains). This repetition of the consonants 'ayin and daleth either as part of the root ידע, or the preposition עד, highlights the folly of accusing God of ignorance. When God answers the nation's queries about time (74.9-10) in the following Psalm 75, the same two consonants are repeated in another temporal reference (מועד, 75.3).

That individual had sought to know 'this' (זאת, 73.16), a proleptic reference to the end of the wicked in the following v. 17, and finally did comprehend.[2] In 74.18 God is asked to 'remember this' (זכר זאת), the demonstrative pronoun having no clear antecedent, but referring proleptically to the statements immediately following, where the enemy maligns God's name (18aβ, b). Repetition of the identical imperative in 74.22 and root (חרף) from v. 18 supports prolepsis in the latter:

74.18a – זכר זאת אויב חרף יהוה
74.22b – זכר חרפתך

Furthermore, the suffixed noun of v. 22 is feminine, creating a referent of the same gender for זאת in v. 18. This pronoun (זאת) is therefore proleptic in 74.18, as it was in 73.16, where it referred to the end (לאחריתם, 73.17) of the wicked. That end was described with more details in Ps. 74.1-11, and the identical pronoun in 74.18 is part of a request for the end of those reviling God. If Israel's wickedness was judged, then justice requires the same for the reproaching enemy.

Such a reproach included the turning of Israel's temple into ruins (למשאות, 74.3), the very punishment said to have fallen upon the wicked of 73.18 (למשואות). As stated before, the wicked of Psalm 73 are members of the chosen nation itself, whose punishment in 74 is thereby explained. Israel's temple and sanctuary(ies) are referred to variously in Psalm 74:

---

2.   Compare the same proleptic use of this pronoun (זאת) and referent (לאחריתם) in Deut. 32.29.

בקדש...מועדך...מקדשך...משכן־שמך...מועדי־אל – vv. 3, 4, 7, 8

Their destruction explains how the speaker of 73.17 finally understood the end of the wicked after coming to the sanctuaries of God (מקדשי־אל). References to the 'sanctuaries of God' and 'ruins' in successive verses of 73.17 and 18 do not make explicit the connection between the two. Only in 74.3-8 does the reader understand that the ruined sanctuaries are evidence of God's punishment upon the wicked of Psalm 73.

The violence (חמס) perpetrated by the wicked in 73.6 is spread throughout the land itself in 74.20 (חמס). God's people joined the wicked in 73 and now suffer at the hands of the enemy. Their din rises continually (תמיד) against God in 74.23. Arrogant words by the wicked (in the heavens and on earth, 73.9) initially anguished the individual of Psalm 73. Nonetheless, he became confident of God's continual (תמיד, 73.23) presence, knowing his own hand (ביד־ימיני, 73.23) was being held. Although his flesh 'failed' (כלה, 73.26) him, he was confident of God's sustaining power. In contrast to the speaker of 73, the cry of the nation in 74.11 is that God 'cease' (כלה) withholding his hand (יד וימינך) of help.

The final strophe (vv. 18-23) of Psalm 74 exhibits striking parallels with Psalm 72, to the point that it is essentially a prayer for its fulfilment. Psalm 72 had promised justice and relief for the oppressed in vv. 2 (ועניך), 4 (עניי...אביון), 12 (אביון...ועני) and 13 (ואביון). Therefore with good reason the request in 74.19 (ענייך) and 21 (עני ואביון) is for the same group of people. Promised in 72.14 was an end to violence (חמס) and so comes the petition in 74.20 for God to take note of violence (חמס) in the land. Instead of blessings, prayers and offerings ascending to God all the day, as promised in 72.15 (כל־היום), the deity is scorned all the day in 74.22 (כל־היום). That reproach is continual (תמיד) in 74.23, as opposed to the continual prayer of 72.15 (תמיד). Consequently, Psalms 74 and 73 similarily lament the contradictory situation between the present and the promises of 72. However, the wickedness of Psalm 73 turns out to be that of Israel, and so the nation received deserved judgment (Psalm 74) instead of peace.

Psalm 74 does not have the series of particles marking major divisions as in Psalm 73, but these are indicated by other means. Strophe II (vv. 12-17) is clearly marked by the sixfold repetition of the second person singular masculine pronoun (אתה), while in strophe III (vv. 18-23) there is alternation between imperatives and the negative command

(אֵל־). Strophe I (vv. 1-11) is bound on either end by terms such as נֶצַח,
לָמָה (vv. 1, 10-11), and by repetition of the second person masculine
singular pronominal suffix.

Similarities between the first and third strophes are striking. Verbal
parallels between the two, including the ubiquitous נֶצַח are numerous,
and this reflects the strong emphasis on time. References to the enemy's
derision and violence dominate both I and III, but strophe II appeals to
God's past mighty works as a reason for intervention in the present. In
fact, v.10 near the end of strophe I is quite similar in vocabulary and
meaning to the opening v. 18 of strophe III:

$$\text{יְחָרֶף...יְנָאֵץ אוֹיֵב שִׁמֶךָ} - \text{v. 10}$$
$$\text{אוֹיֵב חֵרֵף...נִאֲצוּ שְׁמֶךָ} - \text{v. 18}$$

In spite of overt similarities between strophes I and III, transitions to
and from strophe II are also evident. So, for instance, the noun קֶרֶב
('midst') in the final v. 11 of strophe I is followed by the same form in
v. 12 at the outset of strophe II. The divine name אֱלֹהִים (vocative) in
v. 10 is repeated in v. 12, and in vv. 13-17 by a string of second person
masculine singular pronouns directed to God.[3] At the other end of strophe II the two boundary cola (v. 17b and 18a) contain the same root
חֹרֶף, first as the noun 'winter' and then as the verb 'deride'.

Evidence of unity across the entire psalm can also be found. Reference to pasture and flock in v. 1 of strophe I corresponds to another
animal, the turtledove, in v. 19a of strophe III. Between are the fierce
sea monsters of strophe II (vv. 13, 14) which God destroys. Animal
imagery thus unites all three strophes. The domesticated creatures in
strophes I and III represent the chosen nation. The speaker of v. 19
(strophe III) entreats God that wild beasts (a reference presumably to
those untamed beasts of strophe II), not be given the life of his turtledove. Israel asks the deity in v. 2 to remember (זָכַר) his congregation,
and the final strophe (vv. 18-23) is bounded on either end by the same
imperatival form (זְכֹר, vv. 18, 22). Again, strophes I and III show remarkable similarities and yet the second strophe coheres well with them.

Verses 1-11 can be considered one whole strophe which bemoans the
present distress, recognizing the role of God and the enemy in it. Note
that the enemy (אוֹיֵב...צֹרְרֶיךָ, vv. 3-4) appears near the beginning of the
strophe and its conclusion (צָר...אוֹיֵב, v. 10). God is addressed directly

---

3.   One could argue that the initial divine name of v. 12 is also vocative, given
the direct address of vv. 13-17.

at the beginning (vv. 1-3a) and the end (vv. 10-11), while the destructive actions of the enemy occur in the middle (vv. 3b-9). The fire set by the enemy in vv. 7a, 8b (שְׁרָפוּ...בָּאֵשׁ שִׁלְחוּ) has its origin in the 'burning' anger of God of v. 1 (יֶעְשַׁן אַפְּךָ). Hence, the nation recognizes that the destruction wrought by the destroyers is ultimately allowed by the deity. For this reason the speakers seek to redirect God's anger against the enemy who reviles his name (vv. 7, 10), rather than against the chosen nation. Israel's foes are called 'your foes' (v. 4a) as the nation complains to God.

Strophe I is further unified at either end by various examples of inclusio. The interrogative particle (לָמָה) opens and closes it (vv. 1, 11). Another interrogative in v. 10 includes the divine name (אֱלֹהִים) and the temporal expression (לָנֶצַח), so that three out of four terms in the initial clause of v. 1 (לָמָה אֱלֹהִים זָנַחְתָּ לָנֶצַח) are repeated in vv. 10-11. At both beginning and end of strophe I, the question is essentially the same regarding the endurance of distress. The psalm's initial question, 'Why oh God have you rejected perpetually?' (v. 1a), acknowledges the justice of God's judgment and anger described in the previous psalm. Can God reject the people forever however deserving they are? These temporal questions are the first in a series of such queries that dominate the whole of Book III.

This use of לָמָה at the beginning of Psalm 74 questioning God's ways is like that found at the opening of Psalm 2. Psalm 1 concludes with the assurance that the wicked will not stand in the judgment with the righteous because Yahweh knows their way. Psalm 2 begins with a questioning of that promise in the same way seen in Psalm 74 (לָמָה, Ps. 2.1). If the wicked are not to stand in the judgment with the righteous (Ps. 1.5-6), why are the wicked nations in revolt taking a stand against God and his anointed (Ps. 2.1-2)? Psalm 74 wonders why the wicked nations are allowed to reproach continually if the wicked are to be destroyed, according to the latter half of 73 (and 72).

Unlike the juncture of Psalms 73 and 74 where the superscription of Psalm 74 intervenes, none appears between Psalms 1 and 2. However, if the lack of superscription in Psalm 2 provides continuity with Psalm 1, the use of superscriptions with the common name Asaph provides continuity between 74 and the previous 73.

Nouns pronominally suffixed with the second person masculine singular (ךָ-) dominate the first strophe of Psalm 74 from beginning to end, appearing in seven verses (vv. 1, 2, 3, 4, 7, 10, 11) out of eleven. This suffix is replaced by the independent pronoun (אתה) in strophe II (vv. 12-17) and imperatives, whether negative (אל־) or positive, in strophe III. The divine name אלהים is strategically located in this psalm as it was in Psalm 73. It opens (v. 1) and closes (v. 22) the whole poem, practically closes strophe I (v. 10) and opens strophe II (v. 12). At the opening of the third and final strophe is the only instance of the Tetragrammaton (v. 18), resembling the single appearance in the previous Psalm 73. One other form of divine name is found as part of a construct chain in v. 8 (מועדי־אל). This instance is a variation on the form in v. 4 (מועדך) and also serves as a link to the following Psalm 75 (v. 3).

Similarities between vv. 1 and 22 extend beyond the divine name. The initial interrogative particle in v. 1 (למה אלהים) and the lengthened imperative in the same position of v. 22 (קומה אלהים) strengthen the effect of the inclusio through sound. They also reveal a change in outlook between beginning and end. The speaker asks, 'Why?' in v. 1, but after descriptions of the destruction (strophe I), and of God's past deeds (strophe II), he feels justified in asking God to act in the final strophe III, 'arise...contend' (קומה...ריבה, v. 22a).

The fourfold repetition of the noun נצח ('perpetuity', vv. 1, 3, 10, 19) highlights the temporal emphasis in this psalm. The interrogative in v. 10, (עד־מתי, 'how long?') expresses hope that the desolation has an eventual end, and the same question is expressed in the immediately preceding v. 9 (עד־מה). At the end of v. 10 the further use of נצח creates closure for the first strophe.

Other temporal terms found across the psalm show again the importance of time for this poem, being the first example of a consistent refrain in Book III.[4] Just as in the distant past (קדם, v. 2) God had intervened on behalf of his people, so there is hope for the same in the not too distant future. Verse 12 repeats reference to the past (מקדם) as in v. 2, but this time more remotely to creation, as subsequent verses in strophe II reveal. Strophe III utilizes three distinct temporal terms stressing the perpetual distress of the present (לנצח, v. 19; כל־היום, v. 22; תמיד, v. 23). The latter two create a semantic inclusio with the first across strophe III, as well as the entire psalm. God's continual anger of v. 1 parallels the enemy's continual blasphemy in vv. 22-23.

---

4. Granted, the use of עולם in 73.12 shows that this theme was introduced already, but the first examples of entire questions of a temporal nature are found here in 74.1, 9, 10.

His perpetual (לנצח) anger of v. 1 also parallels the apparent perpetual (לנצח) forgetfulness of v. 19.

Reproach against God is quite vocal as the adversary roars in v. 4a, and the din is heard again in 23b by means of similar forms. Identical suffixed plural nouns alongside shin–aleph initial forms create a striking correspondence around the psalm:

$$\text{שאגו צרריך...} - \text{v. 4}$$
$$\text{צרריך שאון...} - \text{v. 23}$$

Verse 7 states that God's name (שמך) was defiled and v. 10 of the same strophe I wonders how long such blasphemy (ינאץ...שמך) will continue. Verse 18 repeats the same verb and suffixed noun (נאצו שמך) in another interrogative. References to the divine name in vv. 7, 21 are likewise linked by verbs that are close phonetically, but opposite semantically, resulting in a neat chiastic pattern between strophes I and III:

$$\text{חללו...שמך} - \text{v. 7}$$
$$\text{ינאץ...שמך} - \text{v. 10}$$
$$\text{נאצו שמך} - \text{v. 18}$$
$$\text{יהללו שמך} - \text{v. 21}$$

The interrogative 'How Long?' (עד־מה or עד־מתי) in vv. 9, 10 begins a string that dominates Book III. (Temporal questions in different form that express the same complaint are found as well in places such as 77.8-10; 85.6.) It appears at Pss. 79.5, 80.5, 82.2 and finally at 89.47, because the distress presented in Psalm 74 endures to the end of Book III. In Psalm 89.47 the question is repeated using vocabulary and metaphor (anger described as fire in 74.1, and literal fire in v. 7) similar to that in Psalm 74:

$$\text{עד־מה: עד־מתי....לנצח} - \text{74.9-10}$$
$$\text{עד־מה יהוה תסתר לנצח תבער כמו־אש חמתך} - \text{89.47}$$

This bicola of 89.47 is almost verbatim that found in 79.5.[5] Furthermore, the ubiquitous נצח ('perpetuity') of 74 (vv. 1, 3, 10, 19) echoes across Book III (77.9; 79.5; 89.47).

Another common term from Psalm 74, the imperative 'remember' (זכר, vv. 2, 18, 22) is repeated twice in Psalm 89 (vv. 48, 51), immediately following the interrogative v. 47. Psalm 89.52 repeats more terminology common to Psalm 74, 'enemy' and 'reproach' (אויב, vv. 3, 10,

---

5. See Chapter 7.

18; חרף, vv. 10, 18). The result is an inclusio of temporal interrogatives, references to divine anger and a taunting enemy formed around Book III by Psalms 74 and 89.47-52. These examples in Book III all follow the promise in Ps. 72.7 that the kingdom of peace and righteousness would last 'until there was no moon' (עד בלי ירח). If the promise was of eternal peace, how long would the present distress last (עד־מה, 74.9)?

Psalm 74.8 quotes the thoughts of the enemy as they planned to carry out their destruction. They say in their hearts (בלבם אמרו) they will oppress, and as a result all the meeting-places of God (אל) in the land are burned (v. 8a, b). In Ps. 73.7 the wicked had spoken arrogantly in their hearts (לבב), and in the same strophe questioned God's ability to know (ואמרו...אל, 73.11). Therefore, when Israel joined the wicked in Psalm 73, they brought on themselves the judgment described generally in 73.18-28 and in more detail by the first strophe of 74.

The reference to God's hand in v. 11 supplies the semantic tie to a litany of deeds performed in the following strophe II (vv. 12-17). The second person pronoun אתה dominates these verses (seven times in six verses). In Ps. 89.10-13, 18, 39, a series of the same pronoun precedes a request to remember (89.48, 51), even as this strophe II precedes an identical request (74.18, 22). Around strophe II is an inclusio formed by reference to the land within which he performed these deeds (הארץ, v. 12), being the same one whose borders he marked off (גבולות־ארץ, v. 17).

Strophe II concludes with reference to 'winter' (חרף, v. 17b), anticipating the verb 'reproach' of identical consonants in v. 18a (חרף) in the following strophe III. The latter is bordered at either end (vv. 18, 22b) by the adjective 'foolish' (נבל) and same root חרף. Adding to this unity are the double imperatives (positive and negative) of v. 18a and 19b, both being repeated in the final two verses:

זכר...אל־תשכח – vv. 18-19
זכר...אל־תשכח – vv. 22-23

Four times in this last strophe the deity is commanded to remember. The initial verse (18) and final two (vv. 22, 23) remind him of the taunting enemy, while the middle three (vv. 19-21) remind him of his afflicted people.

Verse 20 is a command to look at the covenant, one of various parallels with Psalm 89, where the covenant is a major theme (vv. 4, 29, 35, 40). Accompanying common terminology between 89 and 74 show that this is the Davidic covenant in 74.20. Both the pleas to 'remember' (זכר) in Ps. 89.48, 51 and references to the 'reproaches' (חרפה) caused by the enemy (89.42, 53, 52) repeat that found in 74.18, 22. All these parallels are found in the final strophe of each psalm. Psalm 89.40 accuses God of spurning his covenant with David, resulting in reproach (חרפה) upon him by all his neighbors (89.42). The psalmist asks if the desolation will last continually (לנצח) and refers to God's fiery and burning anger (89.47), terms and themes reminiscent of Ps. 74.1, 7-8. Parallels in Ps. 74.19-21 with Psalm 72, discussed above, confirm this identification with the Davidic covenant. What 74.19-21 requests is the fulfilment of Psalm 72, another version of the promise to David, and thereby creating another enveloping theme around Book III.

The initial command of 74.22 (קומה) is formed by a root repeated in v. 23b, referring to those who have risen up against God (קמיך). It only seems proper that God should rise up against those who do the same against him. This lengthened imperative of v. 22 is found again in 82.8 (קומה אלהים) when God is again asked to rise up against wicked.[6]

In conclusion, Psalm 74 is a complaint to God about the continual anger and abandonment of his flock. The speaker appeals to God's own honor, since the enemy has dishonored both his name and sanctuary. God's great exploits in the past are rehearsed as an incentive to do the same on behalf of the afflicted nation. At the same time, the destruction and perplexity described in detail by the first strophe of Psalm 74 explain the consequences of the wickedness embraced by the same nation in the previous 73. Assured destruction of the wicked shown to the speaker in 73 upon entering the sanctuaries is revealed to be that of Israel itself in 74.

Finally, the speaker appeals to the afflicted and humble nature of his people, and the promise made to them of a kingdom of justice and peace (Psalm 72), as the basis for arising and contending against the enemy. A direct answer to this latter request is given in Ps. 76.10, but without a specific timetable. Psalm 75 also responds, if only vaguely, to the time of God's intervention (v. 3). Such vagueness provokes various permutations of the question, 'How long?' throughout Book III (77.8-10; 79.5; 80.5; 82.2; 89.47).

---

6.   These two instances of this particular long form of the imperative and divine name (קומה אלהים) are the only examples in the entire Hebrew Bible (see further discussion in the Appendix).

Chapter 3

PSALM 75

The superscription of Psalm 75 is rather lengthy compared to the previous two and may point to its close correspondence with them. The initial למנצח is a common form in superscriptions, and undoubtedly serves as a link to the ubiquitous 'perpetuity' (נצח) in the previous psalm (74.1, 3, 10, 19). The latter adverbial construction was one example of the 'time' theme repeated throughout the poem. Its use here in 75.1 provides a link on the canonical level to temporal references of 74 and not necessarily to musical direction.[1] Since Psalm 75 contains divine answers to the time questions of 74, it may very well be that למנצח refers to the 'eternal one'.[2] As such, he can answer queries and complaints regarding time such as those in 74 using the parallel term לנצח (vv. 1, 3, 10, 19). This same form is repeated in three successive titles (Psalms 75–77). In a similar sequencing, Psalm 80 includes the same term in the superscription following לנצח of 79.5, and is followed in 81.1 again by למנצח.

The following phrase in the superscription, 'do not destroy' appears formally to be a simple negative command, much like those found in the last strophe of the previous psalm (74.19-23). The most frequent of those in Psalm 74 is 'do not forget' (vv. 19, 23). The former of these two (74.19) is followed by a temporal construction and reads, 'do not forget forever'. As just argued, the title of 75.1 is addressed to 'the eternal one' and so there is formal and conceptual continuity with 74.19:

אל תשכח לנצח – 74.19 – 'do not forget forever'
למנצח אל תשחת – 75.1 – 'to the eternal one do not destroy'

---

1. See BDB, s.v. נצח, pp. 663-64.
2. This is presumably a piel masculine singular participle (מנצח).

The pleas not to forget (74.18, 23), and not to give the lives of his afflicted ones to the enemy (74.19), continue in the superscription of 75.[3]

This particular phrase (אל־תשחת) is found in the superscriptions of three successive previous psalms (57–59), proving its role as a linking device. Here in Psalms 74–75 the link is not between superscriptions only but includes vocabulary in the text of the previous Psalm 74. Thus it is surely not coincidental that Ps. 75.5, 6 likewise repeat negative commands, only in these instances directed at the arrogant and the wicked. As a result, the form in 75's superscription that resembles a negative command is preceded in 74 by similar constructions and followed by more in the text of 75 itself.

If the first two items of the superscription (למנצח אל־תשחת) provide linkage to the content of the previous Psalm 74, the following two are identical to the superscription of Psalm 73 (מזמור לאסף). An even closer parallel is found with the following Psalm 76 where the title's final three forms repeat the final three of 75 (מזמור לאסף שיר). Part of 75's superscription also serves as a structuring device within the psalm itself. The term מזמור is identical in root to the long imperfect form of v. 10 (אזמרה), framing most of the poem. The psalm begins with praise (vv. 1, 2) and ends likewise (v. 10). Between these two declarations of praise is the primary reason for them, that is, God's judgment of the wicked.

The major questions of Psalm 74 were, 'How long?' (vv. 9-10) and 'Why?' (vv. 1, 11). In response to the first, 75.3 declares that a time (מועד) has been chosen in which God will judge with equity. In 74.4, 8 is found the identical term twice (מועדך, מועדי) referring to either an appointed time(s) as in 75.3, or place(s), as the context of 74.3-8 implies. Within the canonical context of Psalm 74 it appears that this ambiguity is deliberate in order to create correspondence with 75. Although the traditionally appointed times/places have been destroyed (74.4, 8), God is capable of setting up another (75.3) in which he will avenge the previous destruction. Repetition of identical consonants strengthens the semantic correspondence between the temporal questions of 74.9-10 and answer of 75.3:

---

3.   The same phrase אל־תשחת is found in Deut. 9.26, meaning 'do not destroy (your people)'. See also in Ps. 78.38 the indicative form ולא־ישחית.

עַד־מָה: עַד־מָתִי – 74.9-10
מוֹעֵד – 75.3

Reiterated assertions of God's righteous and sovereign judgment in vv. 3 (אֶשְׁפֹּט) and 8 (שֹׁפֵט) explain indirectly the 'Why?' interrogatives of 74.1, 11. He exalts and debases according to his own will (75.8), and consequently the present lowly state of the nation is by God's own just decision. For those enemies who filled (מָלְאוּ) the land with violence in 74.20, they will themselves be forced to drink to the dregs the full (מָלֵא, 75.9) mixture of the wine of God's judgment. God's hand that has been withdrawn in 74.11 (יָדְךָ) will be bared in 75.9 (בְּיַד־יְהוָה) to judge the wicked.

Psalm 75 also responds to questions raised in 73. The wicked (רְשָׁעִים) of 73.3, 12 are arrogant and proud, but in 75.5 (וְלָרְשָׁעִים) they are warned against haughty behavior and then cut down in vv. 9, 11. In fact, the word pair of 73.3 is repeated here in 75.5:

...בְּהוֹלְלִים...רְשָׁעִים – 73.3
...לְהוֹלְלִים...וְלָרְשָׁעִים – 75.5

Psalm 75 also refers to the pride of the wicked in terms reminiscent of 73. Those for whom 'pride is their necklace' (עֲנָקַתְמוֹ גַאֲוָה, 73.6) are surely identical to those who speak 'with arrogant necks' (בְּצַוָּאר עָתָק, 75.6). The individual speaking in 75.5 (אָמַרְתִּי) has warned the boastful to cease. Canonically speaking, the same person was tempted to join the haughty ones (אִם־אָמַרְתִּי) in 73.15, and speak like them (אֲסַפְּרָה כְמוֹ), but resisted the doubts and eventually recounted (לְסַפֵּר) the great works of God in 73.28, to whom he remained close (קִרְבַת). Now in 75.2 he declares that all those close (וְקָרוֹב) to God's name[4] will recount (סִפְּרוּ) his wondrous deeds. Given these close and numerous parallels between the end of 73 and 75's opening, it is probable that the resemblance between the two plural feminine nouns referring to divine works contributes to canonical cohesion.[5]

מַלְאֲכוֹתֶיךָ – 73.28
נִפְלְאוֹתֶיךָ – 75.2

There exists also an important difference between these two texts, in that the individual speaking in 73.28 (וַאֲנִי) is now expanded to a group

4.   The parallel confession of 73.28 contains three different divine names: אֱלֹהִים...בַּאדֹנָי יְהוִה.
5.   A similar correspondence between feminine plural nouns referring to divine exploits is found in 86.10 (נִפְלָאוֹת) and 87.3 (נִכְבָּדוֹת).

in 75.2b (ספרו). Just as the single righteous individual in Ps. 1.1-3 is joined by a congregation of righteous in 1.5, so the single righteous individual of Psalm 73 is now joined by others in 75.1.

Part of the judgment of vv. 3-4 is described in v. 4 as 'righting' (תכנתי) the pillars of the earth. Previous Psalms 73 and 74 had questioned the upside down moral order and now is heard the promise of eventual rectification. This restoration is complete as evidenced by the repetition of the noun 'all' (כל) across the psalm. 'All' (וכל) inhabitants of 'earth' (ארץ) melt in the judgment of v. 4, and this includes 'all' the wicked made to drink in v. 9 (כל), with 'all' finally falling hewn to the ground in the end in v. 11 (וכל). This divine rectification upon the entire earth can only be carried out by the one in 74.17 who established 'all' (כל) the regions of the 'earth' (ארץ). The creator of earth's physical order is also concerned to restore its moral order.

Psalm 74 uses this same noun 'all' (כל) to describe the total destruction carried out on the temple (74.3) and meeting-places of the land (74.8). It also relates the enemies' 'unceasing' (כל־היום) reproach in 74.22. In response to this, Psalm 75 again provides assurance that all the wicked of the earth will drink the wine of judgment (v. 9) and be hewn down (v. 11). Wicked Israel's temple was wholly destroyed, but eventually all the wicked will be judged justly.

Psalm 75 is difficult to analyze strophically, lacking any explicit formal dividers. However a theme of righteous judgment can be discerned at three distinct points. Strophe I, stretching from vv. 2-4 confesses community praise to God, followed by divine words promising equitable judgment. Strophe II from vv. 5-9 warns the wicked before describing divine judgment, and strophe III from vv. 10-11 declares individual praise and participation in righteous judgment. The justness of this judgment is asserted in v. 3 (of strophe I) by the term 'equity' (מישרים). A warning to the wicked and arrogant of vv. 5-6 (of strophe II) explains God's reasons for exaltation and debasing in v. 8 and so reveals justice. The final v. 11 (of strophe III) states explicitly that the wicked will be hewn down and the righteous one exalted. In view of the questions raised in Psalms 73 and 74, 75 is a clear and reassuring answer of eventual justice.

Across the psalm there is lexical repetition that highlights its message. Twice the verb 'judge' (שפט, vv. 3, 8) is found and each time in a context emphasizing God's own standard of justice. Strophe II begins and ends with reference the wicked (רשעים, vv. 5, 9), and another in v. 11

brings the total to three within this short psalm. This group is warned throughout strophe II and also labelled as 'boastful' by the twofold use of the root הלל in v. 5. After five verses of warning (vv. 5-9) they are assured destruction in v. 11.

The threefold use of the root רום (vv. 5-6), meaning 'be exalted', is used as warning against pride. As the fourth example of this root in v. 8 explains, it is God who decides who will be exalted. The final v. 11 identifies the one who will be exalted as the 'righteous one' and promises the cutting down of the wicked. Each occurrence of the verb רום (except for v. 8) is accompanied by the noun 'horn' (קרן, as part of a Hebrew idiom). Clearly this psalm underscores the certainty of God's just judgment on the wicked.

Verse 2 is unique in that it is spoken in the first person plural, which never occurs again in the psalm. As mentioned above, those close to God's name now include a group along with the individual of 73.28. Colon B (according to the MT) then declares that 'they recount your wondrous deeds'. Reasons for this thanksgiving must be the ensuing assurances of God's just judgment in response to the communal lament of Psalm 74.

The three strophes making up Psalm 75 all begin with verbs of speaking (vv. 2, 5, 10), but only the initial one is in first person plural (הודינו). Immediately following in v. 3 there is a change to first person which dominates the rest of the poem. The repeated first person singular pronoun אני in vv. 3 and 10 envelopes the bulk of the psalm and the rarer form אנכי in v. 4b confirms the intentional use of this pronoun. Following in v. 5 is further first person speech (אמרתי).

The identity of this first person speaker is difficult to discern. In vv. 3-4 it is clearly the judge (אשפט) of the world who speaks, which v. 8 (שפט) identifies as the deity. In v. 10 the speaker who praises God also takes part in the judgment of v. 11. The same independent first person singular pronoun repeated in vv. 3 and 10 leads one to think that they are identical individuals. In fact, the judgment promised in v. 3 appears to be taking place in vv. 10-11. However, the same speaker praises God in v. 10. Does he hew down the wicked as an instrument of God? Furthermore, the speech begun in v. 5 in the first person (אמרתי) ends in vv. 7-9 referring to the deity in third person. Given the numerous parallels already noted between Psalms 75 and 73, the repetition of this pronoun אני at either end of both Psalms 73 and 75 seems to point to the same individual. If so, the complaints of 73 have been replaced by confidence to the point that the individual takes part in the judgment of the wicked as the instrument of God. The Davidic prince of Psalm 72 was also to judge (שׁפט, vv. 1, 2, 4) with the judgments and righteous-ness (צדק) given to him by God, and so Psalm 75 is a reaffirmation of that promise. Psalm 72 implies a merging of roles between the deity and the prince (vv. 15, 17-19), and the same occurs here in 75. Later in Psalm 89 the righteousness and justice (צדק ומשׁפט) attributed to the divine throne (v. 15) are identical characteristics of the Davidic throne in 72.1, 2, 4. These and other evidence of this merging will be seen in the discussion of Psalms 87–89.

References to a horn (קרן) in Book III are found only here in Psalm 75 (vv. 5, 6, 11-twice) and then twice in Psalm 89 (vv. 18, 25). In Psalm 89 it is object of the verb 'raise' (רום), identical to that found in Psalm 75. The horn restored in 89.25 clearly belongs to the promised Davidic king. Presumably then, the raised horns (תרוממנה קרנות) in 75.11 belong to the righteous Davidide. Supporting this identification is the fact that references to the wicked in Psalm 75 are inevitably plural (vv. 5, 9, 11). However, parallel to the last example in v. 11a is the unexpected singular 'righteous one' of v. 11b. Note that in Ps. 1.5, 6, the plural noun 'wicked ones' is paired twice with the plural 'righteous ones'. This anomaly fits the canonical presentation of a righteous one standing out from the wicked nation in Book III. The first example was Psalm 73, where the wicked ones are twice named (vv. 3, 12) in con-trast to the righteous individual (ואני, 'But I…' vv. 2, 22, 23, 28).

Similar language to Psalm 75 dominates the psalm of 1 Sam. 2.1-10 at its opening ('my horn is exalted', רמה קרני, v. 1) and at its conclu-sion ('he exalts the horn of his anointed', וירם קרן משׁיחו, v. 10). The arrogant speech of Ps. 75.6 (תדברו...עתק) is closely parallel to 1 Sam. 2.3 (תדברו...עתק), as is the idea of God's establishing the foundations of the earth in a context of justice against the wicked (Ps. 75.4; 1 Sam. 2.8, 9).[6] God is the one who raises up in Ps. 75.8 (רום—same root as found in 75.5, 6, 8, 11; 1 Sam. 2.1, 7, 8, 10) and brings down (שׁפל, Ps. 75.8; 1 Sam. 2.7). At the other end of the book, 2 Samuel 22 takes up many of the themes and terms of 1 Samuel 2 while reaffirming the Davidic covenant in the face of chaos in the royal family. Psalm 75 also

---

6.   The similarity of this psalm to 1 Sam. 2 has been recognized by others. See M.E. Tate, *Psalms 51–100* (WBC, 20; Dallas: Word Books, 1990), p. 258; Gunkel, *Die Psalmen*, p. 327.

plays the role of affirmation to promises previously given (Ps. 72) concerning David's house.

As noted already, the term used for appointed time (מועד) is identical to that used in 74.4, 8, referring presumably to some sort of meeting places which the enemies had burnt. Now God as speaker appoints one of these (מועד, 75.3) to judge them. Not only does מועד create direct links to the previous Psalm 74, it also resonates consonantally with the final noun of 75.4b, raising the possibility that the rarer first person pronoun also was chosen to create phonetic parallels:

כִּי אֶקַּח מוֹעֵד... – v. 3a
...אָנֹכִי תִכַּנְתִּי עַמּוּדֶיהָ – v. 4b

The pillars of the earth (עמודיה) will be set right at the appointed time (מועד). Note that both are direct objects of the verb and occupy the final position in each clause. When Ps. 75.3, 4 declare that God will right the pillars of justice in the earth, the upside-down moral world of Psalm 73 is rectified, as is the humiliating situation of Psalm 74.

The wicked are addressed in 75.5 by the identical word pair (הוללים/רשעים) of 73.3, where they enjoyed perpetual peace and prosperity. Now they are warned and then hewn down after drinking of God's wrath (75.9, 11). The poet designates them initially by the word pair and then further references to them are by the more common member (רשעים, vv. 9, 11). Likewise, Ps. 73.3 refers to the wicked using the same pair of masculine plural nouns in identical order, and then subsequently uses the more common term (73.12). God has answered quite directly previous complaints and queries in Psalms 73–74 through the words of 75.

The address to the wicked continues in 75.6, recalling 73.8 where they had spoken from on high, repeating the same noun and verb:

73.8b – וידברו...ממרום ידברו
75.6 – אל־תרימו למרום...תדברו

Psalm 73 describes the arrogance and 75.6 warns against it before describing its consequences in vv. 8-11. It becomes clear that 75.5, 6 function canonically as a direct answer to the complaint of 73.3-12.

Psalm 73.10b had stated that the waters of the wicked were fully drained out to the wayward chosen people. The vocabulary used regarding those waters in 73.10b is close to that of 75.9 in reference to the wine, mixed and drained to the dregs by the wicked:

73.10b – ומי מלא ימצו למו
75.9 – ויין...מלא...ימצו

The verb used here (מצה, 'drain out'), in niphal first and then qal, is a rare form. Its two occurences here are the only examples in the entire Psalter. Their appearance so close to each other in Book III is not fortuitous. Assuredly, those in 73 who imbibed the waters of the wicked will also imbibe the wine of judgment in 75.

Psalm 75.9c also repeats a particle (אך) which was seen to sustain the structure of the entire Psalm 73 (vv. 1, 13, 18). Psalm 73 questioned whether God was treating the wicked righteously and the first statement that God was 'surely' (אך, v. 1) good to Israel was said perhaps without full confidence. The second instance in 73.13 commenced an expression of the opposite, namely that maintaining purity was certainly futile, but finally in 73.18 confidence returns that the wicked are to be judged. By use of this same particle in 75.9c, the speaker expresses certainty of full punishment for the wicked. They will be poured the wine of judgment to the dregs, assuring complete judgment (אך שמריה ימצו). Consequently, within the single v. 9 are two formal parallels to Psalm 73 that affirm punishment on the wicked.

The independent pronoun and disjunctive waw of 75.10 (ואני) was also seen repeatedly in Psalm 73 (vv. 2, 22, 23, 28). There may be an attempt to identify the righteous individual of Psalm 73 with the speaker here in 75. The disjunctive or contrastive waw before the pronoun in Psalm 73 generally contrasted this individual with the wicked and the same is true here in 75.10. It is the wicked of the earth who have been made to drink God's wine of judgment in v. 9d, and then the text reads, 'but I [ואני] will declare forever.' He places himself opposite the wicked as a faithful mouthpiece of God's praise. He does not join the wicked in disbelief in Psalm 73 and is not judged along with them in Psalm 75. His praise of God is eternal (לעולם) here in 75.10a, which repeats his declaration that God was his portion forever (לעולם) in 73.26.

Admittedly, common forms such as the particle אך and pronoun אני found in consecutive or nearly consecutive psalms may not always be signs of canonical intent. However, after repeated instances of less common forms such as those shown in 75.9, 10 (ביד־יהוה, מלא, ימצו, רשעי), which contribute overtly to the dialogue already begun previously in Psalm 73, more common forms such as אך or אני that are also consistent with and adding to the message cannot be ignored.

The lengthened first person imperfect of v. 10 (אזמרה) is of the identical root as the noun in the superscription mentioned already (מזמור). Together they form an inclusio around the psalm. This same verb expresses on the part of the individual essentially what the group declared in v. 2 (הודינו), another inclusio on the semantic level.

The God to whom the individual gives praise (v. 10b) is the God of Jacob (אלהי יעקב), a title used in the subsequent psalm as well (76.7). There he rebukes and vanquishes men of war. In Psalm 75 the God of Jacob is praised in the midst of warning to the wicked, while in 76 the destruction is wrought by rebuke from the God of Jacob's mouth. Undoubtedly, the divine epithet at the end of Psalm 75 is playing an anticipatory role to the following psalm.

The concluding verse of Psalm 75 again repeats themes seen in previous verses and also those of previous psalms. All the horns of the wicked will be cut down while those of the righteous one are raised. Beginning with Psalm 1, the contrast of fates between the wicked and righteous is a major theme of the Psalter.[7] This was also true in Psalm 73 at the outset of Book III, where the wicked seemed to be perpetually prosperous, contrary to Psalm 1's assertions. Psalm 73 was also set in contrast to Psalm 72 where righteousness was to reign universally (vv. 1-3, 7) in a Davidic kingdom. Psalm 74 longed for judgment on the enemy who had destroyed Zion (v. 2), the very place where God's anointed king would destroy the enemy (Ps. 2.6-12). Psalm 75 promises (vv. 3, 4, 8-10) this long-awaited judgment on the wicked, and thereby rekindles hope in the eventual fulfillment of Psalms 1–2 and 72. This answer is not time-specific, and so by the end of Book III (Ps. 89.25) God is still reminded of the promised exaltation of the horn of the righteous.

---

7. See P.D. Miller, 'The Beginning of the Psalter', in McCann (ed.), *The Shape and Shaping of the Psalter*, pp. 83-92 (85). He states that this theme is especially dominant in the first book of the Psalms.

Chapter 4

PSALM 76

The superscription of Psalm 76 differs in only one point from that of
the previous psalm. What is hypothesized as a reference to instrumental
music (נגינת) by commentators, replaces what has been discussed earlier
as a command not to destroy of Ps. 75.1 (אל־תשחת).[1] This latter term
served as a catchword to the previous Psalm 74 and across Psalms 57–
59 served as a link in the superscriptions between the psalms. Similarily, the term נגינת in this superscription appears to be a link not to the
previous psalm's content, but to the following Ps. 77.7 where the same
term in the singular (pronominally suffixed) is found (נגינתי). Thus, it
(נגינת) provides a forward link, while the remaining terms look back-
ward and forward (למנצח...מזמור לאסף), except for שיר, which is found
in the previous but not subsequent superscription. As will be shown,
this particular term in the superscription is consistent formally with the
content of the psalm itself.

Dominating this psalm are niphal participles (vv. 1, 5, 7, 8, 13) and
added to this are two nun-initial indicative verbs (vv. 6, 12).[2] The psalm
opens and closes with niphal participles (vv. 2a, 13b), both in reference
to the deity—God is 'known' (נודע) in Judah, but 'feared' (נורא) by all
the kings of the earth. If God is known in v. 2, vows are made to him in
v. 12 (נדרו, נדר ע), with consonance adding to the stated concept of
greatness. Here the second form נדרו is an indicative verb, not a participle, but the similarity of form adds to the aforementioned parallel.
These rhetorical features highlight the move from the first strophe (vv.
2-4), describing God in the midst of Israel, to the last (vv. 12-13),
describing him in the midst of the rulers of the earth.

Both first and last strophes refer to God in the third person, but the

---

1. Gunkel, *Die Psalmen*, p. 329; Tate, *Psalms 51–100*, p. 260; M. Dahood,
Psalms II: 51–100 (AB, 17; Garden City, NY: Doubleday, 1968), p. 217.
2. See Tate, *Psalms 51–100*, p. 264.

intervening two (vv. 5-7, 8-11) are direct address (except for v. 10), the first portraying him as warrior and the second as judge. These two middle strophes are also introduced by nun-initial participles, character-izing God as 'resplendent' (נָאוֹר, v. 5) and as 'feared' (נוֹרָא, v. 8).

At strategic points in the psalm then, these phonetically similar par-ticiples create a chain of expressions that extol God in various roles (נוֹרָא...נָאוֹר...נוֹדָע). Each strophe specifies the name אלהים once (vv. 2, 7, 10, 12), as has been true of most psalms in Book III up to this point. The Tetragrammaton found once near the end (v. 12) is another characteristic of the first four psalms in this Book. On the basis of these features, the psalm can be outlined as follows:

I.   vv. 2-4 – God's fame within Israel (נוֹדָע)
II. vv. 5-7 – God as victorious warrior (נָאוֹר)
III. vv. 8-11 – God as fearsome judge (נוֹרָא)
IV. vv. 12-13 – God as fearsome to surrounding rulers (נדרו)

Consequently, either a niphal participle or nun-initial indicative verb introduce each strophe. The second and third rearrange the consonants resh, aleph and long (ô) vowel (נוֹרָא, נָאוֹר).

The choice of Zion as revealed by v. 3 is a repeated theme in Book III of the Psalter. We read in Ps. 78.68b of the choice of Mount Zion and in 84.8 that faithful ones appear before God in Zion. The entire poem of Psalm 87 is a 'song of Zion' (cf. Ps. 137.3, שִׁיר לָנוּ מִשִּׁיר צִיּוֹן), emphasizing its choice above all other dwellings of Jacob (v. 2).[3] Implied in these references from Psalm 76 onward is a confidence that the Zion destroyed in 74.2 did not cease to exist forever. Psalm 76 is an answer to previous laments in Book III and 72 (as was Psalm 75), and portrays a Zion where God dwells (76.3), assuring its eternal existence.

Parallel to God's renown (נוֹדָע) in v. 2a is his great name in 2b (שְׁמוֹ גָּדוֹל). The name of God was a repeated theme in Psalm 74, where the enemy reviled it constantly, but here its fame is restored. It was the afflicted and poor that praised his name (74.21), followed in 75.2 with those close to that name recounting wonders. Those afflicted and poor ones close to his name of the previous psalms, are the same in Judah and Israel (76.2) who now know God's greatness. The use of the proper name Judah (יהודה), meaning 'praise', repeats the idea of renown (נוֹדָע), aided by the consonance of daleth. Repeated daleths link all the vocabulary related to fame of v. 2 (נוֹדָע בִיהוּדָה...גָּדוֹל). The reason for

---

3.   Gunkel, *Die Psalmen*, p. 330, regards Ps. 76 as a Zion song.

this fame will be given in the rest of the psalm, where exploits in war and judgment are enumerated.

It is in Zion (שָׁמָּה, v. 4) that the weapons of war are to be shattered by God, including arrows, shields and swords. This explains how the peace (שָׁלוֹם) of 72.7 can be enduring and abundant, as the archaic name Salem (שָׁלֵם, 76.3a) suggests. This root likewise is used in the sense of recompense or the related concept of payment,[4] as in 76.12 where all are admonished to pay (שַׁלְּמוּ) their vows to Yahweh. Salem/Zion here in 76.3 recalls those who destroyed it in Ps. 74.2 and reviled the name (74.7, 10, 18). That recompense is paid immediately in 76.4a, where the shattering of war implements is described with the help of repeated shin (שָׁמָּה שִׁבַּר רִשְׁפֵּי־קָשֶׁת).[5] In fact, both the shin and mem of Salem in 3a are repeated in the adverbial 'there' (שָׁמָּה) of the following 4a. One could postulate that shin and mem unite the entirety of strophe I (vv. 2-4), since in each the combination is repeated (שְׁמוֹ, שָׁלֵם, שָׁמָּה). Thus, in restored Zion/Salem God will put an end to warfare and the vituperation of his name described previously in Psalm 74.

Verses 9a and 10a will continue alliteration, using the same two consonants mem and shin. The judgment God pours out on the earth is from heaven (מִשָּׁמַיִם, 9a), implying through sound and similar content that שָׁמָּה of v. 4a is in heaven. Thus, God's name (שְׁמוֹ) and dwelling (שָׁלֵם) are there (שָׁמָּה) in heaven (שָׁמַיִם), from which war will be ended and justice established (vv. 2, 3, 4, 9, 10). Undoubtedly Zion/Salem is to be understood as an eschatological extramundane city.

God's power in victory over the enemy had already been insinuated in 74.13, using the identical verbal root שׁבַרְתָּ ('break') as that in 76.4 (שָׁבַר).[6] The resulting peace established in Zion will be portrayed later in Psalm 87 where different nationalities are living together harmoniously as part of its citizenry. Warfare against Zion in 74.2-8 had resulted in the city's desolation, but now war and Zion's enemies in

---

4.   BDB, s.v. שָׁלֵם, p. 1022.

5.   In four out of the five instances of shin in vv. 3, 4, it is followed by a bilabial consonant. The same repeated use of shin is found in Ps. 46.9-10, another Zion song (אֲשֶׁר שָׂם שַׁמּוֹת...מַשְׁבִּית...קֶשֶׁת יְשַׁבֵּר), in a similar context. Psalm 46 also describes Zion as God's dwelling (vv. 5, 6), he utters his voice (cf. 46.7; 76.7), and shatters the war implements (46.10; 76.4). It is the same 'God of Jacob' who performs these deeds in both psalms (76.7; 46.12). See the discussion in Tate, *Psalms 51–100*, pp. 264-65.

6.   The same root is found in Ps. 46.10.

general have come to an end. This second naming in Book III of Zion (76.3) is an appropriate response to the lament and questions of Psalm 74. The warring enemies and their implements described in Ps. 74.3-8, will be smashed by the God who dwells in Zion (76.3, 4).

Psalm 75 promised that God had chosen a time to judge the wicked, and now in the following 76 we see a more detailed and vivid outworking of those words. At the same time, each point of Psalm 74 is being answered by 75 and 76. In 74 the central strophe (vv. 12-17) remembered God's powerful exploits in the past, appealing directly to him repeatedly by the second person independent personal masculine pronoun (אתה). The identical pronoun is used three times across the two central strophes of Psalm 76 (vv. 5-7, 8-11), referring to divine deeds of vengeance for Zion and the afflicted. In fact, its twofold occurrence in v. 8 appears redundant and is missing from the LXX, but the repetition here in 76 strengthens the link with exploits enumerated in 74.12-17.

In another link to Psalm 74, the afflicted were mentioned there repeatedly (vv. 19-21, עני, ענייך), pleading for deliverance. Now in 76.10 they are promised salvation (ענוי), reaffirming the words of Psalm 72.2, 4, 12. Nonetheless, since the time of that described deliverance is not known, the question, 'How long?' surfaces repeatedly throughout Book III (77.8, 9; 79.5; 82.2; 89.47).

The sleep described in Psalm 76 is clearly a picture of death, as commentators have recognized.[7] As stated in Ps. 76.6, it is divinely caused in its context and as read canonically in the light of Ps. 75.9. In the latter, Yahweh made the wicked drink wine to the dregs and it is for this reason they sleep in Psalm 76. The inability to find their hands (ידיהם) in 76.6b conjures the image of one completely under the influence of alcohol who can be plundered easily (76.6a). Because of being made to drink from the cup in the hand of Yahweh (כוס ביד־יהוה, 75.9), their power has been nullified. Despite being stouthearted and men of valor they are not able to resist the intoxication of death served up to them. By the power of God's hand, the hands of warriors are rendered useless.

It is said here in 76.6 that all (כל) the valiant warriors are incapable of action. Likewise, all (כל) the wicked in 75.9b drink the wine prepared for them by Yahweh. Clearly the sleeping warriors of Psalm 76 are included among the wicked of 75.9. One wonders if there may not

7.   Gunkel, *Die Psalmen*, p. 331; Tate, *Psalms 51–100*, p. 262. See Jer. 51.39, 57.

be editorially induced canonical paronomasia between the inability of the warriors to find their hands (לֹא מָצְאוּ, 76.6) and the drinking of 75.9 (יִמְצוּ, 75.9). The former would be the result of the latter. Consonance between the rare form אֶשְׁתּוֹלְלוּ of 76.6 ('plundered') and יִשְׁתּוּ in 75.9 likewise serves to underscore the results of divinely induced drinking and destruction.

The term 'all' (כֹּל) contributes to a contrast here in Psalm 76. In v. 10 it is *all* the afflicted and humble of the earth who will be saved, contrasting with *all* the men of valor of v. 6b who cannot find their hands. Because of this display of divine power and justice, *all* those surrounding God in v. 12 are to pay their debts to him. They are exhorted to learn from the two previous groups and offer obeisance to Yahweh. This address in the final two verses of the psalm is apparently directed to the kings and rulers of the earth (cf. v. 13).

Warnings to kings following a scene of military subjugation is precisely that found at the conclusion of Psalm 2. The kings are warned in 2.10-12, following the destruction of v. 9, and told to serve Yahweh with fear (בְּיִרְאָה), a root repeated once in each of the two final verses of Psalm 76 (נוֹרָא, v. 13; לַמּוֹרָא, v. 12). In either psalm the divine judgment originates in heaven (2.4; 76.9), and both emphasize the heavenly Zion's role in that conflict (2.6; 76.3). Both psalms are preceded by those promising the judgment on the wicked (1.5, 6; 75.9, 11) and reward for the righteous (1.5, 6; 75.11). Undoubtedly, Psalm 76 refers to the same eschatological conflict found in the Psalter's introduction.

Strophe II begins with a direct second person address to God (76.5), and ends with the same (v. 7). Between the two is v. 6, describing in third person those warriors who are cast into sleep. Instead of addressing God by the second person independent pronoun (אַתָּה), as in v. 5, he is called the God of Jacob (אֱלֹהֵי־יַעֲקֹב) in v. 7. This latter epithet is also part of the pattern of repeated divine names in each of four strophes in the psalm (vv. 2, 7, 10, 12). It repeats the exact name of God used in Ps. 75.10, to whom the psalmist directs praise following an image of the wicked imbibing divinely prepared wine. Likewise in 76.7, this particular epithet also follows an image of warriors in the state of wine induced sleep.

As a conquering warrior in v. 5 (opening strophe II), God was seen as 'resplendent' (נָאוֹר), but now as a wrathful and 'feared' (נוֹרָא) judge at the outset of strophe III (v. 8). The latter is part of a string of four examples of the root יָרֵא ('to fear'), found from this point onward in the poem, that reveals a major theme of the final two strophes (נורא, v. 8; יראה, v. 9; למורא, v. 12; נורא, v. 13). Given in v. 8b is a reason for fearing God. No one can stand before 'your wrath' (אפך), and this serves to confirm the reality of that same wrath against Israel (אפך) of 74.1. However, it also confirms that a final judgment awaits all, including those who despised the God of Israel in 74.10, 18, 22, 23.

Consonance of mem and shin opens v. 9 (משמים השמעת). God makes judgment (דין) to be known from heaven, a concept repeated in the following v. 10a, where the semantic cohesion is augmented by repetition of the same consonants (למשפט). This pair of terms denoting judgment signals a restoration of the justice described in Psalm 72, where the identical roots are found in the same bicola (במשפט...ידין, 72.2). As noted above, the heavens (משמים) from which judgment descends (v. 9), is the place where war implements are shattered (שמה–v. 4), being also where Salem (שלם) is located.

The infinitive construct בקום ('when arises') of v. 10 is a direct answer to the plea in Ps. 74.22 for God to arise (קומה). While the infinitive construct בקום hearkens back to Psalm 74, the two following forms, '...God to judge' (למשפט אלהים) confirm the promise in Psalm 75 that God is a judge (אלהים שפט, 75.8), and will judge (אשפט, 75.3) with equity. As noted previously, the twin terms for judgment (דין, משפט) in 76.9, 10 remind the reader of the promise of the same in Ps. 72.1, 2, where God is to grant such authority to the king. This root שפט is repeated three times in Psalm 72 (vv. 1, 2, 4), the parallels indicating that both Psalms 76 and 72 promise restoration of the same kingdom.

The allusions to Psalm 72 continue in 76.9, 10. Included in God's work of judgment is the saving of all the afflicted of the earth (דין...להושיע כל-ענוי-ארץ). These same afflicted were cause for pleading in 74.19-21, as noted previously, the speaker not forgetting the promised justice for them in 72. They are a dominant theme in Psalm 72 (vv. 2, ועניך; 4, עני עם יושיע; 12, משוע ועני). Their deliverance is likewise promised in Psalm 72 utilizing the identical verbal root several times over (ישע, vv. 4, 13) as that here in 76.10. From a canonical perspective, 76.10 is a crucial answer to the doubts expressed in the preceding psalms (73–74) of Psalm 72's peaceful and just kingdom ever appearing.

Verse 10b also provides a canonical contrast with the preceding psalm. Psalm 75 promised the judgment of all the wicked of the earth, with little being said about the poor and afflicted. In 76.10 the afflicted of the earth are to be saved and the vocabulary is reminiscent of 75.9d's description of the wicked:

יִשָּׁתוּ כֹּל רִשְׁעֵי־אָרֶץ - 75.9d
לְהוֹשִׁיעַ כָּל־עַנְוֵי־אֶרֶץ - 76.10b

This comparison confirms the statement of 75.3 that judgment will be in equity. The wicked drink the dregs of God's judgment and are cut down (Psalm 75), but the afflicted and poor (who praise the name in 74.21) are delivered (Psalm 76).

In 76.11 human anger praises God (תוֹדֶךָ), and praise in 76.2 is also implied by the proper name 'Judah' (יְהוּדָה). The double use of this root ידה in 75.2 corresponds to the proper name of 76.2 and the same root in 76.11. Both psalms declare praise to God for being victor over the wicked in Psalm 75, and armed warriors in 76. This is a change from the laments of 73–74 where overt praise is scarce.

Praise in 76.2 is expressed by the proper noun already mentioned (יְהוּדָה), along with the participle 'he is known' (נוֹדָע) and the adjective 'great' (גָּדוֹל). The latter two forms are those that also express praise in the following Psalm 77. The same adjective describing God occurs in 77.14b (גָּדוֹל) at the opening of a list of mighty deeds performed (vv. 14-21). In the immediately following verse (77.15b), God makes known (הוֹדַעְתָּ) his strength among the nations. The one known in Judah (76.2) is now known among the nations (77.15). Consequently, 76.2 creates strong links both backwards and forwards in Book III, much as was true of 75.2.

The phrase 'all who surround him' in 76.12 certainly includes those in Judah and Zion of vv. 2-3, but also others who are commanded to bring homage.[8] Kings are mentioned directly in the following 76.13 (לְמַלְכֵי אָרֶץ), presumably included among those bearing gifts. Such a scenario again recalls Psalm 72 directly. The exhortation to all (כֹּל) those surrounding Yahweh to do homage, including kings in 76.12, looks forward to the era described in Psalm 72 where all (כֹּל) kings and nations will do the same (72.10-11). The reason for such homage in Psalm 72 is given in vv. 12-15 (כִּי), being that the righteous king will defend the afflicted (וְעָנִי, v. 12). He will do this through righteous

---

8.   Such a statement (יוֹבִילוּ שַׁי) corresponds closely to Ps. 68.30, where the kings of the earth bring gifts of homage to Yahweh (לְךָ יוֹבִילוּ מְלָכִים שָׁי). Furthermore, just as in Ps. 76.8 and 13, God is 'fearsome' (נוֹרָא) in 68.36. Compare also the rebuke (גָּעַר) of 68.31 against enemies and the same in 76.7 (מִגַּעֲרָתְךָ).

judgment (במשפט ועניך...ידין, v. 2). Likewise, in Psalm 76, the salvation of the afflicted ones (להושיע כל ענוי, v. 10) through a fearful divine
judgment (דין ארץ יראה...למשפט, v. 9-10), provides a basis for the
command to all (v. 12), including kings (v. 13), to pay homage. Consequently, Psalm 76 reiterates the promise of a future kingdom of peace
and justice seen in Psalm 72. However, unlike Psalms 72, 76 adds a
description of the conflict which will precede the universal peace.

As can be seen, each psalm from 73 to 76 has made direct reference
to the content of 72, either by way of complaint (73, 74), or by way of
reaffirmation (75, 76). Nonetheless, the following Psalm 77 takes up a
complaint much like Psalm 74, since this promised redemption is still
far off. The smoking anger seen in 74.1 (אף), and described as invin-
cible in 76.8 (אפך), is still burning continually against Israel in 77.10
(באף). Good reason for this continued wrath will be detailed at length in
Psalm 78.

Chapter 5

PSALM 77

The superscription of this psalm is the third in a series opening with the form למנצח (Psalms 75–77) and then followed by a construction which is similar to vocabulary in either the previous or following psalm. The first two items of Psalm 75's superscription (למנצח אל־תשחת) provided strong links to Psalm 74's content, while only one element (לאסף) was common to the previous superscription. Apparently, links between the superscription of 75 and 74's content provide cohesiveness lacking between their respective headings. Between 73 and 74, only the ascribed author (לאסף) is common to their headings (as between 74 and 75), but no parallels are evident between superscription and content of each. Of course, the bodies of each poem are closely linked, as shown above.

Between the titles of 75 and 76, four out of five elements are identical and so the binding is strong. Between the headings of Psalms 76 and 77 are three common vocabulary items, while the remaining elements correspond to the other's content. The second item in 76 (בנגינת) parallels נגינתי of 77.7. In 77's superscription itself, the second form is על־ידיתון (*kethib*), whose meaning is uncertain.[1] It may be derived from the root ידה, which would create ties to the previous psalm in two places (76.11, תודך; 76.2, יהודה).[2] As a result, the unique form of 76's heading (בנגינת) would link to the following 77's content and that of 77's heading (על־ידיתון) to the previous 76's content. It appears then that, whenever possible, the redactor of the Psalter utilized elements in the successive superscriptions to create cohesion between the psalms.[3]

---

1. See Tate, *Psalms 51–100*, p. 120 for a sample of views.
2. BDB, s.v. ידה, p. 393.
3. This becomes quite obvious in the superscription of Psalm 88. Such evidence also makes all the more striking the complete lack of correspondence between headings at the juncture between books (Pss. 72–73 and 89–90).

Parallel vocabulary to Psalm 77 in both 76 and 74 reveal continued discussion of the desired redemption. In the previous Psalms 74 (vv. 13-17) and 76 (vv. 5, 8),[4] the same masculine singular second person independent pronoun (אתה) used here in 77.15 is found in contexts narrating God's powerful exploits. In 74.13 the poet addresses God (אתה), remembering his power (בעזך) over the waters (מים) and their inhabitants. Here in 77.15 he is addressed in the same manner (אתה) concerning his power (עז), including victory over the waters (מים) in vv. 17, 18, 20. These deeds are from the past (מקדם, קדם), as noted in 74.2, 12, and likewise, the speaker in 77.6, 12 recalls the same exploits of old (מקדם). In fact, the temporal form and identical verbal root together confirm the common subject matter between 77 and 74,

$$מקדם פעל \quad – \quad 74.12$$
$$מקדם...פעלך \quad – \quad 77.12b\text{-}13a$$

Based on these past actions, the speaker in 74 had twice asked God not to forget (אל־תשכח, vv. 19, 23), while in 77.10 an interrogative expresses the same sentiment (השכח). Not only has he seemingly forgotten former deeds done on behalf of his people, he is angry with them in the present (יזנח,77.8; זנחת, 74.1). The question is whether this anger will persist forever (לנצח, 77.9; 74.1, 10, 19). Another temporal term, 'yet' (עוד), is likewise found in both 74.9 and 77.8, expressing the divine rejection.[5]

Order is important in understanding the correspondence between Psalms 74 and 77. The A colon in each successive verse of 77.8-10 contains terminology that provides a direct link to questions and pleadings already seen in Psalm 74. Verse 8 asks if God has 'spurned' (זנח) forever, essentially the same question of 74.1 (למה אלהים זנחת לנצח).[6] The following 77.9 uses another very common term from Psalm 74, including the clause just quoted, לנצח. In 74.19 this latter temporal phrase was part of a request that God not forget forever (אל־תשכח לנצח). The following v. 10 (Psalm 77) repeats the verb (השכח), meaning that phonetic

---

4.   However, as seen in the previous chapter, Psalm 76 apparently describes a future salvation prophesied in 73, while 74 recalls the past.

5.   It will also be an important part of the divine answer to 77's questions in the following Psalm 78 (vv. 17, 32).

6.   The verb זנח is utilized in 74.1, 77.9 and finally 89.39, all complaining of the apparent rejection by God of his people and his covenant with David.

resonance (sibilants plus ḥeth) is maintained through the three A-cola of vv. 8-10, using the same terminology and order as in Psalm 74:

יזנח – 77.8a
לנצח – 77.9a
השכח – 77.10a

זנחת לנצח – 74.1
תשכח לנצח – 74.19

In fact, the three interrogatives at the middle of Psalm 77 neatly encapsulate Psalm 74, by repeating elements from either end.

The individual speaker of 77.7 muses within (לבבי) over the distressing state of the nation. In similar fashion, 73.13, 21, 26 meditated within (לבבי) over the seeming contradiction between present distress and previously given promises. Apparently the questions of Psalm 73 have not been entirely resolved, as can be seen in the parallels between 73.11 and 77.10-11. Both are interrogatives, the first uttered by the faithless nation questioning God's knowledge, and the second by a righteous individual questioning divine compassion:

אל...בעליון – 73.11
אל...עליון – 77.10-11

Psalm 76 has assured a future destruction of God's enemies, and the musings of 77 yearn for its accomplishment. The aforementioned pronoun אתה of 77.15 carries on the threefold repetiton of the same in 76.5, 8, in similar contexts of divine exploits against the enemy. While the speaker of 76.8 asks who (מי) can stand before God's wrath, the same interrogative form (מי) in 77.14 proclaims his inimitability. Such is the divine grandeur that the earth feared in 76.9 (ארץ יראה) and similarily shook (ותרעש הארץ) in 77.19. His greatness is declared in 76.2 (גדול), as it is in 77.14 (גדול). If he is known in Israel and Judah (נודע), according to 76.2, so his power is made known to the nations (הודעת) in 77.15. His resplendence in 76.5 (נאור) is reiterated in 77.19 (האירו). Therefore, the coming great deliverance portrayed in Psalm 76 will be similar to the one recalled in Psalm 77.

It is God's wrath (אפך) in 76.8 that inspires destruction of enemies, but in 77.10 that wrath (באף) is still directed against Israel. This recalls how God's own people joined the wicked in 73.10, and thus are not exempt from wrath and judgment as portrayed in Psalm 76. The conditions of Psalm 72 will be realized, but a wicked nation (73.10) cannot be a participant. The lengthy rehearsal of continual rebellion by Israel in the subsequent Psalm 78 reiterates this idea. Nonetheless, the speaker remembers and yearns for the redemption of the sons of Jacob described in 77.16 (בני־יעקב), by the same God of Jacob named in 76.7 (אלהי יעקב).

While the speaker remembers past salvation, past failures cannot be ignored. The divine wrath mentioned in 77.10 (באף) provides a resumption of what 76.8 (אפך) already expressed, '…and who can stand before your anger?' Not even Israel can escape that anger, as 77.10 proves, whereupon Psalm 78 describes it in greater detail (vv. 21, 31, 38, 49, 50—all examples of אף). Psalm 74.1 had previously described how God's anger (אפך) burned against his own flock, and it continues in 79.5 (תאנף), and throughout Book III (אפך, 85.4, 6; אפים, 86.15), using various synonyms (עשנת, 80.5, cf. 74.1; חמתך, 89.47, 88.8; 79.6; עבר, 89.39; 78.21, 49, 59, 62; בער, 89.47; 79.5).

Gunkel, in typical fashion, divides the psalm according to form-critical categories, finding a lament in vv. 1-11 (*Klagelied*) and a hymn in vv. 12-21 (*Hymnus*).[7] However, Kselman is correct in calling the poem a unity from the hand of a 'gifted poet'.[8] We find the term יד in vv. 3 and 21, creating inclusio across the whole of the poem. The hand extended to God in petition of v. 3 parallels the hope for a hand of guidance, as provided in v. 21. The present lack of action on God's part (strophe I) is contrasted with a past mighty intervention (strophe II).[9]

The first strophe of the poem (vv. 1-13) is also defined by this hand of v. 3 and a close parallel in v. 11 (ימין). The poet's hand is extended to God, sensing that the divine right hand has been withdrawn. Likewise, parallel imagery surrounds the second strophe (vv. 14-21). God's former work known to the nations (בעמים, v. 15) and on behalf of his own nation (עמך, v. 16), was accomplished by his own arm (בזרוע, v.16). Included in that former work was the guidance of his people (עמך, v. 21) through the water, using the hands of Moses and Aaron (ביד, v. 21).

In v. 2 there are two references to the voice of the poet (קולי) crying out to God, which are paralleled twice (vv. 18, 19, קול) by the divine voice. The voice of the poet is expressed in crying out (אצעקה, v. 2),

---

7.   Gunkel, *Die Psalmen*, p. 333.

8.   J.S. Kselman, 'Psalm 77 and the Book of Exodus', *JANESCU* 15 (1983), pp. 51-58 (58).

9.   Kselman, 'Psalm 77', p. 56.

and the divine voice likewise thunders in the clouds (שְׁחָקִים, v. 18).[10] The exploits of the past (vv. 14-21) are remembered in the hope of a future redemption. Whether the hiphil verb (והאזין אלי) in v. 2 is taken as a simple perfect, imperative, infinitive or waw consecutive form, the expectation of an answer is present in this psalm.[11] This verb form provides a connection to Ps. 78.1a where the hiphil form is clearly imperative (האזינה). Psalm 78 provides answers to the questions and lament of 77, proving that God has indeed lent an ear. However, the appeal to past exploits in the exodus of strophe II (78.14-21) as a motivation for divine action in the present, can elicit unexpected responses. Gracious deliverance at that time was accompanied by continual disobedience on Israel's part, as remembered by the speaker of Psalm 78. For this reason the present Israel is commanded to give an ear (חטו אזנכם, 78.1b) and not be as former generations (78.8).

Psalm 77 can be divided into two strophes, as mentioned above, vv. 2-13 and 14-21. Not only does the double use of the same divine name (אלהים) at the beginning of each strophe support the division (vv. 2, 14), but the prominence of first person speech in strophe I distinguishes it from strophe II, where second person masculine pronominal forms abound. In strophe I the emphasis is on the individual speaker's own meditation and remembrance, as revealed by the first person verbs dominating every verse except the three interrogatives of vv. 8-10. Nonetheless, these queries are an integral part of that meditation and so are to be included in the first strophe. The backbone of strophe I is the fourfold repetition of the root זכר ('remember', vv. 4, 7, 12 twice), inevitably in the first person. Accompanying are three parallel instances of the semantically similar form שׂיח ('muse', vv. 4, 7, 13). Kselman has observed that the verb 'forget' (שׁכח) is found precisely in the middle of these four occurrences of 'remember'.[12] The speaker remembers and wonders if God has forgotten.[13]

Kselman has also pointed out that vv. 16 and 21 are very similar in

---

10. A similar sequence of sibilant, guttural and qoph occurs in the root of each.

11. See GKC §63o, and BDB p. 24 for waw-consecutive, Dahood, *Psalms II*, p. 223 for imperative and Ibn Ezra, *Miqraot gedolot* (New York: Shulsinger Bros., 1945), p. 48a (מה) read it as an infinitive.

12. Kselman, 'Psalm 77', p. 57.

13. Another example of consonance is present in the contrast between the poet's meditation (שׂיח) in vv. 4, 7, 13 and apparent divine forgetfulness (שׁכח) in v. 10.

vocabulary and style.[14] Verses 14-16 describe redemption of God's own people and revealed power to peoples in general. Verses 17-20 speak of the deity's power over the seas, the heavens and earth, while v. 21 resumes again reference to the people. At least one reason for placing the bicolon of v. 21 at the psalm's end and not following v. 16 is its relation to Psalm 78 which follows. The subject of Israel's redemption from Egypt and the trek through the desert is the major theme of Psalm 78, although Moses' and Aaron's names are never mentioned. Psalm 78.72 concludes with David guiding (ינחם) Israel by his hands (כפיו), as did Moses and Aaron in 77.21 (נחה) with their hands (ביד). As a result, David takes Moses' place in the subsequent psalm as shepherd of the people (78.72). The strategic placement of this verb at the end of the psalm in each case is surely not coincidental. Psalm 77.21 is clearly anticipating the subsequent psalm, and perhaps separated from v. 16 for that purpose.[15]

At the same time it should be noted that vv. 17-20 resemble closely Ps. 18.8-18, a psalm ascribed in its superscription to the time when David was delivered from his enemies.[16] Therefore, Psalm 78, which recounts events under Moses, and is rounded off with a portrayal of David as the ideal shepherd, is consistent with 77. The latter surrounds vv. 17-20 with overt references to the exodus and wilderness trek under Moses in vv. 16 and 21. Furthermore, Psalm 76 also portrays the eschatological battle from Zion to restore the peace and justice promised in 72, using imagery from Exodus 15. The horse and rider of 76.7 (וסוס ורכב) begin (Exod. 15.1) and end (Exod. 15.19, 21) the song sung by Israel, being just two of many parallels between the two.[17] Consequently, Psalm 76 to 78 is a string of psalms that share references to the

---

14. Kselman, 'Psalm 77', p. 55.

15. Chronological ordering may be present in first mentioning the redemption of Israel from Egypt (77.16), followed by a description of the parting of the seas (77.17-20) and concluded by the subsequent shepherding through the desert (77.21). In either case, 77.21 is an appropriate introduction to Psalm 78's content.

16. Tate, *Psalms 51–100*, p. 274 notes that fifty-two percent of the vocabulary in 77.17-20 is found in Ps. 18.8-18.

17. The war (מלחמה, Ps. 76.4; Exod. 15.3), sword (חרב, Ps. 76.4; Exod. 15.9), fearsomeness (נורא, Ps. 76.8, 13; Exod. 15.11), rhetorical question concerning God's greatness (מי, Ps. 76.8; Exod. 15.11), name of God (שמו, Ps. 76. 2; Exod. 15.3), spoil (אשתוללל/שלל, Ps. 76.6; Exod. 15.9), majesty (אדיר/אדר, Ps. 76.5; Exod. 15.6, 11), might (חיל, Ps. 76.6, Exod. 15.4), salvation (ישע, Ps. 76.10; Exod. 15.2), and greatness (גדול, Ps. 76.2; Exod. 15.16) are common vocabulary to each.

exodus, while engaged in a dialogue concerning restoration of the Davidic promise as stated in Psalm 72. The expected eschatological fulfillment to the house of David will apparently resemble the deliverance accomplished under Moses.

The final verb of v. 2 (וְהַאֲזִין) begins a string of the same through Psalms 77, 78 and 80, revealing a dialogue between God and the people at the canonical level. Psalm 77.2 either declares that God has hearkened to the speaker (assuming a perfect verb form) or requests the same (imperative), while the speaker in Ps. 78.1 asks the people to hearken to the divine response. The response of 78 answers complaints voiced in 77, but due to the nature of that response Ps. 80.2 (הַאֲזִינָה) again asks for a hearing. For example, 77.8b wondered if God would yet *again* grant favor, and so 78.17a explains how the nation sinned yet *again* and *again*:

$$\text{וְלֹא־יֹסִיף לִרְצוֹת עוֹד} \quad - \quad 77.8\text{b}$$
$$\text{וַיּוֹסִיפוּ עוֹד לַחֲטֹא־לוֹ} \quad - \quad 78.17\text{a, (cf. 32a)}$$

If the verb form of 77.2 (וְהַאֲזִין אֵלַי) is perfect, then the second strophe (vv. 14-21) could possibly be construed as a divine answer to the psalmist. The power and guidance described therein would portray a future deliverance and this would explain the close parallels to the battle and victory of Psalm 76. In other words, meditation on past redemption (77.16) has been divinely inspired and constitutes a prophecy of future redemption.

Both Psalms 77 and 78 conclude with references to the shepherds who guided Israel by their hands (כַּפָּיו, בְּיַד), using the same verb (נחה), and so each psalm opens and ends in like manner. The hiphil pattern verb (הַאֲזִינָה/הַאֲזִין) is placed at or near the beginning of each and the same root (יִנְחֵם/נְחִית) concludes each psalm. These and other parallels confirm the intentional juxtaposition. Clearly, Psalm 78 is positioned to be read in the light of 77.

Throughout Book III of the Psalter, the interrogative construction עַד מָתַי/מָה is repeated often (74.9, 10; 79.5; 80.5; 89.47) to question how long the present distress will endure. Now other versions of essentially the same query are repeated in 77.8-10. The different versions often share the same terminology, such as לָנֶצַח, found in 89.47, 77.9 and 74.1, strengthening the semantic connection through formal means.

The fourfold use of זכר in this psalm recalls the threefold use in Psalm 74, a text of similar content, as already noted. In Psalm 74 all three are imperatives directed toward God. The last two (vv. 18, 22) ask that God remember the reviling of the enemy, while the first (v. 2) asks, rememberance of the congregation redeemed long ago (זכר...קדם). Now the speaker is again recalling those days of past redemption (77.12), using essentially the same terminology (אזכרה, מקדם). Psalm 78 shows that Israel itself has forgotten the deeds of its God (vv. 11, 42a), but the individual speaking (78.1-2 are spoken in first person singular) has not forgotten them, as the lengthy psalm itself proves. The memory of Israel itself proved to be very short (78.35, 36), but the individual speaking there and in Psalm 77 has been faithful. In other words, Psalm 77 reveals a faithful speaker who remembers God's past works as opposed to the forgetful nation in 78, while Psalm 78 itself consists of the words of one who recalls former deliverances. At the same time, Psalm 78 answers the complaints raised in the first half of 77. Apparently one and the same speaker asks (Psalm 77), and then answers (Psalm 78), becoming a true mediator between Yahweh and Israel. Note how this voice calls Israel to 'hearken' to his torah, and to 'the words of my mouth' in 78.1, words reminiscent of Deut. 32.1. The righteous individual of Book III has become a figure like Moses.

This same phenomenon of a righteous individual distinguished from a wayward nation was heard in Psalm 73. Within that one psalm the speaker both questioned God (vv. 1-12) and then expressed answers to those same doubts (vv. 17-28). That same speaker promised to recount God's wondrous deeds in 73.28c (לספר), a good introduction to the middle strophe of Psalm 74 (vv.12-17). However, the first strophe (vv. 1-11) came from the community, as the first person plural in vv. 9-10 confirms. Psalm 75.1 indicated that the individual of 73.28 was speaking again, but this was accompanied by many others, as the plural (ספרו) indicated. However, an individual (ואני/אנכי, vv. 3-4, 10-11) again speaks in Psalm 75 acting in concert with the deity in judgment (רשעים אגדע, 75.11a; cf. v. 9d, where God judges the same wicked). That violent judgment against the wicked is detailed in Psalm 76, and so presumably the same individual of 75 will take part. However, in Psalm 77 we return apparently to the present pre-judgment time, since the complaints of Psalm 74 are raised again. Have the reassurances of Psalms 75–76 that 72's kingdom will indeed come been forgotten? It is more probable that the long delayed fulfillment of those promises arouses further laments. Indeed, the dominant theme of Book III is the prolonged postponement of expectations that Psalm 72 aroused.

In Ps. 77.12, the speaker recalls the wonders (פלא) of the past. A

change of perspective occurs in v. 15, where God continues to do wonders (עשׂה פלא), the participle indicating a hope for the present and
future.[18] Past salvation recounted in vv. 14-21 is expected in the future
as well. However, reminding Yahweh or being reminded by him of past
salvation could also bring to mind past rebellion, and such is the result
in Psalm 78. Israel's fathers forgot (78.11) the wonders performed (פלא
עשׂה, 78.12), and so there is good reason for the delay.

Verse 13 describes the meditation (הגיתי) of the speaker on all the
past works of God. This verb is important, found in the Psalter's introduction describing the ideal man (ובתורתו יהגה, Ps. 1.2). He meditates
on the Torah day and night, and the same is true of the speaker in Psalm
77. He spends days and the whole night in pleading, remembering and
meditating (vv. 3-7, 12-13) on the exploits of ancient days and years,
narrated in the Torah (vv. 6, 12-21). Consequently, the speaker of
Psalm 77 fits the profile given of the man (אישׁ) in Psalm 1.[19]

Read canonically, Psalm 77 is another plea for the promised future
restoration by an individual distinguished from a disobedient nation.
Psalm 76 had predicted a deliverance in Zion and now the question is
how long before it takes place, if ever. The speaker expects a future
redemption based on the character of the God who performed wonders
in the past. Psalm 78 will describe how continual rebellion accompanied the previous wonders and thereby explains the present continual
divine wrath of 77.

18. GKC, §116a.
19. This is not the first resemblance between Book III and Psalm 1. The individual of Psalm 73 rejected the company of the wicked (רשׁעים, vv. 3, 12), as did
the man of Ps. 1.1 (רשׁעים).

Chapter 6

PSALM 78

Psalm 78's superscription continues the list of Asaphite psalms begun in 73 and continuing to 83. The generic title מַשְׂכִּיל breaks with those of 77 or 79 on either side, labelled מִזְמוֹר. The root שׂכל is common in wisdom literature such as Proverbs (מִשְׁלֵי), and we find the psalm itself called a proverb (מָשָׁל) in v. 2. In this case, the semantic relation to wisdom is clear in both terms, while the designation of 'riddles' (חִידוֹת) in v. 2b presents another sapiential parallel to the superscription. In contrast to Psalm 78, the other headings in Book III containing the same element מַשְׂכִּיל (Psalms 74, 88, 89) do not correspond to overt wisdom features in the body of the psalms themselves. Furthermore, the preceding Psalms 76–77 demonstrated how terms in the superscriptions were connected formally to the body of the neighboring psalm, but such is not the case in Psalm 78.

As stated in the previous chapter, Ps. 77.21 could serve as a fitting title for the bulk of Psalm 78. From vv. 12-54 the poet recalls the exodus from Egypt and the trek through the desert led by Moses and Aaron. There are numerous formal similarities accompanying those of content. Both psalms begin and end with identical roots (נחה, אזן). Each psalm also concludes naming a shepherd whose hands led the flock (בְּיַד, 77.21; כַּפָּיו, 78.72), that is, Moses and Aaron in 77 and David in 78. The shepherd imagery is made explicit at each psalm's end by the use of צֹאן at 77.21 and 78.70 (at 78.72 the root רעה expresses the same). Consequently, a cursory examination of both psalms demonstrates that their contiguity is not fortuitous.

A verse by verse examination of 77 reveals abundant evidence of how Psalm 78 responds to it. Psalm 77.1 stated either that God had answered or should answer the speaker (הַאֲזִין אֵלַי), and in 78.1 an extended answer is announced by a request for the people to listen (עַמִּי

(הַאֲזִינָה).[1] In Ps. 77.3 the petitioner describes how he extended his hand
(יד׳) in the time of his distress (בִיום צרתי) without being comforted.
The reason for the delay in rescue from distress may be found in 78.42,
where the nation does not remember the hand of God (יד׳), which at
one time (יום) redeemed them from the hand of the enemy (צר). This
distress in 77.3 continues day and night (בִיום...לילה), perhaps because
the nation had forgotten (78.11) how God had led them day and night in
the desert (יומם...וכל הלילה, 78.14). The speaker in 77.3 refuses (מֵאֲנָה)
to be comforted, while in 78.10 it is recalled that Israel refused (מֵאֲנוּ) to
walk in his counsel.[2] Apparently it was distress that caused the poet to
seek (דרשתי) the Lord (77.3), and distress caused Israel to do the same
in 78.34 (וּדרשׁוהוּ). However, soon thereafter Israel treacherously
deceived its God (78.36-37), and for this reason mercy is delayed in
Psalm 77. The speaker's seeking in Psalm 77 is continual and unceasing, even when no answer is forthcoming. On the other hand, the seeking of the nation in 78.34 is shortlived indeed, and so this individual in
77 again distinguishes himself from the wayward people.

In 77.4 a series of the root זכר begins (vv. 4, 7, 12 twice), where the
poet remembers God's past mercy (vv. 8-10) and miracles (vv. 12-13).
Yahweh's command to Israel in 78.5-7 warned against forgetting (ולא
ישׁכחו) the miracles of the past (v. 7b), which is precisely what they pro-
ceeded to do (וישׁכחו, 78.11). Ironically, the poet in 77.10 asked if God
had forgotten (השׁכח), on behalf of a forgetful nation. There was a point
in the past when Israel did remember (ויזכרו, 78.35), but eventually
forgot the work of his mighty hand in redemption (לא זכרו) in 78.42,
and meanwhile God himself was remembering them and their frailty
(ויזכר) in 78.39. Thus, the speaker in Psalm 77 did not forget what God
had commanded to remember and stands out from the nation as an
example of obedience.

More examples of this individual's distinction from the nation at large
continue. While the poet's spirit (רוח׳) in 77.4, 7 rightly remembers and
seeks God, the spirit (רוחו) of a rebellious generation in 78.8 does not
prove faithful. In 77.5 the speaker had become speechless in anguished
vigil (לא אדבר), which is not true of the rebellious generation who

---

1.   This same form is found three more times in Book III (80.2; 84.9; 86.6),
revealing repeated requests for God to listen and implying that the extended answer
of Ps. 78 did not placate the supplicant(s).
2.   In the whole of the Psalter this root is found only in these two consecutive
psalms.

spoke against God (וידברו באלהים) in 78.19. When the same individual of 77.6, 12 reflects on the great deeds of the days of yore (מקדם), it reflects obedience to the words of Psalm 78 which teach the remembrance and transmission of past traditions (מני־קדם, 78.2). This reflection takes place in the heart of the constant individual (עם־לבבי, 77.7), a practice the past generations failed to carry out (78.8, 18, 37, לב or לבב). It is only the last instance of this term in 78.72 where we are told of David's faithful heart (לבבו), matching the heart of the speaker in 77.7.

Three consecutive verses of Psalm 77 (8-10) ask questions without answers in the psalm itself, but for which remarkable responses are found in Psalm 78. Verse 8 uses the epithet 'Lord' (אדני) when asking if he will be angry (cf. 74.1) forever. The same epithet is used once in the following psalm (78.65) describing how Adonay awoke to free them from their enemies (78.66, צריו; compare also 74.10, צר). Given the promises of eventual salvation for Israel in Psalms 75–76, the deliverance described in 78.65-72 assures the reader that it will happen again. Colon B of 77.8 continues the question begun in A, asking if the Lord will ever again be favorable. The answers of 78.17, 32 are remarkably similar to the question:

$$
\begin{array}{rl}
\text{ולא־יסיף לרצות עוד} & -\ \text{77.8b} \\
\text{ויוסיפו עוד לחטא־לו} & -\ \text{78.17a} \\
\text{בכל זאת חטאו־עוד ולא} & -\ \text{78.32a}
\end{array}
$$

In addition to the corresponding underlined forms, both clauses of 77.8 and 78.17 include an infinitival form. The speaker in Psalm 77 wonders if God will ever again be gracious to his people, and the answer in Psalm 78 is that Israel itself was sinful time and again. God was patient in the face of Israel's waywardness, and so Israel should be patient in the midst of wrath. The idea of repeated sin by Israel is stated again in 78.32a, using the identical עוד.[3] In this manner, Psalm 78 recalls the repeated sin of Israel by repeated and parallel references. Lexical correspondences are accompanied by the fact that each of these vv. 17 and 32 are at the opening of new strophes.[4] The sheer length of Psalm 78

---

3. A third time across this lengthy psalm and thus more distant from the previous Ps. 77, a summary statement highlighting repeated sin is given in the form of an exclamation (כמה ימרוהו במדבר, 78.40a), without any specific parallel to Ps. 77.

4. The psalm is taken here to consist of seven strophes, with divisions occurring at vv. 9, 17, 32, 40, 56 and 65, following *BHS*.

serves also to reveal the continual nature of Israel's rebellion. God's continual anger is matched by the nation's continual obstinacy.

In 77.9 the question is whether God's promise has ceased to endure from generation to generation (לדור ודור). Immediately in the first strophe of Psalm 78, a major theme is the recounting of past exploits to succeeding generations (דור, 78.4, 6, 8). It becomes clear in the body of Psalm 78 that succeeding generations did not pass down the memory of those deeds executed on behalf of the nation, and so God has responded in kind by withholding graciousness for many generations (77.9). The speaker in 77.9b wonders if God's promise (אמר) has ceased to be valid, but the problem is rather that the words of 78.1 (לאמרי־פי) have not been heeded by the nation. Admittedly, the root אמר is extremely common in biblical texts. Nonetheless, its appearance at strategic points in either psalm (78.1 and in the midst of the distinctive three-verse interrogative of 77.8-10) which undoubtedly are juxtaposed in order to be read in tandem supports the comparison. Furthermore, the comparison is consistent with the message evident from numerous other parallels already shown.

In 77.10 the poet wonders if God has forgotten (השכח) to be gracious. In reality it is not God who has forgotten but Israel in general (לא־זכרו, 78.42), and the sons of Ephraim in particular (וישכחו, 78.11), in spite of the fact that they were commanded not to forget (ולא ישכחו, 78.7). As can be seen from the long rehearsal, this forgetfulness endured for an extensive period. In the same verse (77.10) the poet wonders whether God has shut off his compassion in anger (אף). The following Psalm 78 does not deny that God's anger (אף) has burned against Israel (vv. 21, 31). However, he sought to restrain his anger (להשיב אפו, v. 38c) in the midst of unfaithfulness, and so the present anger must be for good reason. The same v. 38a of Psalm 78 states that God is compassionate (והוא רחום), in spite of the deception practiced by Israel as described in vv. 36-37. Psalm 77.10b had previously questioned God's compassion (רחמיו). As a result, 77.10b is answered directly in 78.38, as demonstrated by parallel vocabulary (רחם, אף). Psalm 78.38 (and 39) will prove a key verse as well in the following lament of Psalm 79.

It is remarkable how in 77.8-10 ideas and terminology corresponding to Psalm 74 are reiterated, while at the same time pointing directly to the following Psalm 78. Consequently, these interrogatives become key to the structure and message of Book III up to this point. Essentially the same type of question will be expressed in 79.5 with close ties to 74, 77, 78 and the final 89.

The following v. 11 (Psalm 77) similarily reveals purposeful links to 78, as did the previous three interrogatives. The question here is whether the right hand (ימינו) of the Most High (עליון) has changed. In Psalm 78 it is seen that the Most High (עליון) was their redeemer (78.35) and is still gracious (v. 38a, the divine epithet עליון of 35 is the ultimate antecedent of the pronoun הוא). In fact, a threefold correspondence can be detected between these texts:

77.10-11 – אל...רחמיו...עליון
78.35, 38. – ואל עליון...רחום

It is affirmed later in response to 77.11b that his right hand (ימינו, 78. 54) continues being capable of prodigious feats.

Israel's unfaithfulness is noted again in 78.19-20 where they question God in a manner that parallels formally the interrogatives of 77.8-10. There the poet asks if God has forgotten (השכח, v. 10a) how to be gracious to his people and then continues in 10b (אם) wondering if mercy has been shut up in anger. Likewise in 78.20cd, the sequence is of interrogative heh (הגם) followed by the same particle (אם). Here the people question whether God can provide food. The recollection of such doubt on the part of the nation in 78.20cd serves as an appropriate answer to the question of whether God had forgotten to be gracious in 77.10. He certainly remembered past graciousness, including the spurning of it (78.19-20), and so withholds it in the present (77.10).

Between Ps. 77.12 and 13 is found a pair of words derived from the same root עלל, referring to past deeds the poet recalls (מעלליה ובעלילותיך...). This same pair is found in Psalm 78 in two noncontiguous, albeit closely contrasting verses (7b, 11a).[5] (The identical root שכח in the latter two confirms the contrast between command and disobedience to that command.) The speaker of 77.12a has followed the command given in 78.7 as the following shows:

77.12a – אזכיר מעללי־יה
78.7b. – ולא ישכחו מעללי־אל

The same individual has distinguished himself from the sons of Ephraim by musing on God's works:

5. This pair occurs in Book III only in these two psalms.

77.13b – ובעלילותיך אשיחה
78.11a – וישכחו עלילותיו

Both verbs reveal phonetic similarity as well by repeated sibilants and ḥeth.

The second colon of 78.11 uses a closely parallel form (ונפלאותיו) to that just mentioned in colon A (עלילות), based on the same root as the noun in 77.12 (פלאך), and the identical noun follows immediately in 78.12a (פלא). As a result, in the two consecutive vv. 12b, 13b of Psalm 77 the order is פלאך...ובעלילותיך, while in vv. 11a, 12a of Psalm 78 the opposite sequence occurs, עלילותיו...פלא. Furthermore, two examples of the root זכר ('to remember') in 77.12 contrast with two examples of שכח ('to forget') in 78.7, 11. Taken together, these verses present a deliberate distinguishing of the righteous individual speaker of Psalm 77 from the nation of 78.

The questions of 78.19-20 cast doubt on God's ability to provide, while the question of 77.14b expresses faith in divine power:

77.14-15a – אלהים...מי אל גדול...האל
78.19 – באלהים...היוכל אל

Therefore, this individual in Psalm 77 stands out as an example of faith and obedience to the commands given to the nation in 78.1-8. He remembers (Psalm 77), and passes on (Ps. 78.1-8) the former deeds in contrast to the forgetful generations of 78.

Across the first strophe of 78 (vv.1-8) are repeated admonitions to recount (ספר, vv. 3, 4, 6) to future generations what had been handed down. In fact, there are specific instructions to repeat the wondrous deeds Yahweh had done (v. 4). This command echoes an indicative statement from Psalm 75:

75.2 – ספרו נפלאותיך
78.4 – מספרים...ונפלאותיו

The speaker of Psalm 78 is performing this command, that is, recounting the works of God, fulfilling his promise of 73.28 to do the same (לספר כל מלאכותיך). The nation speaking in 79.13 will make a similar vow (נספר תהלתך), answering directly 78.4 (תהלות).

It was seen previously that Ps. 77.14-16, 21 made reference to the exodus in terminology similar to that of Exodus 15. In Psalm 78 the exodus and march through the desert are the major topic of discussion. We read in Ps. 77.15a that God is a doer of wonders (עשׂה פלא) in the exact words of Exod. 15.11. Psalm 78.12 then repeats these words using the perfect verb form (עָשָׂה פֶלֶא). Again, Israel forgot the wonders done in Egypt (וַיִּשְׁכְּחוּ, 78.11-12), but the speaker of Psalm 77 remembers (זָכַר, 77.4, 7, 12).

In 77.15 the two parallel nouns referring to divine works of power in redemption are פֶלֶא and עֹז, which parallel closely עֲזוּזוֹ and נִפְלְאוֹתָיו of 78.4cd in a command to recount them. It was his power that also fed Israel in the desert (עֹז, 78.26), but later because of continual rebellion his 'power' (עֹז, 78.61) was taken captive.[6] Rebellion therefore explains the sad situation of the nation in Psalm 77. The same 77.15 declares that God made known (הוֹדַעְתָּ) his power among the nations by delivering Israel. What was made known to the nations was supposed to be made known (נֹדְעָם, לְהוֹדִיעָם, יֵדְעוּ, 78.3, 5, 6) to the future generations of Israel but they failed, as the ensuing verses confirm.

The speaker of 77.16 also recalls that Israel was redeemed (גָּאַלְתָּ) by the strong arm of Yahweh, as did Israel recall for a short time their redeemer (גֹּאֲלָם) in 78.35, but then quickly forgot again (78.36, 42). Redeemed Israel is called 'your people' (עַמְּךָ) not coincidentally in the latter part of 77 (vv. 16, 21), and it is addressed by this noun in 78.1 (עַמִּי) when asked to hearken. This same people asks scornfully if Yahweh was capable of preparing meat for them in the desert (לְעַמּוֹ, 78.20d). They (עַמּוֹ) were led through the desert like a flock (78.52), but rebelled nevertheless and were given over to the sword (עַמּוֹ, 78.62). After all that was done for them, their continued rebellion could only produce judgment. David was finally chosen to shepherd the people (עַמּוֹ, 78.71), apparently more successfully than Moses and Aaron, who are absent from the entire Psalm 78.

As stated in the previous chapter, Ps. 77.17-19 is remniscent of the words of David in Ps. 18.7-16, being surrounded by explicit references to the exodus under Moses in 77.14-16, 21. Now in Psalm 78 there is a long rehearsal of the exodus and trek to Canaan without ever mentioning Moses' name, only David's (78.65-72). The exodus and pilgrimage under Moses and Aaron had resulted in stubborness and rebellion, but the new leader at least was a man of perfect heart and wise guidance (78.72). Just as the speaker of Psalm 77 stands out from the people in Psalm 78 for remembering past wonders in his heart (לְבָבִי), so David in vv. 70-72 is exemplary among the people for his perfect heart (לְבָבוֹ), in contrast to their faithless one (לִבָּם, לִבּוֹ, לָבֶם, 78.8, 18, 37). At 78's beginning

---

6.   A reference apparently to the ark, according to the context of 78.61.

(vv. 1, 2) is found an individual faithful in the words of his mouth (פי), and at the end (v. 72), one faithful in his heart (לבבו), creating an inclusio of faithfulness around the psalm.

Israel was given the name 'sons [בני] of Jacob and Joseph' in 77.17. Jacob is a name given Israel throughout Psalm 78 (vv. 5, 21, 31, 71). It was however these same sons (בני) who were commanded to pass on the faith and memory of their fathers (78.4, 5, 6), and failed. The first concrete example of this faithlessness in Psalm 78 is found at v. 9, where the sons of Ephraim (בני אפרים) are guilty of not keeping the covenant. Ephraim's sons were faithless and he was a son of Joseph, making the link between Pss. 77.16b (בני יעקב ויוסף) and 78.9 (אפרים בני) quite transparent. For this reason we read that Ephraim/Joseph was eventually rejected (78.67), while Judah, David's tribe, was chosen (v. 68). Thus, the sons of Jacob and Joseph who were redeemed in 77.16 are faithless, and finally rejected in favor of Judah and his son David (78.9, 67, 70).[7]

The choice of Zion as an eternal dwelling, and eternal shame given to God's enemies (78.66, 70) reiterates promises given in 76.2-4. Zion/Salem was the divine dwelling place, and there battle implements were to be destroyed in a conflict that would usher in the conditions of Psalm 72. It would also reverse the conditions so lamented in Psalm 74. For example, eternal shame upon the Lord's enemies in 78.66 (צריו...חרפת עולם) avenges the situation described in 74.10, 18, 22 (יחרף צר...לנצח חרף יהוה...חרפתך...). The sanctuary of 74.3, 7 (בקדש, מקדשך) and 73.17 (מקדשי־אל) that lay in ruins and ashes, is rebuilt forever in 78.70 (מקדשו). Mount Zion of 74.2 (הר־ציון), wherein God dwelt, is also restored in 78.68 (הר ציון). Therefore, within Book III the final strophe of Psalm 78 (vv. 65-72) is more than a rehearsing of God's covenant with David, but rather becomes the pledge of an eventual restoration of Zion which now lies in ruins and of another shepherd like David. In the midst of complaints and laments, the promises of Psalms 72, 75 and 76 have been reaffirmed. Further on in Book III this restored Zion will be described again in overtly eschatological terms by Psalm 87.

From 77.17 to 20 the particular reference to waters (מים) overcome by God is repeated four times. His work involving waters (מים) in 78.13, 16, 20 was an answer in the past, saving the people from Pharoah and

---

7. Ephraim and Judah are the only tribes mentioned in this long history. Ephraim is singled out especially as disobedient and rejected (78.9, 67, also Shiloh in v. 60) while Judah/Zion and David are specially chosen (vv. 68, 70).

thirst in the desert. Other terms for water in Psalm 77 (תהמות, v. 17; מ,
v. 20) are repeated in the same vicinity of 78 (מ, v. 13a; כתהמות,
v. 15b). In either psalm the waters respond to the power and presence of
God. These waters flow forth (זרמו) from the clouds in 77.18, while
waters likewise flow forth from the rocks in 78.16 (נוזלים) and 78.20
(ויזובו).[8] The waters saw (ראוך) God in 77.19 as he displayed power,
and likewise wonders were shown (הראם) to Israel in 78.11. Thus, the
many parallels between the final strophe of Psalm 77 and the wilderness
wanderings narrated in 78 imply that 77.14-21 are references to the
exodus as well. However, numerous links between 76, with its
eschatological victory, and the final strophe of 77 also show that the old
deliverance under Moses is to be repeated in the future.

Ties between Psalm 77's final strophe and 78 continue by means of
the term שחקים ('clouds') in 77.18 and 78.23.[9] In the musings of Psalm
77, God's voice (קול, vv. 18, 19) in the clouds was apparently a
response to the calls of the individual (קולי, v. 2).[10] A cynical call given
by the people in 78.20cd (הגם לחם יוכל תת, 'Is he also able to give
bread?') also elicits a divine response from the clouds (שחקים, 78.23).
Nevertheless, the nation still did not believe or become obedient even
after the divine provision (v. 32). Once again, the individual in 77 is
portrayed as faithful in contrast to the nation of 78.

As shown thus far, 77.21 has numerous contacts with Psalm 78,
being an appropriate precursor to it. The verb נחה of 77.21 at the
psalm's end is a major theme of 78 (vv. 14, 53, 72), as is the metaphor
of Israel as a flock (צאן, 77.21; 78.52, 70). Guidance by Moses of his
people (עמך) in 77.21 is revealed to have its source in God (78.14, 53,
וינחם), and the new shepherd of that people (עמו) becomes David in
78.71-72. Between 77.21 and 78.52 the parallels are especially obvious:

77.21a – נחית כצאן עמך
78.52-53a – ויסע כצאן עמו...וינחם

However, the guidance by Moses and Aaron announced in 77.21 and
then detailed in Psalm 78 was obviously not effective in producing a

---

8. Repeated zayin (voiced alveolar fricative) connects the references to moving
water.
9. This term is found in the plural only in these two psalms of Book III. Twice
in Ps. 89.7, 38 the singular is used.
10. Again showing how 77.14-21 is a pledge of a future deliverance in response
to the previous lament of 77.2-13. Through musings on past salvation, the speaker
is seeing a picture of the same in the future.

faithful flock. David takes over this flock (צאן, 78.70b), or nation (עמו, 78.71b) finally, when God arises to deliver his people (78.65-72). His hands (כפיו, 78.72) replace those of Moses and Aaron (ביד, 77.21), all of which were only instruments of the divine hand (ידו, 78.42). The obvious failure of the flock under Moses, as Psalm 78 amply shows, leads to the choice of David. In Psalm 79 the flock appears once again (עמך וצאן, v. 13), but this time with a different attitude. They promise to repeat from generation to generation what past generations had neglected to do and claim to be the flock (מרעיתך, 79.13; וירעם, 78.72) under faithful David, and God's own inheritance (בנחלתך, 79.1; נחלתו, 78.71). If Psalm 78 is the divine answer to complaints in Psalm 77, then 79 voices the people's response to 78. Faithful David at the end of 78 contrasts with the just-described faithless nation, but Psalm 79 voices the plea of a nation that identifies with David.

As for the rhetorical qualities and structure of Psalm 78 itself, inclusio is evident at the beginning and end of this lengthy poem, confirming its unity as presently shaped. The people addressed in v. 1 (עמי) appear throughout the poem (vv. 20, 37, 52, 62), and then finally in the penultimate v. 71 (עמו). That same nation is called by the pair of proper names with preposition beth (ביעקב...בישראל) in vv. 5 and 71. Found also at either end with a singular masculine pronominal suffix is 'heart' (לבבו, לבו, vv. 8, 72), and with the plural suffix twice more in the body of the psalm (vv. 18, 37). The mouth of the faithful speaker in vv. 1, 2 (פי) sets up a correspondence with the heart of the faithful David at the psalm's end (לבבו, v. 72). If beginning and end portray faithfulness, the exact center (vv. 36-37) of the entire psalm reveals the opposite character, but in the same sequence; unfaithful mouths, unfaithful hearts:

פי – faithful (vv. 1-2)

פיהם – unfaithful (v. 36)
לבם – unfaithful (v. 37)

לבבו – faithful (v. 72)

As seen often since Psalm 73, a stark contrast becomes evident between the faithful Davidide and the unrighteous nation.

The strophic division of the psalm has been accurately portrayed by the editor of *BHS*. Seven strophes are divided at vv. 9, 17, 32, 40, 56 and 65. Strophe II opens in vv. 9-11 with the first concrete example of sin like that of the fathers as described in strophe I. In spite of numerous warnings about teaching sons (בנים, vv. 4, 5, 6) in the first strophe, so they would not be like their fathers (v. 8), the sons (בני, v. 9) of Ephraim are the unfaithful ones named at the outset of strophe II. In v. 11 we read that these sons of Ephraim forgot (וישכחו) his works, in direct disobedience to the injunction of v. 7a (ולא ישכחו) of the first strophe. In fact, those works are named in v. 11 by two plural nouns (ונפלאותיו עלילותיו) practically identical to those found in v. 4 (ונפלאותיו) and v. 7 (מעללי־אל). Rejection of his Torah by Ephraim in v. 10b (בתורתו) directly defied another command of the opening strophe in vv. 1 (האזינה...תורתי) and 5 (ותורה...אשר צוה). The strictures in strophe I resemble formally the summary statements of sin beginning each new strophe across the psalm except for the last, where Adonay intervenes to reverse a continual trend. In other words, the prohibitions of strophe I are disobeyed 'to the letter', according to the opening verses of each successive strophe.

Verse 17 opens the third strophe and again refers directly back to strophe I. The nation was not to be rebellious (מרה, v. 8b) like their fathers, but committed that very sin (למרות, v. 17b). At the opening of the fourth strophe (vv. 32-39) we read that they did not believe (לא־האמינו, v. 32), directly imitating their faithless fathers (לא־נאמנה, v. 8d). The object of their unbelief was the miraculous deeds (בנפלאותיו), in direct violation again of strophe I (ונפלאותיו, v. 4). Verse 32 opens this strophe IV by repeating similar terminology given at the outset of strophe III. If v. 17 declared that they continued to sin against God (עוד לחטא־לו), nothing had changed in 32 (הטאו־עוד).[11] The sins of the fathers described in vv. 7-8 of strophe I as a warning were repeated over and over again. For this reason, the fifth strophe opens with evident exasperation, 'How often they rebelled against him...!' (כמה ימרוהו, v. 40), again using a verb from strophe I's final v. 8.[12] Strophe V's initial description of disobedience is continued to v. 42, where the people did not remember (לא זכרו) his hand, a direct violation of the command not to forget (ולא ישכחו) in v. 7. The continual nature of the rebellion and unbelief is repeated at each of these strophe–initial verses, either by stating it directly (עוד, vv. 17, 32) or by repetition of the same

11. These forms עוד and יסף placed at strophe–initial junctures were shown previously to provide answers to the questions posed in Ps. 77.9-10.

12. Strophes III, IV, V and VI all open their descriptions of disobedience making direct reference to v. 8 at the conclusion of strophe I. Strophe II by its third verse (11) has quoted v. 7 directly, so that each strophe from II to VI has made reference to either v. 7 or 8.

verb (מרה, vv. 40, 56). In this manner the central theme of the psalm is reiterated at important junctures.

In both vv. 17 and 40 the verb מרה ('to rebel') is followed in vv. 18 and 41 by נסה ('to test'). These two verbal roots come together in v. 56 to open the penultimate sixth strophe (וינסו וימרו). Again, the rebellion of the fathers in v. 8 (מרה) is repeated, as is the testing seen in previous strophes. In another direct violation of strophe I, the testimony (עדות) set up in v. 4 is not kept in v. 56 (עדותיו). For a fifth time, the sins of the fathers are repeated, using the same terminology used to describe that generation in v. 8.

An indirect reference is made to Ephraim in v. 57, before the more explicit mention in v. 67 and even v. 60. Ephraim's disloyalty in v. 9, where the tribe is named directly, is compared to archers who turn back at the time of battle. Verse 57 in the penultimate sixth strophe compares the sin of the nation in a general manner as a treacherous bow which 'turns aside'.[13] When these two descriptions are compared in the original it becomes clear that Ephraim is also the subject of the second:

$$\text{v. 9 – רומי־קשת הפכו}$$
$$\text{v. 57 – נהפכו כקשת רמיה}$$

The sheer length of this psalm (72 verses) contributes further to the feeling of continual disobedience. Not only is sin described by the usual terminology (רמי, בגד, סוג, סרר, מרי, חטא), but the negative particle is used repeatedly to describe the omission of those positive acts required of the nation, as in לא האמינו or לא שמרו (vv. 10, 22, 30, 32, 37, 42, 56). This cycle is finally put to an end in v. 65, where the Lord intervenes to turn back the enemies and raise up a faithful leader to shepherd the wandering flock.

Along with the individual speaker of Psalm 78 there is heard a community of the faithful, since vv. 3 and 4 speak in the first person plural. That community was heard previously in 75.2 (הודינו, ספרו), and even in the lament of 74.1-11. A community of voices will reappear in the following Ps. 79.13 where they promise to pass on the praises of their God from generation to generation, using terminology very close to that of 78.4:

$$\text{78.4bc – לדר אחרון מספרים תהלות יהוה}$$
$$\text{79.13c – לדר ודר נספר תהלתך}$$

13. Following BDB, s.v. הפך, p. 245.

The double promise of 79.13 to 'praise' and to 'recount' (נודה...נספר)
of this community identifies them as the same group speaking in 75.2
(הודינו...הודינו...ספרו). Perhaps not coincidentally, the promise to praise
of 79.13 follows the lament of the first twelve verses, just as the praise
of 75.2 follows directly the lament of Psalm 74.

The phrase in 78.4, 'to the following generation' is essentially equivalent to that of 79.13, 'generation to generation', while the 'praises of
Yahweh' in 78.4 parallel 'your praises' in 79.13. In other words, the
last clause of 79.13 reflects the first strophe of 78. At the same time, the
first two clauses of 79.13 repeat vocabulary from the last four verses of
Psalm 78:

78.69-72 – לעולם...צאן...לרעות...עמו...וירעם
79.13a – ואנחנו עמך וצאן מרעיתך...לעולם

Therefore the speakers in 79.13 are claiming to be the faithful of 78.3-4
and of David's flock.

Psalm 78.65 opens the final strophe (VII) of the lengthy poem by
responding not only to the defeats of previous strophes but to the
previous psalm as well. Here is found the only instance of the epithet
אדני ('Lord') in all of Psalm 78, following the twofold use in Psalm 77
(vv. 3, 8). The speaker asks in 77.8 if the Lord will be angry forever,
since there appears to be no answer. When he arises to do war in 78.65
it is an answer to that complaint of the previous psalm.[14] In the case of
Psalm 78, any response on God's part is only out of compassion in light
of the continual rebellion shown by Israel.

Psalm 77.8 asked Adonay if his anger would endure forever
(הלעולמים), and again the final strophe of Psalm 78 provides an answer.
Zion will be established forever (לעולם, 78.69). The city may appear to
have been forgotten, given its present desolation (74.2), but the Zion
built by God is eternal according to 78.69 (cf. Ps. 87.1, 5). It is built as
'heights' (רמים) according to v. 69, another way of referring to the
enduring heavens where God dwells (Ps. 18.17; 93.4; 102.20).[15] Psalm
76.3 had already named heavenly Zion/Salem as the divine abode.

Parallel to the idea of permanence implied in v. 69a is the same idea
expressed more explicitly in 69b (לעולם). In contrast to the house at
Shiloh which was rejected (v. 60), the abode of Zion will not be cast

14. This same divine epithet אדני is used in the appeal of Ps. 79.12 to judge surrounding enemies.

15. See Hakham, *Sefer tehillim*, p. 60 (ס).

down and is firmly established as the earth. It is described more fully in Psalm 87 of this same Book III as having its foundation (יְסוּדָתוֹ, 87.1. cf. 78.69b, יִסַּד), in the mountains (בְּהַרְרֵי, 87.1; cf. הַר, 78.68) of holiness (קֹדֶשׁ, 87.1; cf. מִקְדָּשׁ, 78.69). Furthermore, God's love for this same city is expressed in 78.67 (אהב) as it is in 87.2 (אהב). At the canonical level, eschatological heavenly Zion of Psalm 78 is clearly identical to the city of 87, and of the previous 76. Again, in Ps. 84.8 the Zion of divine abode appears (אֶל אֱלֹהִים בְּצִיּוֹן), and assures the reader that the ruins of 74.2-8 are not eternal.

Psalm 78 has responded to 77's lament concerning continual divine anger by pointing out that Israel's rebellion was continual as well. Nonetheless, hope is kept alive by the promise in 78.65-72 that the Davidic covenant is not forgotten. A heavenly, eternal and divinely constructed Zion along with a Davidic shepherd are assured by the speaker. Such a hope is brought back to the rude reality of the present in the lament of Psalm 79, which opens with another description of ruined and desecrated Jerusalem similar to Psalm 74. The chasm between the dismal present (Psalm 79) and the promised future (Ps. 78.65-72) can only prompt the same question as before, 'How long?' (79.5).

Chapter 7

PSALM 79

The string of Asaphite psalms continues here in 79, as it will up to 83, and this name provides the only link with Psalm 78. Since both 79 and 80 are so much alike as laments over the present situation of the nation (cf. 79.5, 10 with 80.5, 13), the use of the genre designation מזמור ('psalm') appears to bind them as a pair and separate them generically from the surrounding Psalms 81 and 78. On the other hand, the distribution of מזמור across Book III in its entirety provides unity beyond any other superscriptional element, never being absent in two successive psalms. At the borders of Book III there is a conspicuous absence of this term (Psalms 68–72, 89–91),[1] as the following demonstrates:

מזמור	–	Psalm 67
———	–	Psalm 68
———	–	Psalm 69
———	–	Psalm 70
———	–	Psalm 71
———	–	Psalm 72
מזמור	–	Psalm 73 (Book III begins)
———	–	Psalm 74
מזמור	–	Psalm 75
מזמור	–	Psalm 76
מזמור	–	Psalm 77
———	–	Psalm 78
מזמור	–	Psalm 79
מזמור	–	Psalm 80
———	–	Psalm 81
מזמור	–	Psalm 82
מזמור	–	Psalm 83
מזמור	–	Psalm 84

1. See Wilson, *The Editing*, pp. 163-67, for the role played by מזמור in the grouping of psalms. The use of this term in Book III confirms his conclusions.

מזמור	– Psalm 85
——	– Psalm 86
מזמור	– Psalm 87
מזמור	– Psalm 88
——	– Psalm 89 (Book III ends)
——	– Psalm 90
——	– Psalm 91
מזמור	– Psalm 92

Clearly the genre designation מזמור functions to bind Book III closely together, and is left out at the transition from the previous Book II and to the following Book IV. The continuous sequence of four from Psalms 82–85 serves to bridge the discontinuity created by the change from Asaphite Psalm 83 to Qorahite Psalm 84. As will be seen later, there are further superscriptional elements used to smooth over this authorial change.

The psalm itself can be divided into two strophes, the first (vv. 1-5) lamenting the reproach suffered at the hands of the nations, including the temple, Jerusalem and her inhabitants, while strophe II (vv. 6-13) decries the reproach of God's name by these same surrounding nations. Requests for divine intervention through repeated precative forms across strophe II (vv. 6-12) are based on the situation described in strophe I. Strophe I begins with reference to the nations (v. 1, גוים), that have made Israel food to be consumed (v. 2, מאכל), while strophe II opens with a request that divine anger be poured out on those same nations (v. 6, הגוים) that have consumed Jacob (v. 7, אכל). In the second strophe, a repentant nation is concerned with reproach of Yahweh's name (vv. 6, 9, שמך).

Each strophe closes with verses (5, 13) that are closely related formally and thematically to previous psalms. This is true of v. 8 as well. No forms common to the poem such as גוים ('nations', vv. 1, 6, 10 twice), שמך ('your name', vv. 6, 9 twice) or any others are found in vv. 8 and 13.[2] In other words, a rhetorical analysis of Psalm 79 reveals that vv. 5, 8 and 13 are distinct to the poem. As such they are possibly additions by the canonical redactor of Book III or the Psalter as a whole. Common to both vv. 5 and 13 are the semantically related forms לנצח and לעולם, seen before either in the lament of Psalm 77 (vv. 8, 9), or

---

2.   Even the comon particle -כ found in vv. 3 and 11 is not utilized, but rather the lengthened form כמו (v. 5). The latter is repeated twice in the previous psalm (78.13, 69).

Psalm 74 (vv. 1, 3, 10, 19). Furthermore, all three verses 5, 8 and 13 answer directly to statements made in the previous Psalm 78, as will be seen shortly.

In spite of the uniqueness of vocabulary in 79.5, 13 (and v. 8) to the psalm itself, the verses are consistent with the message of the poem and the immediate context in which they are found. Verse 5 appropriately asks how long the desolation of vv. 1-4 will endure. Verse 8 is placed in the midst of requests for salvation (vv. 6-12) and contains good reasons for Yahweh to intervene. Past sins are confessed and known divine mercy is requested. Verse 13 quotes the self-confessed faithful remnant of the nation, promising praise once the previous requests of vv. 6-12 are granted.

At the beginning and end of this psalm, the nation identifies itself quite explicitly with its god (vv. 1, בנחלתך;[3] 13, מרעיתך...עמך). Furthermore, the nations have entered (v. 1, באו) into his inheritance, and near the conclusion request is made that the cry of the imprisoned ones be allowed to enter (v. 11, תבוא) before him. References to the nations (גוים) dominate this complaint psalm (vv. 1, 6, 10 twice). At the beginning of the psalm they have shed the blood of God's servants (שפכו דם...עבדיך, vv. 2-3) and near the end vengeance is asked for that same blood (דם עבדיך השפוך, v. 10). At the outset Israel complains that it has become shameful to its neighbors (חרפה לשכנינו, v. 4), and then prays at the end that shame be returned upon those same neighbors (לשכנינו...חרפתם, v. 12). Consequently, there exists a unity across this entire psalm. However, there is also consistency between its content and that of the preceding psalm.

Psalm 78 presented David as liberator of the nation and an eternal temple was to be built in Zion (vv. 65-72). The situation in Psalm 79 seems to be the opposite of that promised. David was brought in (הביאו, 78.71) to shepherd the inheritance (נחלתו, 78.71), but immediately following in 79.1 Israel complains that the gentile nations have invaded (באו) that same inheritance (בנחלתך). Israel is designated by the word pair עם...נחלה in 78.71, and this word pair is divided up across Psalm 79 as an inclusio between vv. 1 (נחלתך) and 13 (עמך). In addition, the promise to recount God's praise (נספר תהלתך) in 79.13 makes clear that this confessing nation identifies with David's flock and not the disobedient nation described in Psalm 78.8-64. They join themselves to the

---

3. 'Your inheritance' read in light of the immediately preceding Ps. 78.71 is a reference to the nation.

faithful ones of 78.3, 4, a community that recounts (מספרים סַפְּרוּ) the praises (תהלות) of Yahweh. Such a pledge in 79.13 to be faithful not only identifies them with the flock of David in 78 but also the individual in Psalm 73 who stood out from the wayward nation:

73.28 – וַאֲנִי...לְסַפֵּר כָּל־מַלְאֲכוֹתֶיךָ
79.13 – וַאֲנַחְנוּ...נְסַפֵּר תְּהִלָּתֶךָ

A major theme of Psalm 79 can be discerned by the fourfold repetition of גּוֹיִם across the poem (vv. 1, 6, 10 twice).[4] These nations have gained the upper hand over Israel and have devastated the divine inheritance, temple, capital (all in v. 1) and servants (vv. 2-3). This represents a complete reversal of the victory over the nations in the conclusion of the preceding 78. A defiled temple in 79.1b (הֵיכַל קָדְשֶׁךָ) contrasts with the temple which was to be built like the heights forever in 78.69 (מִקְדָּשׁוֹ). If Mount Zion (הַר צִיּוֹן, 78.68) was so loved, how could its city (יְרוּשָׁלַםִ, 79.1) be in ruins? If Israel his inheritance (נַחֲלָתוֹ, 78.71) was to be led by David, how could that same inheritance (בְּנַחֲלָתֶךָ, 79.1) be violated by the nations? The promise of 78.65 was to drive back the enemy into everlasting shame (חֶרְפַּת עוֹלָם נָתַן לָמוֹ) and raise up God's servant as shepherd over the nation (עַבְדּוֹ, 78.70). Instead, the bodies of his servants are food for the fowl of heaven (נָתְנוּ...עֲבָדֶיךָ, 79.2), while the nation is suffering shame from its neighbors (חֶרְפָּה, 79.4). In the present juxtaposition of 78 and 79, the opening words of the latter are a direct response to the final strophe of the former.

The complaints of Psalm 79 respond as well to 78 as a whole. Provision of food in the desert, including the flesh of fowl (עוֹף), came from heaven (שָׁמַיִם), and was consumed (וַיֹּאכְלוּ) by the nation, as recounted in 78.26, 27, 29. Now, in a complete reversal, it is the nation itself that has become food for the fowl of the heavens (מַאֲכָל לְעוֹף הַשָּׁמָיִם, 79.2b). In 78.50 the Egyptians had their lives and livestock (חַיָּתָם) turned over to the plague, and now the flesh of God's own people has been given to the beasts of the earth in 79.2c (לְחַיְתוֹ). If Egypt's rivers had been turned into blood (וַיַּהֲפֹךְ לְדָם יְאֹרֵיהֶם) in 78.44, the blood of God's own people has been poured out like water in 79.3 (שָׁפְכוּ דָמָם כַּמַּיִם). Note the consonance between שָׁפַךְ and הָפַךְ strengthening the contrast.

Given these opposing circumstances, it is no coincidence that in 79.5 the poet asks how long God's anger will burn against Israel. This question of time is equivalent to those raised in the interrogatives of 77.8-

---

4.   Following *qere* in v. 10c.

10. These latter three have already been shown to parallel 74.1, 10 closely. The interrogative form used here in 79.5, 'How long?' (עד־מה) repeats exactly the expression of 74.9b (עד־מה), and is close to עד־מתי of 74.10a.

The anger of Yahweh in this same 79.5 (תאנף) has been seen before. The noun form (אף) appeared in 74.1 as part of another interrogative sentence, and so the two interrogatives of Psalm 74 (vv. 1, 9-10) are combined in 79.5b. As part of the same question in 74.1 is the temporal phrase לנצח, also repeated in 79.5b. The metaphor of anger as fire in 74.1 continues here in 79.5 (and then in 80.5 and 89.47). In 76.8b, another interrogative clause, God's anger was described (אף), as it was in 77.10b (אף), likewise an interrogative. Throughout Psalm 78, the anger of Yahweh (אף/אפ) was revealed against Israel (vv. 21, 31) and Egypt (vv. 49, 50). The sad desolation of Israel across this book is due to divine anger. Since its duration is unknown, the question is asked over and over again. The linking of such interrogatives across the book becomes unquestionable when 79.5, 6 is compared with 89.47:

79.5-6a – עד־מה יהוה תאנף לנצח תבער כמו־אש קנאתך:...חמתך
89.47[5] – עד־מה יהוה תסתר לנצח תבער כמו־אש חמתך

This question and others like it are never fully answered in Book III. In 75.3, as seen previously, it was confirmed that a time had been chosen to judge in righteousness, but without specificity.

When the poet uses the lengthened poetic preposition כמו in 79.5, it recalls the twofold use of the same in Psalm 78 (vv. 13, 69), recounting miracles done on behalf of the nation, either in parting the waters of the sea or building a temple. The full phrase of 79.5b (כמו־אש) repeats terminology from two successive verses (78.13, 14) that recount the

---

5. Note that the term utilized for 'anger' in 79.5 (קנאתך) does not match that used in 89.47 (חמתך), so that the latter can be used in 79.6 (חמתך). Furthermore, the form חמתך in 89.47 provides a direct link to the same used in 88.8. The variation between תאנף of 79.5 and תסתר of 89.47 can also be explained at the canonical level. In 79.5, תאנף continues reference to the same root of the previous 78.21, 31, 38, 49, 50; 79.10; 74.1. The combination of חמת (79.6) and אנף (79.5) together creates a direct link to 78.38, as will be seen. As for תסתר of 89.47, it creates another of many direct links back to 88 (v. 15, תסתיר). The combination of two interrogatives as here in 79.5, 10, one beginning with למה and the other with עד מה, is found in 74.1, 9-10 and 80.5, 13. The linking of 88.15 (למה) and 89.47 (עד מה) by means of the root סתר, accomplishes between 88 and 89 what is found three times previously within single psalms.

provision for Israel by means of the two corresponding elements, water and fire. The two elements are likewise connected in 79.3, 5 by like prepositions:

מַיִם כְּמוֹ־נֵד...בְּאוּר אֵשׁ – 78.13, 14.
כְּמַיִם...כְּמוֹ־אֵשׁ – 79.3, 5

Manipulation of the elements for the provision of Israel in Psalm 78 contrasts with the opposite of Psalm 79, where they are used (figuratively) in the destruction of the nation.

The wrath of Yahweh as expressed by two terms in 79.5a, 6a (תֶּאֱנַף, חֲמָתְךָ), corresponds to the same in 78.38cd (אַפּוֹ, חֲמָתוֹ) of the central strophe IV. Taken in their respective contexts, these parallels represent a contrast between the long-enduring restraint of divine wrath in Psalm 78 and the long-enduring time of its expression in Psalm 79. At the same time, egregious and continual disobedience explains such incessant divine anger.

When the nation in 79.8 requests that God not remember (אַל־תִּזְכָּר) their sins, they are appealing on the basis of a statement made in 78.39. Because God remembered (78.39, וַיִּזְכֹּר) that they were only flesh, he did not judge them immediately, and thus honored their remembrance in 78.35 (וַיִּזְכְּרוּ). Their memory turned out to be short-lived, for in 78.42 they forgot (לֹא זָכְרוּ) the mighty works in Egypt. Now in 79.8 they ask that their iniquity (עֲוֹנֹת) be forgotten. This request is based on the statement of 78.38a (between the 'remembrance' of vv. 35 and 39) that God covers iniquity (כַּפֶּר עָוֹן). The latter verb of 78.38a is repeated in the same series of requests for forgiveness of Psalm 79 (v.9c, וְכַפֶּר) in precative mood. A further parallel between these two series of verses (79.8-9 and 78.38-39) is found in the description of God as merciful in 78.38a (רַחוּם) and the request that he demonstrate his mercies (רַחֲמֶיךָ) in 79.8b. Consequently, repeated appeal is made by 79.8-9 to strophe IV at the heart of Psalm 78 (vv. 32-39), where God's merciful character is affirmed in the midst of rebellion.

Forgiveness and mercy are requested in 79.8ab because of the extremely (מְאֹד) low condition of the nation in v. 8c. This was not the nation's condition in the desert when God sent food in abundance, so that they were well (מְאֹד, 78.29) satisfied. Rather, it was a result of the utter (מְאֹד, 78.59) rejection of the nation by its god. Once again, 79.8 is found to resonate with and respond to Psalm 78.

Psalm 79.9 is a call for help from the God of their salvation (יִשְׁעֵנוּ), a confidence not present in the desert generation (בִּישׁוּעָתוֹ, 78.22). In

v. 9b there is concern for the glory of God's name (שמך), a concern seen throughout Psalm 74 (vv. 7, 10, 18, 21), especially its reproach by the enemy. Such zeal for the name is ultimately grounded in the promise that it would increase and endure universally, as promised in Ps. 72.17, 19, during the eschatological reign of peace. In fact, the name is forever glorious in 72.19 (שם כבודו לעולם), the same concern of the speakers in 79.9 (כבוד־שמך). The same name is important to the righteous in 75.2, and renowned in 76.2 within Israel. Consequently, when Israel is solicitous in 79.6d, 9ab for the divine name among the nations (along with wrath requested on those who do not know it, 79.6), they are simply requesting fulfillment of Psalm 72's promises.

It is for the sake of that name that Israel requests again the covering (כפר, 79.9b) of sins, based on 78.38 (יכפר). The noun designating these sins (חטאתינו, 79.9b), was seen twice at important summations in the previous psalm (78.17, 32). Since these latter two verses are important in explaining the continuing desolation, it is appropriate for the nation to ask that these sins be covered in 79.9b. Again, Psalm 79 appeals to the compassion of God, detailed in the central strophe IV (vv. 32-39) of Psalm 78.

In 79.10, the similarities to Psalm 74 and the following Psalm 80 are made clear. The first strophe of Psalm 74 began and ended with two interrogative clauses introduced by the particle למה ('Why?', vv. 1, 12). Between them in 74.9-10 were two more nearly identical interrogative constructions, עד־מה, עד־מתי ('How long?'). Now in Psalm 79 the first interrogative of v. 5 opens with עד־מה and the second in v. 10 with למה. The same pattern repeats itself in the following Psalm 80 with עד־מתי in v. 5 and למה in v. 13. In addition, all three of these psalms (74, 79, 80) are communal laments. They repeat the dominant concern of Book III: Why and how long will the present desolation endure?

Requests continue in v. 11, but this time for a deliverance of the prisoner by God's powerful arm (כגדל זרועך), terminology used in the description of the conquest of Exod. 15.16 (בגדל זרועך). It also resembles closely the vocabulary of two clauses, Ps. 77.14 and 16, which display consonance (גאלת בזרוע, אל גדול), likewise found in a context filled with allusions to Exodus 15. As a result, the request in 79.11 is essentially one for a new deliverance on a par with the previous from Egypt.

Appeals continue in 79.12, asking for the reproach of the enemy (חרפתם) to be turned back upon them. The promise previously given in

Ps. 78.66b was of eternal reproach (חרפה) upon Adonay's enemies. Repeated correlation of Psalm 78's strophe VII (vv. 65-72) and 79.12, continues with the common use of the divine epithet already mentioned (אדני). It is Adonay who arises and brings about the deliverance of 78.65, and to him the prayer of 79.12 is directed. It can be no coincidence that the same divine epithet and noun from consecutive vv. 65, 66 of Psalm 78 are repeated in the single phrase of 79.12b:

78.65 – אדני...חרפת
79.12 – חרפתם אשר חרפוך אדני

The prayers of 79 essentially ask for accomplishment of the deliverance described at the end of 78. This is further confirmed by the close relation between 79.13 and strophe VII of 78. The speakers of v. 13 are claiming to be David's flock, who promise to faithfully praise and recount God's praises unto every generation. They identify themselves as, 'your people, the flock of your pasture' (עמך וצאן מרעיתך, 79.13a). This vocabulary repeats that found in the last three verses of 78. David is taken from the flock (צאן, v. 70) to pasture (לרעות, v. 71) his people (עמו, v. 71), a task he does (וירעם, v. 72) with integrity of heart. An expectation is thus created in 78 to be led to security, just as the nation of old in the wilderness, described in 78.52 (כצאן עמו). However, the flock has been consumed and its pastures destroyed, as 79.7 declares, creating another contrast with Psalm 78. Furthermore, Jacob is portrayed as abiding in a ruined pasture (יעקב ואת־נוהו, 79.7b), recalling 78's conclusion in a similar pastoral context (לרעות ביעקב, 78.71). If God can provide a Davidic shepherd over Jacob who will lead them faithfully, why are Jacob and his place of pasture now destroyed?

These same speakers of 79.13 continue their references to the last strophe of Psalm 78. As Adonay's flock they promise to praise him forever (לעולם), based on the fact that they were promised in Zion an eternal temple (מקדשו...לעולם, 78.69). They then identify with the speakers of 78.3-4. From generation to generation they promise to recount praises, in imitation of, and obedience to, the speakers of strophe I in the previous psalm:

78.4 – לדור...מספרים תהלות
78.6 – דור...ויספרו
79.13c – לדר ודר נספר תהלתך

The noun 'generation', repeated in 78.4, 6 is qualified by the same adjective 'next' in both cases (דור אחרון), which is semantically close

to לדר ודר ('from generation to generation') of 79.13. The speakers of
79.13 insist that they are not as the generation of the fathers described
in the intervening strophes of Psalm 78 (II to VI). They rather identify
with those faithful guardians of the tradition in 78.1-8 and request that
the promises of deliverance as described in 78.65-72 be fulfilled. The
final verse (13) of Psalm 79 takes elements from the beginning and end
of the previous psalm in response to it.

It is remarkable that the vocabulary of 79.13 contains no parallels
with the previous twelve verses of the same psalm. The same can be
said about v. 8 (except for the ubiquitous particle כי), and has been
noted for v. 5.[6] All three are candidates for the editorial hand responsible for the Psalter's final shape. Both vv. 8 and 13 are filled with verbal
parallels to the immediately previous Psalm 78. Verse 8 asks for forgiveness on behalf of the nation for past offences (עונת ראשנים), as
narrated through the middle bulk of Psalm 78 (vv. 9-64; cf. עון in 78.38,
at the very center of the psalm), and then v. 13 identifies with those
faithful who belong to David's flock at the two extremes (78.1-8 and
65-72). Consequently, the whole of Psalm 78 is summed up in the
canonical additions of 79.8 and 13. At the same time they are added
with an eye to 79's message as well. Psalm 79.8, which requests forgiveness for the offences of past generations, provides justification for
divine salvation in the subsequent vv. 9-12. Once Yahweh's deliverance has been accomplished as requested in vv. 9-12, the self-confessed
faithful nation promises to retell his praises (79.13).

The canonical dialogue continued in Psalm 79 includes themes from
psalms before 78 as well. Both the terms 'Jerusalem' and 'environs/
neighbors' (סביבות ירושלם) of v. 3b create parallels to Psalm 76. Psalms
75 and 76 assured the lamenting poet of 74 that eventually God would
vindicate his reproached name with righteous judgment and peace.
According to 76.2-3, God's name (שמו) is great in Israel and Judah, and
he dwells in Salem (שלם) where the instruments of war are destroyed.
To Yahweh in Salem will all those surrounding kings (סביביו, 76.12)
bring offerings. Nothing could be more different to this situation
described in Psalm 76 as the one narrated in 79, where Jerusalem/
Salem's (ירושלם) inhabitants are slain, and God's name (שמך, 79.6, 9,
10) is disgraced. What surround Jerusalem are not tribute-laden kings
(סביביו, 76.12) but corpses of the slain (סביבות, 79.3). Based on the

---

6. Verse 5 was shown above to resonate closely with the following Ps. 89 and
the previous Pss. 74, 77.

promises of Psalm 76 (which answer complaints in Psalm 74 similar to 79), the speakers of 79 can legitimately question the permanence of defeat, disgrace and desolation. Even the preceding 78 promised the eternal choice of Zion in Judah that God loves (78.68), and establishment there of his temple forever (78.69). How can this same city and temple continue in ruins (79.1) in the face of such promises?

If previous promises are recalled in Psalm 79, so are previous complaints. Except for the Tetragrammaton, every member of v. 5a is repeated in the interrogatives of Ps. 74.1, 9-10:

$$
\begin{array}{ll}
79.5a - & \text{עד־מה יהוה תאנף לנצח} \\
74.1 - & \text{לנצח...אפך} \\
74.9\text{-}10 - & \text{עד־מה: עד־מתי...לנצח}
\end{array}
$$

The promised answer to Psalm 74's questions in Psalms 75–76 has not materialized as yet, and so the questioning continues, as it will until the end of Book III.[7]

Two parallel imperatives of 79.9ab recall a promise made in Ps. 72.12 concerning the kingdom of peace and justice. Its king was to deliver (יציל) the poor, the needy and those without help (עזר). When the plea for help and deliverance is made in 79.9 (עזרנו...והצילנו), it is nothing less than a request for the implementation of conditions assured in 72. Furthermore, in 72.11 it is predicted that all kings (מלכים) and nations (גוים) would bow down to him. This prediction is further explained in 72.17 as a time when his name (שמו) would eternally endure blessed by all nations (גוים). The speakers of 79.6 request that God pour out his wrath upon the nations (הגוים) and the kingdoms (ממלכות) who do not call on God's name (בשמך). Their petition is well founded, since this is precisely what 72 had promised.

Links forward to Psalm 80 are also prominent in 79. To the reproach of 79.4a (חרפה לשכנינו) is added in 4b two more descriptions of the nation's debasement (לעג וקלס). The identical root לעג and prepositional phrase לשכנינו are repeated in Ps. 80.7, demonstrating that the lamented and embarrassing situation continues. Another clear link with Psalm 80 occurs in 79.6, where the speakers seek judgment on the nations which do not call on God's name. In 80.19, the presumably identical community promises to practice precisely what their enemies have not:

---

7.   As noted above, Ps. 89.47 is remarkably similar to v. 5.

79.6b – בשמך לא קראו
80.19b – ובשמך נקרא

The pastoral theme found in 79.13 (צאן מרעיתך, 'flock of your pasture') continues at the outset of 80, where the shepherd of the flock (רעה...כצאן, v. 1a) is addressed directly. David is the shepherd portrayed in 78.70-72 (צאן, לרעות, וירעם) and so the two roots צאן and רעה are repeated at strategic points through Psalms 78 (conclusion), 79 (conclusion) and 80 (beginning). The former of these two (צאן) is repeated through four consecutive psalms (77.21; 78.52, 70; 79.13; 80.2). Israel as a flock strays under the shepherds Moses and Aaron (77–78), but seeks reconciliation and restoration (79–80). The faithful shepherd David and his flock of 78.1-8 and 70–72 are those with whom the petitioning community identifies.

Chapter 8

PSALM 80

The use in this superscription of למנצח resembles that of Psalm 75. The closely related form לנצח was found in the body of Psalm 74 three times preceding the following superscription of 75. The appearance of לנצח in 79.5 anticipates the repetition of למנצח in 80.1. Furthermore, the preceding interrogatives of both Psalms 74 and 79 (containing the form לנצח) are introduced by identical or nearly identical particles:

$$
\begin{array}{ll}
74.9\text{-}10 & - \quad \text{עד־מה עד־מתי...לנצח} \\
75.1 & - \quad \text{למנצח} \\
79.5 & - \quad \text{עד־מה...לנצח} \\
80.1 & - \quad \text{למנצח}
\end{array}
$$

Elements in the superscription of Psalm 80 do not appear to have parallels within the psalm itself. Rather, most point to previous and following psalms, as is the case with עדות ('testimony'). The latter is found twice in 78 (vv. 5, 56), and then in the following 81.6. As for מזמור, the same root appears in 81.3 (זמרה), but not in 81's superscription. Both Psalms 79–80 contain the contiguous forms מזמור and לאסף, which do not appear together in 78 or 81 on either end of this pair. As a result, both 79 and 80 acquire special closeness at the level of superscription. At the level of content and genre, both voice the laments of a faithful community. For example, both Pss. 79.5 and 80.5 are interrogatives asking 'How long?' (עד מתי/עד מה), followed later by another opening with 'Why?' (למה, 79.10; 80.13).[1] The enigmatic phrase אל־ששנים resembles previous superscriptions in the Psalter (45.1; 60.1; 69.1), but no connections within the environment of Book III are apparent.

Verse 2a also contains elements that resonate back to Ps. 74.1b.

---

1. This twofold pattern of interrogatives repeats that seen in 74.9-11, as noted previously.

There the psalmist wondered how long God's wrath would continue against the flock of his pasture (בצאן מרעיתך), and now the poet addresses directly the shepherd of the same flock (רעה...כצאן). The same verbal root and noun were seen at 78.52 (צאן), 78.70-72 (צאן לרעות...וירעם), and in 79.13 (וצאן מרעיתך), the latter identical to 74.1b. As a result, when 80.2a opens with רעה and צאן it simply continues the discussion of prior psalms. The nation identifies itself as God's flock in 79.13, and in 80.2 continues in direct address to the divine shepherd. Shepherd imagery continues only through v. 2 and is enough to make evident the link to previous psalms. The progression from Moses and Aaron as shepherds (77.21), to Yahweh (78.52-53) and the eschatological David (78.70-72), extends into Psalm 80. In fact, Ps. 80.2 is a petition (נהג כצאן) for a new redemption and guidance of the flock such as that seen in 78.52 (כצאן...וינהגם).

It was shown in the previous chapter that 79.13 recalls elements from the beginning and end of the previous 78 and now 80.2a repeats the phenomenon. Appeal to the shepherd (רעה) of Israel recalls 78.71-72 (לרעות...וירעם), and the imperative האזינה requesting a hearing recalls the same directed to the people of 78.1 (האזינה). This is further evidence demonstrating the similar functions and forms of Psalms 79 and 80.

The shepherd addressed in 80.2 (רעה) guides the flock of 79.13 (מרעיתך). Indeed, the shepherd of Psalm 79 is Adonay (79.12), but the human instrument used is the eschatological David of 78.71-72 (לרעות...וירעם). Even the faithful community of 79.13, identifying itself as the people and flock of Adonay (עמך וצאן), recognize the David of 78.71-72 as the divinely ordained shepherd (צאן...עמו). A further petition in 80.16, 18 for the son whom God strengthens (אמצת), refers to the Davidic promise, as 89.22 (תאמצנו) will confirm. That twice-mentioned son (בן) of 80.16, 18 is part and parcel of repeated requests for salvation (ונושעה, 80.4, 8, 20; see also v. 3, לישעתה לנו), promised repeatedly in Psalm 72 (ישׁ, vv. 4, 13) through the king's son (לבן־מלך, 72.1).

The salvation so earnestly sought in 80.3b continues the request made in the previous 79.9a:

$$\underline{\text{לנו}}...\underline{\text{עזרנו}}...\underline{\text{ישׁענו}} \quad - \quad 79.8\text{-}9a$$
$$\underline{\text{לישׁעתה}}\ \underline{\text{לנו}} \quad - \quad 80.3b.$$

Both of these confessions are in direct contrast to the description of Israel in 78.22b. There the unfaithful nation did not trust in his salvation

(יְשׁוּעָתוֹ), and the faithful remnant now (Psalms 79–80) seeks to distinguish itself from previous generations.

The two parallel designations given to the nation in 80.2ab are Joseph
and Israel, both rejected in 78.59, 67a, but now pleading for restoration.
Verse 3 requests deliverance for the tribe Ephraim, also rejected (cf.
78.67b). That salvation will be effected through divine might (גְבוּרָתֶךָ,
80.3), recalling the simile of 78.65b where Adonay rises from sleep
as a strong man (כְּגִבּוֹר) to turn back his enemies. As noted above,
the request of 80.3 is for a restoration and fulfilment of the Davidic
covenant promised in Psalm 72 and further described in the last strophe
of 78.[2]

Verse 4 begins a threefold repetition (vv. 4, 8, 20) of the same refrain
across Psalm 80, asking God to return them (or himself in v. 15), utilizing the root שׁוּב, as in a previous request of 79.12a (הָשֵׁב). Both requests
are two sides of the same coin, that is, return reproach on our neighbors
and return us to favor. The same neighbors of Ps. 79.4, 12 are mentioned again in 80.7, reinforcing the close linkage:

$$\text{79.12} - \text{וְהָשֵׁב לִשְׁכֵנֵינוּ}$$
$$\text{80.7-8.} - \text{לִשְׁכֵנֵינוּ...הֲשִׁיבֵנוּ}$$

These neighbors mentioned in each psalm also engage in 'derision'
against the faithful community. The latter is expressed by the noun
form in 79.4 and the verb in 80.7:

$$\text{79.4} - \text{לִשְׁכֵנֵינוּ לַעַג}$$
$$\text{80.7} - \text{לִשְׁכֵנֵינוּ...יִלְעֲגוּ}$$

Consequently, the embarrassing situation described in 79 continues in
the subsequent 80. Both express the afflicted community's plea to God,
but 79 emphasizes vengeance on the enemies (vv. 6, 12), while 80
focuses on Israel's salvation (vv. 3, 4, 8, 15, 20). Promises by the community (first person plural forms) to either utter and recount praise
(79.13) or call on God's name (80.19) conclude each psalm.

Two requests in 79.11, 12 plead that the cry of the prisoner come
before (לְפָנֶיךָ, v. 11) God and that he return (וְהָשֵׁב, v. 12) reproach on
the enemy. The repeated refrain of Psalm 80 (vv. 4, 8, 20) takes both of
these elements and combines them into one bicolon (הֲשִׁיבֵנוּ...פָּנֶיךָ).
Elements of 79.11 are also repeated in the single colon of 80.3a, both of

---

2.   The use of the same root גבר in 89.14, 20, confirms this hope in a restoration
of the Davidic kingdom.

which seek help for Israel. In 79.11a the request is for a cry to come
before God and in 80.3a that God reveal himself *before* the nation.
Relief is requested for the 'sons of death' in 79.11b, but for the 'son of
the right hand' (Benjamin) in 80.3a:

79.11ab – לְפָנֶיךָ...בְּנֵי תְמוּתָה
80.3a – לִפְנֵי...וּבִנְיָמִן

It is Yahweh in 80.5a who is addressed with the question of 'How
long?' (עַד־מָתַי), as in 79.5 where essentially the same divine name and
interrogative (עַד־מָה) were seen. Both psalms then follow several verses
later with a second interrogative identically introduced with the particle
לָמָה (79.10; 80.13). The content of each is essentially the same: 'How
long will God's anger endure against his people?' and 'Why does he
allow the present desolation?' Consequently, both Psalms 80 and 79
continue the series of temporal interrogatives seen first in 74, and which
will continue to the end of Book III. The final phrase of v. 5 ('How long
will you fume against the prayer of your people?') could be a title for
either Psalms 79 or 80. Both are prayers of the community which feels
abandoned. Note as well that the verbal form describing divine anger
(עָשַׁנְתָ) in 80.5 recalls the use of the same root in the interrogative of
74.1 (יֶעְשַׁן). This community seeks to identify itself as God's people in
either psalm (עַמְךָ, 79.13; 80.5).

The twice-mentioned tears of 80.6 rightly characterize the mood of
the present psalm, as they do the previous Psalm 79. However, the
metaphor of being fed the bread and drink of tears is a direct contrast to
the bread and water supplied to the nation in 78.15, 24-25, 29-30. The
identical noun (לֶחֶם) and verbs (שָׁקָה ,אָכַל) are found in Psalms 78 and
80.6. Read canonically, Psalm 80 seems to be addressing the irony of a
past disobedient nation being sustained, while the present faithful suffer
shame.

A major theme of Psalm 78 was the deliverance from Egypt, and 80.9
recalls it again. Israel in 80.9 is pictured as a vine led out (תַּסִּיעַ) of
Egypt in 80.9, as was recounted repeatedly in Psalm 78 (יִסַּע, vv. 26,
52). The place name Egypt (מִצְרַיִם) used here in 80.9 is found three
times in Psalm 78 (vv. 12, 43, 51). After leaving Egypt, Israel dispos-
sessed the Canaanites (78.55) and 80.9 repeats the account:

78.55a – וַיְגָרֶשׁ...גּוֹיִם
80.9b. – תְּגָרֵשׁ גּוֹיִם

In both of these psalms the past salvation from Egypt is used as a basis
for the present request for deliverance. Psalm 80.15 requests that the
same vine led out of Egypt be visited by means of the strengthened
Davidic son (80.16, 18). Likewise, the Davidic deliverance of 78.65-72
is described in terms reminiscent of the deliverance from Egypt recounted in the same psalm.[3]

Between vv. 11-12 is a description of how Israel filled the land upon
which they were settled, repeating vocabulary of Ps. 78.45, 49, 53 narrating Egypt's judgment. In 80.11, the mountains are covered (כסו) with
the vine of Israel, while in 78.53 the sea has covered (כסה) its enemies,
the Egyptians. The same vine has spread as far as the sea (ים) in 80.12,
in contrast to the sea (הים) overtaking its enemies in 78.53. Yahweh had
sent (ישלח) swarms of insects in 78.45 as well as his wrath upon Egypt
in 78.49 (ישלח...משלחת), but extended (תשלח) the vine's branches to
the sea and river in 80.12. Consequently, identical vocabulary is utilized
both to narrate how Yahweh uprooted the vine Israel from Egypt
(78.45-53) and then replant it in Canaan (80.11-12). The same power
used in judgment against its enemy was exercised on behalf of Israel,
and thus the nation of Psalm 80 seeks to stir Yahweh to similar deeds in
the present.

In 80.13, the second interrogative (after v. 5) appears using the same
particle as that seen in 79.10 (למה). Reference to the breaking down of
the protective wall around the vine, and pilfering by passers-by, is
essentially identical to that of 89.41a, 42a, except that the latter two are
indicative, not interrogative clauses:

80.13 –   למה פרצת גדריה וארוה כל־עברי דרך
89.41a, 42a –   פרצת כל־גדרתיו...שסהו כל־עברי דרך

The shame visited upon the nation in 80 is the shame deplored by the
Davidide in 89. In fact, he suffers the same indignities as his people, but
as the only righteous one.

When Israel remembers how God's right hand (ימינך) planted the
nation in the land (80.16), it recalls 78.54 (ימינו). In the latter is recalled
the establishment of the holy mountain by the divine hand, answering
77.11 which wondered if that hand (ימין) had changed. Psalm 78 saw a

---

3.   Compare especially the vocabulary of 78.52-55 and 78.68-72 (הר, נחלה,
קדשו, הביא, עמו, צאן, ינחם). David is brought in (v. 71) to take over the shepherding
in v. 72 (ינחם) accomplished by God in v. 53 (וינחם), through the hands of Moses
and Aaron (נחית, 77.21).

hope for the future through the deliverance by David and establishment of Mount Zion with its holy place (vv. 68-69). Along the same lines, the verb of 80.16b, 18b (אמץ), is that used in reference to David in 89.22, where also the hand of God (יד) repeats the same in 80.18 (ידך). Thus, Psalm 80 requests national salvation through fulfillment of the promise to David, in harmony with Book III up to this point and in the remaining psalms through 89. Redemption is badly needed because the chosen vine has been burnt by fire (באש) in 80.17a, the result of present divine anger (כמו־אש) in 79.5b and felt previously in 78.21 (ואש).

When the speakers of 80.19a declare they will not backslide (נסוג), there is a definite distancing from previous generations who did turn back in 78.57 (ויסגו). Following in 80.19b, the speakers pledge to call on his name (ובשמך נקרא), distancing themselves from those nations worthy of divine wrath in 79.6 that do not call on his name (אשר בשמך לא קראו). The speakers of 80 are not like disobedient Israel, nor any other disobedient nation, and on this basis appeal repeatedly (vv. 4, 8, 15, 20) for God to restore them. This doubly occurring first person plural verb, practically at the end of the psalm (לא־נסוג...נקרא, v. 19), provides another parallel to the end of the immediately previous Psalm 79, where the community voice twice declares loyalty to Yahweh. In v. 13 they will laud (נודה) and will recount (נספר) his praises to all generations. Both 79 and 80 promise not to be as previous generations seen in Psalm 78, hoping to convince God to restore their fortunes.

On the basis of the repeated refrain (vv. 4, 8, 20), Psalm 80 can be divided into three strophes. The first (vv. 2-4) is dominated by imperatives directed toward God, and in the second (vv. 5-8) the present disgraceful condition of the nation gives reasons for divine intervention. The third and final strophe (vv. 9-20) recalls allegorically past deliverance (9-12), and present desolation (13-14), followed by appeals for restoration stretching from vv. 15 to 20. The latter series of direct requests is encapsulated by an extended divine name (אלהים צבאות) and imperatival forms of the root שוב ('return') at either end.

Reference to the prayer of his people in 80.5 (תפלת עמך) is consistent with both Psalms 80 and 79, given their direct appeal to God for deliverance. Both are communal prayers, and the common suffixed noun עמך here in 80.5 and shortly before in 79.13 identify the speakers. Twice more in Book III the same noun (תפלה, 84.9; 86.1, 6) is repeated to identify the prayer of an individual.

As mentioned before, petitions for the nation's salvation (ישע) in

vv. 3, 4, 8 and 20, are based on the promise of a univeral and peaceful Davidic reign portrayed in 72.4, 13 (ישע). Further allusions to the promises of Psalm 72 come from within the vine allegory of 80.9-17. The past condition of fruitfulness and growth described as reaching from sea to river (80.12) is a direct allusion to what had been promised in the future Davidic reign, as spoken in Psalms 72 and 89:

וירד מִיָּם עַד־יָם וּמִנָּהָר עַד אפסי ארץ – 72.8
עַד־יָם וְאֶל־נָהָר יונקותיה – 80.12
וְשַׂמְתִּי בַיָּם ידו וּבַנְּהָרוֹת ימינו – 89.26

Past glories are to be restored when the Davidic covenant is fulfilled. These references to the promised Davidic kingdom in v. 12 are followed, not coincidentally, in v. 13 by another more explicit parallel to 89.41, as mentioned above.

Parallels to Psalm 89 continue in the succeeding verses. As noted already, the unnamed individual of Psalm 80 is of the Davidic line described in 89.22:

וכנה אֲשֶׁר נטעה ימינך ועל בן אִמַּצְתָּה לך – 80.16
תהי יָדְךָ על איש ימינך על בן אדם אִמַּצְתָּ לך – 80.18
אֲשֶׁר יָדִי תכון עמו אף זרועי תְאַמְּצֶנּוּ – 89.22

For the writer of Psalm 80 (or the canonical editor of the Psalter), the restoration of the vine would take place through revitalization of its main stem, the Davidic line. The vine once planted (גֶּפֶן...וַתִּטָּעֶהָ) of v. 9 is to be restored (גֶּפֶן...נְטָעָה) in vv. 15-16 through this individual. The seemingly awkward insertion of v. 16b[4] assures inclusion under the request for restoration of the vine and stem of vv. 15c-16a, the restoration of the Davidic son as well. Key to the revival of the nation is the appearance of this strengthened royal figure. This same son of 80.16b, 18b (בֶּן אִמַּצְתָּה לך) contrasts quite starkly with the helpless sons of 79.11 (בְּנֵי תְמוּתָה). Through this powerful individual, those without strength will be revived (תְּחַיֵּנוּ, 80.19).

The plea for God's hand to be on the man of his right hand (יָדְךָ...יְמִינֶךָ) in v. 18 recalls that it had been withheld since 74.11 (יָדְךָ וִימִינֶךָ). Another reason for this delay of deliverance will be given in the following psalm (יָד, 81.15) directly from the deity. In spite of the delay, the writer of 89.14 does not forget that God's power is still available through that hand (יָד...יְמִינֶךָ). Through divine empowerment, the

---

4.   *BHS* would delete it, considering it as secondary from v. 18.

Davidic scion's hand would eventually rule from the sea to the rivers
(89.26, ‏ידו...ימינו‎).

In summary, Psalm 80 is a another appeal to God by the faithful
community, similar to that of the previous Psalm 79. Both respond
pointedly to issues raised in Psalm 78, but also repeat questions similar
especially to those seen in Psalm 74. Furthermore, promises given in
Psalm 72 are also recalled. Psalm 81 consists mostly of a response
directly from the God of Israel to the pleas of 79 and 80.[5]

5. T. Hieke, 'Psalm 80 and its Neighbors in the Psalter: The Context of the
Psalter as a Background for Interpreting Psalms', *BN* 86 (1997), pp. 36-43, has
come to many of the same conclusions regarding the role of Ps. 80 in its particular
location.

Chapter 9

PSALM 81

Wilson has noted the lack of genre designation in the superscription for
Psalm 81, and sees it rightly as preparatory for the transition between
Asaphite (82–83) and Qorahite (84–85) psalms.[1] From Psalms 73 to 80
are found several different genre designations before 81, which lacks
any, followed by four consecutive psalms (82–85) repeating the same
מזמור ('psalm'). The latter serves to soften the transition between the
two levitical groups named in Psalms 83 and 84. In other words, the
continual string of genre designations continues unbroken from 73 to
80, before a single superscription in 81 creates an abrupt and notable
change, followed by four straight psalms (82–85) of identical designation across the change of authorial ascriptions.

Within Psalm 81's superscription is the enigmatic phrase על הגתית,[2]
found only three times in the whole of the Psalter (Psalms 8, 81, 84). It
is not by chance that two of the three occurrences are so close in the
same Book III. This rare construction in 81 and 84 contributes further
to the continuity across the change in author ascription of 83–84
accomplished by מזמור. In fact, the parallels between 81 and 84's titles
are more numerous than those between 81 and 82, or 83 and 84:

81 – למנצח על־הגתית לאסף
82 – מזמור לאסף
83 – שיר מזמור לאסף
84 – למנצח על־הגתית לבני־קרח מזמור

Only the Asaphite author ascription is common to all four from 81 to
83, while 81 and 84 each contain two identical phrases between them.

1.   Wilson, *The Editing*, pp. 164-65.
2.   See Tate, *Psalms 51–100*, p. 318 for a listing of the three major explanations: 'a type of musical instrument…a musical tune or setting…a festival or cere-
mony of some kind'.

As might be expected, Psalm 81 itself contains many more ties to surrounding psalms in Book III, supporting the evidence of the superscription. The initial imperative of 81.2, 'cry joyfully' (הרנינו), is obeyed in 84.3 by the speaker (ירננו), while the source of Israel's strength (עוזנו) in 81.2 is that of the individual in 84.6 (עוז־לו). It is notable that Psalm 84 begins a series through 89 in which the individual righteous speaker is prominent. Psalm 84 is also the first of the Qorahite series in Book III. That individual's piety is proven by obedience to the commands of 81, in contrast to the nation (81.12-17).

Praise of God, Israel's strength in 81.2, follows the example of the faithful generation speaking in 78.4 (עזוזו) and of the speaker in 77.15 (עזך). Praise is commanded here in Psalm 81 for the victorious 'God of Jacob' who brought Israel out of Egypt (vv. 2, 5). In a similar context, the God of Jacob destroyed his enemies in 76.7 and 75.10. The song lifted to the God of Jacob in 75.10 reveals terminology identical to that of 81.2b-3a, and again reveals the righteousness of the individual heard in 75:

$$
\begin{array}{rl}
\text{אזמרה לאלהי יעקב} & - \text{ 75.10b} \\
\text{לאלהי יעקב...זמרה...לאלהי יעקב} & - \text{ 81.2b-5}
\end{array}
$$

Although the noun זמרה ('song') is of identical root as the common genre designation מזמור, found in both 80 and 82 on either side, it is absent from the superscription of 81.

The 'testimony' of v. 6 (עדות) also repeats a term found in the superscription of the previous 80.1. This testimony of 81.6 was produced when Israel left Egypt and recalls the vine allegory of 80.9-17, in which the vine was taken from Egypt (ממצרים, 80.9). Psalm 81.11 refers to the same deliverance (מארץ מצרים), as part of the response to Israel's complaint in Psalm 80. However, if this 'testimony' (עדות) in 81.6 was ordained for the nation, God 'testifies' (ואעידה) against the nation in 81.9 for its disobedience. Psalm 78.5 also mentioned this testimony in a similar manner:

$$
\begin{array}{rl}
\text{עדות...שם} & - \text{ 78.5} \\
\text{עדות...שמו} & - \text{ 81.6}
\end{array}
$$

The speaker in 81 commands the nation to do precisely what 78.1-5 ordered. Keeping the festival described in 81.4 is a manner of preserving the tradition for future generations as commanded in 78. Israel is being asked to be faithful according to the example set and ordered by the speakers of 78.1-5, by celebrating a festival that recounts the power of God demonstrated in Egypt (cf. 78.12, בְּאֶרֶץ מִצְרַיִם; and 81.6, עַל אֶרֶץ מִצְרָיִם). Thus, Psalms 79, 80 and 81 all continue discussion of issues raised in the lengthy 78.

When the speaker cried to the shepherd in 80.2, it was on behalf of the nation called 'Israel' and 'Joseph', identical to the nation found in 81.5a, 6a, also called 'Israel' and 'Joseph'. The parallel reveals a nation requesting relief from its God in 80.2 and in 81.5-6 reminded of the disobedience to the law of festival celebration as described in the previous vv. 2-4. In fact, Psalm 81 serves principally as a divine answer to the questions of 79–80, just as 78 answered the complaints of 77. In both cases, the nation's rebellion provides the main reason for continued delay of divine deliverance.

When Ps. 81.8 recalls how Israel called out (קָרָאתָ) in distress and was answered, it offers hope to those in 80.19 who have promised to call out (נִקְרָא) in the present desolation. In fact, the answers of the present Psalm 81 to questions raised in 80 prove that God still answers, even if not in the desired manner. Part of the answer to the individual cry of distress (צָרָתִי) in Ps. 77.3 was given in the voice of thunder (רַעַמְךָ, v. 19), and in like manner an answer of thunder was given in 81.8b (אֶעֶנְךָ...רַעַם) to a previous distress (בַצָּרָה, 81.8a). This declaration proves that God does answer distress calls, but at the same time contrasts with the negative answer of 81.12-17.

Beginning in 81.9 is a call for God's people to listen, as if to answer their petition of 80.2 for a hearing. Psalm 80 is a prayer of his people (עַמְּךָ, v.5) and 81 a response to them (עַמִּי, v. 9), a solemn one at that (וְאָעִידָה). The solemnity of this answer to Psalm 80 is demonstrated further by the first person singular pronoun used by the deity (אָנֹכִי, v.11a) in Psalm 81. It was last used by the same speaker in Ps. 75.4 (אָנֹכִי; cf. אֲנִי in v. 3), which was also an answer to the questions raised in Psalm 74. In 74.9-10 the people sought to know how long the enemy would revile, and 75.3 answered that an unspecified time had been chosen by Yahweh for judgment. In a similar manner, the same type of question in 80.5 as to the duration of his anger against Israel is answered in 81.15a. The interrogative עַד־מָתַי of 80.5 asks how long his anger would endure, and is answered in 81.15 promising 'quick' (כִּמְעַט) subjugation of the enemy. Not only do they correspond semantically, but also phonologically (עַד־מָתַי, כִּמְעַט).[3] Recall that the answer to this

---

3. One could add that 'ayin is followed in each case by dental stops *teth* and *daleth*.

same interrogative particle in 74.10 was another phonologically similar form מוֹעֵד in 75.3. Psalm 80 continued the complaint, explaining that because of divine anger (80.5) the enemy (80.7, אוֹיְבֵינוּ) was free to taunt Israel. The divine reply of Psalm 81 assures quick subjugation of the enemy (81.15a, אוֹיְבֵיהֶם), if only obedience were forthcoming (81.14, לוּ עַמִּי שֹׁמֵעַ לִי).

Israel had recalled in 80.12 how God sent out (תְּשַׁלַּח) their branches to fill the land, in an attempt to motivate intervention. Yahweh's rejoinder of 81.13 refers to sending Israel (וָאֲשַׁלְּחֵהוּ) in stubbornness of heart. They recall only past goodness, but he recalls their past rebellion. They asked that he go (לְכָה) to their rescue in 80.3, but the recollection in 81.13-14 is that they had gone (יֵלְכוּ...יְהַלְּכוּ) according to their own counsels. Refusal to walk in 'my ways' (בִּדְרָכַי, 81.14b) explained why the nation was subject to despoiling in its own chosen way, by the passers-by of 80.13b (עֹבְרֵי דָרֶךְ). The conditional particle לוּ of 81.14a also answers the interrogative particle לָמָה of 80.13. Israel wanted to know 'why' (לָמָה) their protection was destroyed (80.13), so Yahweh answers that 'if' (לוּ) they had obeyed their enemies would have been defeated (81.14).

Divine answers to Psalm 80 continue. Just as they asked that Yahweh's hand (יָד) be placed upon the strong one in 80.18, so he responds that upon obedience his hand (יָד) could be turned quickly against their enemies in 81.15. This act of 'turning' (אָשִׁיב) in 81.15 responds to the repeated request of Psalm 80 to do the same (הֲשִׁיבֵנוּ, vv. 4, 8, 20; שׁוּב, v. 15). Then, instead of being fed (הֶאֱכַלְתָּם, 80.6) the 'bread' of tears, they would be fed (וַיַּאֲכִילֵהוּ, 81.17) the finest of 'wheat':

> 80.6a – הֶאֱכַלְתָּם לֶחֶם דִּמְעָה
> 81.17a – וַיַּאֲכִילֵהוּ מֵחֵלֶב חִטָּה

Here 'wheat' is qualified in such a manner as to resound phonetically with the 'bread' of the previous psalm. Reversed consonants correspond to a reversal in the answer.

The vocabulary used to describe how God would potentially punish Israel's enemies in v. 15 (אָשִׁיב יָדִי) resembles very closely that which describes how Israel itself suffered under God's hand in 74.11 (לָמָה תָשִׁיב יָדְךָ). Perhaps for this reason, the individuals in v. 16 named as haters of Yahweh are without ethnic designation. Both plural pronominally suffixed nouns of v. 15 refer to national enemies of Israel, but haters of Yahweh in 16a does not exclude any nationality. Supporting this is the consonance and thus deliberate connection between the related concepts of 'bow down' of v. 10 and 'cringe' of v. 16:

81.10b – ולא תשתחוה לאל נכר
81.16a – יכחשו לו

Those Israelites who disobeyed the prohibition of idolatry in v. 10 will be forced to come cringing in subservience to Yahweh along with other idolaters. It should be added that the use of the national name 'Israel' in the plea to Yahweh of 80.2 (רעה ישראל) inspires a fourfold response using that same name in 81.5, 9, 12, 14. The latter three state either implicitly or explicitly that 'Israel' does not 'listen' (שמע), and consequently God is not inclined to do the same for them when they ask for a hearing (האזינה, 80.2).

Psalm 81 can be divided into two major strophes according to content and form. Within vv. 2-6a, five plural imperatives (vv. 2-4) directed to Israel are followed by reasons for obedience (v. 5). Beginning in v. 6 and stretching to the end of the psalm, the speaker recalls the nation's deliverance from Egypt and subsequent rebellion. Four verse paragraphs opening in each case with forms of the verb שמע (vv. 6, 9, 12, 14), complete the second strophe. Each instance of this verb is accompanied by references to the nation, first as Joseph (יהוסף) in v. 6 and three times as Israel (ישראל) in vv. 9, 12, 14. Psalm 80 opened with an appeal to God using precisely the same combination of Israel and Joseph (v. 2), and so the divine answer (81) corresponds precisely.

Both of the first paragraphs of strophe II (vv.6-8, 9-11) begin not only with forms of שמע, but forms of the root עוד as well. Within each of these first two divisions is found reference to the exodus from the land of Egypt (ארץ מצרים, vv. 6, 11). Both paragraphs stress the goodness of God, either in liberating Israel from bondage (vv.6-8) or supplying sustenance (v. 11). Verse 6 begins with mention of the laws or testimonies given to the nation, and vv. 10-11 of the following paragraph follow suit with the prohibition against idolatry. The final two paragraphs of vv. 12-13 and vv. 14-17 declare the subsequent disobedience to these commands. A progression can be seen from the hope that Israel would listen in v. 9 of the second paragraph, to the fact that they did not listen in v. 12 of paragraph three, to the description in vv. 14-17 of what would have occurred if only they had listened.

The first strophe of the psalm stretches from v. 2 to v. 5 and is bound together tightly by repetition of the divine epithet 'God of Jacob' (אלהי יעקב) at either end. This title does not correspond to the immediately preceding psalms, but instead recalls Pss. 75.10 and 76.7, where judgment of the wicked and triumph over God's enemies are portrayed. In addition, the praise of 75.10 is promised using a verb (אזמרה) of the same root as the noun זמרה in 81.3. As mentioned above, Psalm 75 is an answer to the temporal interrogatives found in the previous 74, and in the context of praise (75.2, 10) assures a time (מועד, 75.3) of judgment upon the wicked. Psalm 81 follows the temporal interrogatives of 79 and 80 with an immediate expression of praise (81.2-5), but Israel's rebellion now stands in the way of its otherwise quick (מעט, 81.15) restoration.

Psalm 81 is, then, principally a divine response to the complaints and questions raised in the previous two psalms, according to a pattern seen previously in Book III. Psalm 82 will continue the divine reply, begun in 81, to complaints in 79 and 80.

Chapter 10

PSALM 82

Psalm 82 is the penultimate Asaphite psalm and thus matches Psalms 83 and 81 in its authorial superscription. The genre designation מזמור, not seen in 81, begins a series of four that reaches across the name change between 83 and 84 to 85, and then ceases again at 86.[1] As for its content, Psalm 82 resumes themes reaching back across Book III and to Psalm 72 as well. Furthermore, difficult interpretive questions raised by this psalm are clarified when seen in the canonical context of Book III.

The 'congregation of God' (בעדת־אל) has already been seen in 74.2 (עדתך), and the judgment of God described in 82.1 (אלהים...ישפט) recalls 81.5 (משפט אלהי). Those judgments of Psalm 81 were disobeyed (v. 12), as they are here in 82.2-3 (תשפטו...שפטו). The final v. 8 asks that God now arise and do (שפטה) what human judges had failed to accomplish. When Israel called for God to remember his congregation in 74.2, it did not expect such an answer. He remembers indeed, and must judge them (82.7) for wickedness. Their deliberate failure to uphold righteousness (הצדיקו, 82.3), and their support of the wicked (רשעים, 82.2, 4), identifies them with the faithless nation of 73.10.[2] The 'gods' (אלהים) of vv. 1b, 6a, are none other than those appointed to judge in Israel, who are rebuked for not dispensing justice.[3] Their

1. Wilson, *The Editing*, pp. 164-65.
2. The just judgment between the righteous and wicked in Ps. 1.5, 6, is in stark contrast to that described here within Israel.
3. Evidence from the canonical context of the Hebrew Bible supports that of Book III. The commands of Lev. 19.15 and other texts from the Pentateuch are strikingly similar to those of this psalm:

Ps. 82.2-3 – עד מתי תשפטו עול ופני רשעים תשאו סלה: שפטו דל יתום עני ורש הצדיקו
Lev. 19.15 – לא תעשו עול במשפט לא תשא פני דל ולא תהדר פני גדול בצדק תשפט עמיתך

Further parallels exist with Exod. 21.6; 22.7, 8. The latter refer to human judges as האלהים in the context of judgment (המשפטים, Exod. 21.1). Psalm 82.3, 4 demand

former status before appointment to judgeship status is assumed in v. 6, and latter judgment stated in v. 7.

Book III has repeated several times the interrogative construction עד־מתי or עד־מה (74.9-10; 79.5; 80.5), or semantically synonymous interrogatives in 77.8-10 (such as...הלעולמים of 77.8, or ...השכח of 77.10). Each of these examples preceding Psalm 82 has been put in the mouth of the distressed nation and questions how long God will prolong his anger against them. Now in response to these repeated questions, the deity makes use of the same interrogative form (עד־מתי, 82.2). In answer to the question of how long the desolation would last, the same is thrown back at the nation asking how long their corrupt judgment would continue. This series of dialoguing interrogatives continues up to the end of Book III in 89.47. Thus, the canonical context of Psalm 82 views the אלהים as judges in Israel, and not a pantheon of foreign gods the nation had just been prohibited from worshipping (81.10).

Lack of justice to the poor and needy, and thereby to the laws divinely given, was the accusation against these judges in Israel. A just treatment of the poor and needy is precisely what characterizes the reign described in Psalm 72. Judgment (שפט) is a major theme in both psalms (72.1, 2, 4 and 82.1, 2, 3, 8), that is, righteousness judgment (צדק, 72.1, 2, 3, 7 and 82.3) and the saving (הציל, 72.12 and 82.4) from the wicked of the poor, needy and afflicted (עני, דל, אביון, 72.2, 4, 12, 13 and 82.3, 4). Israel's judges are being asked in Psalm 82 to follow the pattern of the just and righteous ruler in 72.

A pattern seen in Psalm 73 depicts the success and prosperity of the wicked (רשעים, vv. 3, 12), followed by their downfall in 73.18 (הפלתם). In like fashion, Psalm 82 twice condemns the wicked (רשעים, vv. 2, 4) and then predicts the downfall (תפלו, v. 7) of those who join them.

justice from these 'gods', and presume that they have been placed in the role of judge legitimately (cf. 82.6a), an appointment that could hardly have been attributed to Yahweh by the canonical editor if they constituted the Canaanite pantheon. In Deut. 1.9-18 Moses appoints judges from among the people who are designated as שרי (a construct of 'princes') even as in Ps. 82.7 (השרים). They are to judge righteously in Deut. 1.16 (ושפטתם צדק), a command apparently forgotten in Ps. 82.3 (הצדיקו). They were not to favor the small or the great (כקטן כגדל, Deut. 1.17). These prepositions and complements resemble the language and range of social status described here in Ps. 82.7 (כאדם...כאחד השרים). Favoritism ignored the fact that judgment was ultimately derived from God (כי המשפט לאלהים, Deut. 1.17).

Psalm 73's description of the prosperity of the wicked is now supplemented by details of their justice system. The speaker of Psalm 73's
complaint is now echoed in Psalm 82 by the deity. Psalm 73 expressed
puzzlement over continued violence and oppression, after the assurance
of eventual peace and righteousness given in 72.[4] Now it is revealed in
82 that Israel's leaders themselves have actively aided the growth of
wickedness, and so impeded the implementation of such a kingdom as
envisioned in 72.

Psalm 74.19-22 appealed on behalf of the 'humble and needy' (עני
ואביון), and so was a petition for the ushering in of 72's ideal kingdom
(cf. Ps. 72.2, 4, 12, 13 for three examples each of אביון and עני). When
God is commanded to arise in 74.22 (קומה אלהים), following concerns
for the lowly in the previous three verses, a pattern matching Psalm 82
becomes apparent. Concern for the humble in 82.3-4 (עני...ואביון) is
followed by the identical command in v. 8 (קומה אלהים). In fact, this
collocation of the lengthened imperative and divine name are found
only in 74.22 and 82.8 in the whole of the Hebrew Bible. Such evidence
confirms the canonical intent to relate the two psalms together and
makes clear that Psalm 82 is a divine decrying of the injustices rendered
by Israel's leaders. Its final verse (8) pleads for God to intervene and
usher in that worldwide kingdom of peace and justice. Further proof of
this is found in the numerous lexical parallels already mentioned
between 82 and 72 in reference to the weak (דל, 72.13; 82.3, 4), humble
(עני, 72.2, 4, 12; 82.3) and needy (אביון, 74.4, 12, 13 twice; 82.4). These
unfortunate ones and their treatment by the legal system (note the form
ידין in 72.2) are a major concern of the king portrayed in Psalm 72, and
of the speaker in 82 (vv. 2-4). The present judges are ordered to deliver
the weak and needy (דל ואביון...הצילו, 82.4), judgment the ruler of
72.12-13 will render consistently (יציל אביון...דל ואביון).

Recognition that all the nations (82.8, בכל הגוים) would some day
come under divine dominion reasserts the promise of 72.11, 17 (כל גוים),
concerning those same nations. This final verse of 82 is an imperative
addressed to Elohim, asking explicitly for implementation of Psalm 72,
and at the same time serves as a perfect bridge to Psalm 83. Many of
those foreign nations are in fact named in 83 (cf. vv. 7-12).

In Psalm 75 the same concern for just judgment (שפט) was expressed

---

4.   The promised freedom from oppression (עושק) and violence (חמס) in Ps.
72.4, 14, was the opposite of that seen in Ps. 73.6, 8 (חמס...עשק).

in vv. 3 and 8 as that found in Ps. 82.1, 2, 3, 8 (שפט), along with the
desire that the wicked (רשעים) not be favored (75.5, 9, 11 and 82.2, 4).
In fact, divine just judgment will restore the foundations of the earth in
75.4 (ארץ...עמודיה) and the lack thereof has caused them to be shaken
in 82.5 (מוסדי ארץ). Psalm 75.3, 4 assured the implementation of
righteous judgment and 76.10 expressed confidence that such would be
done. The words of 76.10 (recalling promises of Psalms 72, 75, and the
complaint of 74) are repeated in 82:

76.10 – בקום למשפט אלהים להושיע כל ענוי ארץ
82.3, 8 – עני...קומה אלהים שפטה ארץ כי אתה תנחל בכל הגוים

As can be seen, the imperative of 82.8 simply continues a request
repeated variously in Book III, pleading for the promises of Psalm 72 to
be fulfilled.

The wicked (רשעים) of 75.5, 9, 11, who are certain to be judged, were
seen in 73.3-12 (רשעים) as enjoying prosperity and peace. While these
verses of Psalm 75 assured their judgment, now God in 82.2-4 asks that
those representing divine judgment abstain from favoring the wicked
(רשעים). The continuing situation of injustice and rebellion practiced by
disobedient Israel makes necessary eventual divine intervention (82.8)
in order to establish righteousness.

Closer to Psalm 82 is the command in 81.3 for the nation to lift up
(שאו) a psalm to God, and apparently they were not obedient (81.12).
What they did lift up (תשאו) were the faces of the wicked in 82.2. In
their disobedience, Israelites walked (ילכו) according to their own
counsel and did not walk (יהלכו) in the ways of God (81.13-14). Preceding these two verses in 81.12 is the double use of the negative
particle (לא), accusing them of not listening nor being willing. In a
similar manner, 82.5 in repeating the negative particle (לא) reveals their
ignorance and lack of understanding, and so as a consequence they
walk (יתהלכו) in darkness. The parallel includes these unjust judges of
Psalm 82 as part of disobedient Israel in 81.12-14:

81.12-14 – ולא...לא...ילכו...יהלכו
82.5 – לא...ולא...יתהלכו

Following the description of unknowing and ignorant judges in v. 5
there is recollection of a solemn pronouncement (v. 6). By means of the
independent first person singular pronoun the deity uses the language of
appointment, as a comparison with Ps. 2.7 reveals:

2.7 – אמר אלי בני אתה אני היום ילדתיך

82.6 – אני אמרתי אלהים אתם

Underlined parallel terms reveal that just as this son was appointed, so the 'gods' of 82.6 were designated to their positions. Such language of appointment in 82.6 contrasts pointedly with 81.11, where another form of the first pronoun is used. No appointment language (אמרתי) appears here when describing the timeless position of Yahweh as God:

81.11[5] – אנכי יהוה אלהיך

82.6a – אני אמרתי אלהים אתם

These 'gods' were appointed to their positions, but can quickly be deposed and destroyed, as the following 82.7 declares. The contrast between God and mortals is continued when 82.6b is compared with 83.19. They may have a likeness of the deity in that they are 'sons of the highest', but there is only one 'highest one':

82.6b – אתם ובני עליון כלכם

83.19 – כי אתה שמך יהוה לבדך עליון

Essential to this contrast is the use of the independent second person singular pronoun in 83.19 (אתה) and the plural form in 82.6a (אתם). Consequently, the correspondence between 82.6a and 81.11 defines Yahweh's unique position, while the parallel between 82.6b and 83.19 performs the same function.

The final verse of the following Psalm 83 repeats the same concept seen in the final verse of 82, in a way that can hardly be coincidental:

82.8 – שפטה הארץ כי אתה תנחל בכל הגוים

83.19 – כי אתה שמך יהוה לבדך עליון על כל הארץ

Universal supremacy is reiterated by closely parallel wording in both instances. Furthermore, the final clause of Psalm 82 serves as a perfect introduction to the content of 83. Numerous gentile nations are listed in Psalm 83, and 82.8b is assuring God's eventual inheritance of them. As will be seen in comments on Psalm 87, the list of foreign citizens of Zion in 87.4b matches those of 83.8b quite closely. Therefore, the inclusion of gentiles in the citizenry of Zion (Psalm 87) has already been implied by juxtaposition of 82 and 83.

---

5.   The first person pronoun used by Yahweh in 81.11, and the immediately preceding reference to foreign gods in 81.10b, highlight the contrast through repetition of the same sequence of consonants: לאל נכר: אנכי יהוה.

As shown above, 82.8 is an explicit call on God to fulfill the promises of Psalm 72. The parallels between 82.8 and 83.19 suggest a reference in the latter to 72 as well:

יהוה...<u>לבדו</u>: וברוך <u>שם</u> כבודו לעולם וימלא כבודו את <u>כל הארץ</u> – 72.18-19

וידעו כי אתה <u>שמך</u> יהוה <u>לבדך</u> עליון על <u>כל הארץ</u> – 83.19[6]

In both cases, the incomparability of Yahweh and eventual universal knowledge of him is declared and reaffirmed. As noted in the discussion of Psalm 73, the doxology of 72 is by no means to be understood apart from the eschatological promises in the body of the psalm itself. Therefore, 83.19 expresses faith in what 82.8 requests, and in what 72.18-19 had already prophesied.

Use of both the long (אלהים) and short (אל) forms of the divine name in 82.1a creates another parallel to the entire bicolon of 83.2. Therefore, in a manner similar to Psalms 77 and 78, both 81 and 82 are not only contiguous in order, but resemble each other closely at the opening and close. On the syntactic level, the conclusion of 82 and opening of 83 demonstrate consistency as well. The imperative קומה directed to God in 82.8a is followed in 8b by the particle כי, introducing a reason for him to comply. Likewise, the three precatives of 83.2 are followed in 83.3 by the same particle, giving reasons for God to heed the requests. In addition, the request in 83.2 that God respond to reproaching and conspiring gentile enemies, is based on the immediately preceding statement of 82.8b that all nations will be his inheritance.

After listing these rebellious nations in Ps. 83.7-9, the speaker asks for judgment upon them, as was done during the era of judges to the Canaanites. This would result in their knowing (וידעו) the identity of Yahweh (83.19), a knowledge which ironically had escaped Israel's own judges in 82.5 (לא ידעו). The irony continues between these two psalms. The 'gods' of Ps. 82.6 who ignore God will die 'as men and as one of the princes' (כאדם...כאחד השרים). Using the same preposition-כ, the speaker of Psalm 83 asks that God do to the enemy nations 'as was done to Midian, Sisera, Jabin, Oreb, Zeeb, Zebah and Zalmunna' (כמדין כסיסרא כיבין...כערב וכזאב וכזבח וכצלמנע, v. 10). The bodies of these ancient enemies fell and became dung on the ground (דמן לאדמה, 83.11). Not only the same preposition, but also the same root אדם is repeated between both psalms. Last but not least, the promise that the

---

6. One is tempted to see here the remnants of a doxology concluding the 'Elohistic Psalter' (Pss. 42–83).

Israelite judges would die as one of the 'princes' in 82.7 (הَשָׂרִים)
resonates with the mention of Oreb and Zeeb in 83, two 'princes' of
Midian (שָׁנֵי שָׂרֵי מִדְיָן, Judg. 7.25). Midian is also mentioned by name in
Ps. 83.10. Perhaps unwittingly, the nation's request in 83 for vengeance
on its enemies recalls and assures judgment declared on its own judges
in 82.

Such irony is supported by further evidence. Injustice as described in
Ps. 82.2 is expressed idiomatically as, 'lifting up the faces of the
wicked' (וּפְנֵי רְשָׁעִים תִּשְׂאוּ). A similar idiom is used in 83.3b of Israel's
enemies as, 'those who hate God lift the head' (וּמְשַׂנְאֶיךָ נָשְׂאוּ רֹאשׁ)
against the nation. The point made by this resonance between 82 and 83
is that when Israel's rulers act corruptly, their enemies will treat them in
like manner.

The unity of Psalm 82 itself has been achieved by a typical example
of inclusio or framing device.[7]

$$\text{אֱלֹהִים נִצָּב...יִשְׁפֹּט} \quad - \quad 82.1$$
$$\text{קוּמָה אֱלֹהִים שָׁפְטָה} \quad - \quad 82.8$$

Two semantically, if not formally similar terms in these two verses add
to the parallelism between them: נִצָּב, 'take one's stand' (v. 1) and קוּמָה,
'arise!' (v. 8). A specific judgment of God's own people in vv. 1-7
leads to the request that he judge the whole earth in v. 8. The universal-
ism of the final verse prepares for the lengthy list of gentile nations in
83.7-9. This participle נִצָּב implies more than the simple act of standing,
as Isaiah 3 reveals:

$$\text{נִצָּב לָרִיב יְהוָה וְעֹמֵד לָדִין עַמִּים} \quad - \quad \text{Isa. 3.13}$$
$$\text{יְהוָה בְּמִשְׁפָּט יָבוֹא עִם זִקְנֵי עַמּוֹ וְשָׂרָיו} \quad - \quad \text{Isa. 3.14}$$

The context here denotes a courtroom scene with its attendant legal
proceedings.

The underlined terms are those found in 82.1, 7, and the final reference to his 'princes' (שָׂרָיו) in v. 14 shows the participation of God with
the leaders in the role of judging. That participation in 82.1 is such that
they are called 'gods' (אֱלֹהִים), and those who are unjust in their rulings
will die just like any 'prince' (הَשָׂרִים), according to 82.7b.

Two strophes can be discerned within the psalm based on formal and
thematic evidence. The first four verses consist of God's reproof to the

---

7.   Cf. L. Alonso Schökel, *Treinta salmos: Poesía y oración* (Madrid: Institución San Jerónimo, 2nd edn, 1986), p. 290.

'gods', after an opening description by the narrator of his presence and role as judge among them. The second group of four quotes the divine accusation of ignorance and then death verdict upon them, with a call at the end for God to rise up and judge the whole earth. Cohesion in the first strophe is achieved by repetition of the root שָׁפַט ('to judge') across the first three verses, followed by a similar form פַּלְּטוּ ('deliver'), on the semantic and phonetic levels in v. 4. Forms such as דַּל and רְשָׁעִים in v. 4, are repeated from the previous vv. 2-3 of the same strophe. Strophe II begins (v. 5) and ends (v. 8) with instances of the nouns אֶרֶץ ('earth') and כֹּל ('all'), the latter appearing also in v. 6.

In conclusion, the brief description of rebellion in the previous Ps. 81.13-14, and the wickedness flourishing in 73, are given depth in 82. Reiterated questions asked of Yahweh in previous psalms, wondering how long the desolation will continue, are answered by his own question asking how long injustice will be practiced. Disobedience at the highest levels in Israel will be repaid with the same judgment meted out to enemies of old, as the following Psalm 83 will recount. Injustice found among judges and rulers reveal the exact opposite conditions promised in the future Davidic kingdom of Psalm 72. A final v. 8 asks God to arise and bring about that very kingdom. Thus, the dialogue of Book III continues in 82 by a continuation of the divine answer begun in 81 to the laments of 79 and 80.

Chapter 11

PSALM 83

This last psalm of the 'Elohistic Psalter' (Psalms 42–83) also concludes the Asaphite group of 73–83. As said before, the presence of מזמור in each psalm from 82 to 85 (after a break in 81 from that genre description) softens the transition from Asaphite to Qorahite psalms between 83 and 84. In Chapter 9 it was observed how the rare phrase על־הגתית in conjunction with the more common למנצח enveloped the sequence of Psalms 81–84. If the final two elements of 83's superscription can be explained within Book III, the genre designation שיר ('song') at its beginning is unique within the immediate environment.[1] As such, its purpose in this stretch of seventeen psalms is not apparent.

Another unifying factor is found by comparing the text of Psalms 82–83 themselves with the superscriptions of 84-85. The construct plural noun בני ('sons of') is not found in Psalms 80 and 81, but then appears in 82.6b and 83.9b, followed by the two occurrences in the superscriptions of 84 and 85, and not at all in 86. This sequence is also used to create cohesion and continuity across the author change between 83 and 84:

——	–	Psalm 80
——	–	Psalm 81
ובני עליון	–	Ps. 82.5b
לבני־לוט	–	Ps. 83.9b
לבני־קרח	–	Ps. 84.1b
לבני־קרח	–	Ps. 85.1
——	–	Psalm 86

The form in Ps. 83.9b (immediately preceding the first Qorahite psalms) reveals lamedh as the preposition joined to the plural noun in question.

---

1. The same designation is found in consecutive Pss. 75, 76 and 87, 88 at either end of Book III. Its repetition from Pss. 120 to 134 undoubtedly contributes to the unity across the 'Psalms of Ascent'. The same can be said for the string of four from Psalms 65 to 68; see Wilson, *The Editing*, pp. 163-64.

That is of course the form in 84.1. Similarity is thus closer precisely at the juncture where authorial ascriptions change. It is probably no coincidence that the string of four psalms utilizing מזמור in the heading (82–85), to create cohesion across the author change, matches this string of four exactly. Neither Psalm 81 preceding this group, nor the following Psalm 86, contain instances of מזמור or בני in either the psalms themselves or their titles.

As mentioned before, parallels between Psalms 82 and 83 occur in the initial two verses of each:

אלהים...אל...ופני רשעים תשאו – 82.1a, 2b
אלהים...אל...ומשנאיך נשאו ראש – 83.2, 3b

Both open with the same sequence of divine names, but in the first case (82.1) the mood is indicative, preparing for direct speech from God to the wicked judges, while the second (83.2) is vocative, appealing to God directly. Immediately following in 83.3 the nation complains of how the enemies of God raise their heads, while the speaker of 82 complains in v. 2 of how the nation's judges raise the head of the wicked. As noted above, if God answers this arrogance as they plead, judgment will fall on them as well.

The same type of irony is suggested by the words of Israel in the following 83.4, 5. Foreign nations have plotted and counselled for the purpose of going to destroy them. However, Israel has gone in its own counsels against the will of God, as stated in 81.13:

ילכו במועצותיהם – 81.13b
ויתיעצו...לכו – 83.4b-5a

Foreign plans against them are just retribution for plans contrary to Yahweh's laws. Israel's own words come back to haunt them again.

Psalm 81 contains further parallels to 83 which confirm this idea. If Israel had only obeyed, God would have quickly defeated its enemies (81.15-16), but instead they plot its destruction in 83.3:

אויביהם...משנאי יהוה – 81.15-16
אויביך...ומשנאיך – 83.3

The oppressive situation described in Psalm 83 is a direct result of the disobedience described in 81.

Reference to the cited desire for Israel's destruction as a nation in 83.5 (מגוי) recalls again the previous 82. If Israel's god is to possess all nations (תנחל בכל־הגוים, 82.8), then only he can decide whether Israel is to cease existence as a people. Therefore the plot of 83.5 should not succeed. God's possession of all nations in 82.8 also provides a basis for the plea to punish the long list of nations in 83.7-9. As inheritor of the world he has the power and authority to judge them. In spite of this future dominion, the present threat against Israel in 83.5 is serious on the part of the foreign nations, and they plan to obliterate it from memory forever (עוֹד). Such a threat could only arise because God's chosen congregation has continually (עַד־מָתַי) favored evildoers (82.2).

Israel's desire in 83 is that God judge these latter nations as he did enemy princes in the book of Judges. Perhaps not coincidentally, it is Israel's judges that have just been condemned in the previous Psalm 82. The victories cited in 83.10-12 came about when judges such as Deborah, Barak and Gideon ruled in Israel, but Psalm 82 reveals that such leaders are not now present in Israel. The corrupt Israelite judges of Psalm 82 will fall and die like men and like princes, just as Israel's enemies fell and died to the ground, as noted above.

The fallen princes and nations of 83.10-12 spoke arrogantly, as if they could take possession of God's own property.

$$82.6 - \text{אֲמַרְתִּי אֱלֹהִים אַתֶּם}$$
$$83.13 - \text{אָמְרוּ...נְאוֹת אֱלֹהִים}$$

This attitude in 83.13 displayed by the foreign nations is an affront to Israel's deity, as is that displayed by Israel's own judges in 82 after they were given godlike authority. Destruction and death was the end result of such an attitude in both cases. Again, Israel's own words of pleading for deliverance highlight their own shortcomings.

In 83.12 there are found three instances of the poetic pronominal suffix מוֹ-,[2] asking that these enemies (vv. 7-9) be destroyed. The repetition of this form four times in the space of three verses (12-14) is purposeful. It was also used multiple times in Psalm 73 as a code word for the wicked, among whom were Israel itself (עַמּוֹ, v.10). Likewise, the enemies of God in Psalm 83 turn out to include Israel when read in the light of Psalm 82. However, the parallels go further between 83 and 73. The individual in Psalm 73 realized the end of the wicked (v. 17), which included God putting them (תָּשִׁית לָמוֹ) in slippery places (v. 18). The resemblance of 73.17 to שִׁיתֵמוֹ ('Put them!') of Psalm 83, used twice over (83.12, 14), is instructive.[3] Based on what is stated in Psalm

2. Cf. GKC, §58g.
3. There appears to be a predilection for the use of this particular verbal root and pronominal suffix, as Pss. 21.10, 13; 45.17 demonstrate.

73, the speaker of 83 asks that this judgment be put into effect against God's enemies, which unwittingly or not is asking for the same against Israel. At the canonical level, however, such a condemnation and inclusion of Israel among the wicked is clearly intentional.

Judgment against the wicked had been promised since Ps. 2.3, 5, where they are referred to four times by means of the same suffix pronoun מוֹ-. The latter of these two verses (Ps. 2.5) contains not only the same suffix, but also a verb form found in Psalm 83. The Lord will surely 'terrify them' (יבהלמו, 2.5), a promise that serves as a basis for the requests in 83.12, 14 (שׁיתמו) and 83.16, 18 (תבהלם, ויבהלו). A further request in 83.18 is that they 'perish' (ויאבדו), repeating the verbal root אבד from Psalms 1.6 and 2.12.

Another ironic request is found in 83.17a. God is asked to fill the enemies' faces (פניהם) with shame, while at the same time Israel practiced favoritism by regarding the 'faces of the wicked' (ופני רשׁעים) in 82.2. Consequently, the request of 83.17 is one that could be turned back upon the chosen nation itself. The shame of these enemies should last 'forever' (עדי־עד) according to 83.18, but 'how long' (עד־מתי, 82.2a) should injustice be allowed to flourish in Israel? Perhaps God should honor their request for the placing of eternal shame not only on their enemies, but also on themselves, since their perversion of justice is apparently endless.

As noted in the previous chapter, the shame requested on Israel's enemies (83.17-18) would result in their knowledge (וידעו, 83.19a) of Yahweh's identity, a knowledge that ironically seemed to have escaped the judges of Israel itself (לא ידעו, 82.5), who walked in darkness. As opposed to Israel's rulers and judges, the individual Israelite poet in 82.8 recognized Yahweh's identity as universal judge, and foreign nations in 83 would come to know this only if shamed and defeated (vv. 17-19). Both Israel and foreign nations needed to acknowledge this fact:

כי־אתה...בכל־הגוים – 82.8b
כי־אתה...על־כל־הארץ – 83.19ab

A canonical role is also played by the independent personal pronoun אתה in 83.19a. This form again signifies that much of the psalm is a direct address to God, as did the opening vocative of v. 2 (אלהים). In contrast, the previous Ps. 82.6 used the first person independent singular pronoun 'I' (אני), as God addressed wicked judges (אתם) within the nation. By the end of 82, God is addressed directly ('you', אתה), as if in preparation for the following 83, which continues in the same person. Such a distribution of pronouns demonstrates again that a dialogue is taking place between God and either the nation or its one righteous individual, in the course of these psalms.[4]

Two strophes make up Psalm 83, the first from vv. 2-9 and the second vv. 10-19. The first consists of an initial triad of imperatives in v. 2, followed by two extended reasons (causal כִּי, vv. 3, 6) for God to heed the plea. Strophe II is a series of four imperatives requesting the destruction and humiliation of Israel's enemies. These four are also followed at the psalm's end (v. 19) by the particle כִּי, but unlike vv. 3 and 6 where causal clauses are introduced, it there begins an object clause.

The psalm as a whole is framed by an inclusio in which two divine names in the initial v. 2 (אֱלֹהִים...אַל) are matched by two divine names in the final v. 19 (יהוה...עֶלְיוֹן).[5] One might have expected the repetition of either אַל or אֱלֹהִים in the final verse, as is done in Psalm 82, forming a more transparent inclusio. The reason may be found in the fact that the 'Elohistic Psalter' terminates with Psalm 83, and an example of the Tetragrammaton in 83.19 (twice if v. 17 is included) creates transition to the following 'yahwistic' psalms. Furthermore, the praise of v. 19 is a fitting precursor to the praises of Psalm 84 following.

In summary, Psalm 83 is a complaint to the deity asking for vengeance on the nation's enemies, that ironically brings to the fore Israel's own guilt, as expressed in previous psalms of Book III.

---

4.   Cf. the analysis of E. Zenger, 'Zur redaktionsgeschichtlichen Bedeutung der Korachpsalmen', in K. Seybold and E. Zenger (eds.), *Neue Wege der Psalmenforschung* (Festschrift W. Beyerlin; Herders biblische Studien, 1; Freiburg: Herder, 1995), pp. 175-98 (189) (translation is mine):

Complaint	God's answer	Complaint
74 ('We')	75+76	77 ('I')
79+80	81+82	83 ('I')

Even though he fails to note how the 'weisheitliche Lehre' (wisdom teaching) in Pss. 73 and 78 participate in this dialogue, he does note a canonical dialogue taking place, analogous to the present study.

5.   W.A. Van Gemeren, *Psalms–Song of Songs* (The Expositor's Bible Commentary, 5; Grand Rapids: Zondervan, 1991), p. 537.

Chapter 12

PSALM 84

In previous chapters, the role of Psalm 84's superscription has been discussed, and so here a short summary will suffice. The sons of Qorah appear here for the first time in Book III after exclusively Asaphite psalms since 73, the transition being smoothed by the common term מזמור ('psalm'). This can be seen by the fact that it appears in the headings of the final two Asaphite psalms (82, 83) and the initial two Qorahite psalms (84, 85). Furthermore, it does not appear in the previous Psalm 81, nor in the following 86, at either end of this group of four. The rare form על־הגתית strengthened continuity with the previous string of psalms back to Psalm 81, the only other occurrence in Book III. Four examples of the construct plural בני creates a tight unity between Psalms 82–85 (82.6; 83.9; 84.1; 85.1), matching exactly the four occurrences of מזמור. Thus, 84 is bound closely to the preceding psalms, and, as will be seen, constitutes a continuation of the dialogue in Book III by responding to 83.

Across Psalm 84 are at least seven direct references to the dwelling-place(s) of God (vv. 2, 3, 4, 5, 8, 11 twice). Emphasis is put on the longing to dwell with God (vv. 2-5, 11) and shunning of the wicked's tents (באהלי־רשע, v. 11b). The tents of the wicked have been identified in 83.7 as those of Edom and its allies (אהלי אדום וישמעאלים..., 83.7-9). In Psalm 84 the speaker takes great pains to distance himself from the enemies and haters of God in the previous psalm who will surely suffer judgment. One would think that surely an Israelite need not fear being identified with the gentile nations arrayed against God and his people. However, it has already been shown that the vocabulary of Psalm 83 indicts the wicked in Israel as well by its relation to Psalms 81–82. The contrast between the dwellings in 83 and 84 is repeated in the formal similarity between יושבי ביתך ('inhabitants of your house') of 84.5 and ישבי צור ('inhabitants of Tyre') of 83.8 (note the plural construct repeated in these examples, as in the reference to tents), the latter included among the enemies of God.[1] The individual speaker of 84 clearly distinguishes himself from those who hate God in 83.

It was recalled in 83.11 that Israel's enemies were destroyed at the 'spring of Dor' (בעין־דאר), but for those who trust in Yahweh a 'spring' (מעין, 84.7) is provided on their journey. Provision of water in 84.7 is narrated by use of the verb ישׁיתוהו ('they make it'),[2] the same found twice in 83.12, 14 where the destruction of the enemy is solicited by the imperative שׁיתמו ('make them'). In fact, the verb is also found twice in Psalm 84, once in v. 7 already noted, and also in v. 4 (שׁתה) relating the protection afforded a bird with its nest near the altars of the Lord. As a result, two calls for destruction of the enemy in 83 are counterbalanced by two promises of provision and protection in 84.

The twice-mentioned man (אדם, vv. 6, 13) who seeks protection in Yahweh is blessed in contrast to the inhabitants of Edom (אדום, 83.7), who along with their allies will become dung for the ground (לאדמה, 83.11). These latter enemies of God were to fall to their death, as was predicted for the wicked judges of 82.7 (כאדם), so that a deliberate contrast is created between the blessed men of 84.6, 13 and the individuals of the two previous psalms. These same blessed men of Psalm 84 who dwell in Yahweh's house remain (עוד, v. 5) alive to praise him, meaning they escape the threat given in 83.5 against Israel to forever (עוד) blot out its name from memory. Praise in 84.5 (יהללוך) is a sound pleasing to Yahweh, as opposed to the arrogant sounds made by the enemy in 83.3 (אויביך יהמיון). Bolstering the more obvious semantic contrast are the underlined consonantal parallels.

Whereas the conspirators of Psalm 83 took counsel in their hearts (לב, v.6) to covenant against God, the heart of the faithful speaker in 84 exults in Yahweh (לבי, v. 3) and in the hearts of such individuals are the ways of blessing (בלבבם, v. 6). These faithful ones described in Psalm 84 'walk' (ילכו, v. 8) increasing in strength, and 'walk' (להולכים, v. 12) in integrity, as opposed to those who purpose to 'walk' (לכו) in conspiracy against God's people (83.5), being eventually destroyed (83.17-19). In fact, those who walk faithfully in 84.8, 12 are in contrast with the wicked seen in every psalm since 81. In the latter it was God's

---

1.   Hakham, *Sefer tehillim*, p. 109 (קט) n. 29.
2.   Although the springs apparently appear as a result of those passing through the 'Valley of Weeping' (בעמק הבכא), the context implies that this provision is ultimately from Yahweh.

people who walked according to their own counsel (81.13, 14), followed by the wicked judges of 82.5 who walked in darkness. Then the
plotters who go/walk against God and his people in 83.5 are followed
by those of a faithful walk in 84.8, 12. Righteousness personified walks
before Yahweh in 85.14, and the David of 86.11 walks according to his
teaching as well. Consequently, the individual speaker across each of
these three psalms (84–86) represents the faithful walk, in contrast to
those of 81–83 who walk in disobedience. Once again, a righteous
individual speaker emerges from Book III who has not been a participant in the failures of the nation.

A request is made that the faces of the enemies be filled with shame
in 83.17 (פניהם), but in 84.10 that the anointed's face (פני משיחך) be
regarded by God. Undoubtedly, the anointed one is the very individual
uttering these words in vv. 9-13, and is the same Davidic figure who
will lament the situation described in 89.39 (משיחך). It is hoped that the
arrogance of God's enemies will end, so that instead of their heads
being raised (נשאו ראש, 83.3b), or those of the wicked (פני...תשאו,
82.2), the face of God's anointed will be regarded. The latter prays in
the first person singular (תפלתי, 84.9) and will be heard again in 86.6
(תפלתי) and 88.3, 14 (תפלתי).

Further contrast between the desires of those nations in 83 and the
individual in 84 is highlighted in the use of terms synonymous with
God's dwelling place and utilizing the feminine plural noun morpheme
ות-:

נאות – 83.13[3]
משכנותיך – 84.2
חצרות – 84.3
מזבחותיך – 84.4

The respect and love given for God's dwellings and presence by the
individual of Psalm 84 is evident if only by the plentiful vocabulary,
and contrasts markedly with the destructive intentions of the enemy in
Psalm 83. Essentially the same contrast between the speaker of 84 and
those of 83 was effected by use of 'tents' in 83.7 and 84.11, as discussed above. Clearly an important, if not the most important, purpose
of Psalm 84 in its present location is to distinguish the individual
speaker from the wicked of 83.

Other parallels further removed from the immediate vicinity of Psalm

---

3.   Taking this noun from the root נוה, meaning 'to dwell'.

84 include an unmistakable parallel between 80.5 and 84.9. Both address God using a rare epithet,[4] asking for answers to prayer uttered by the nation in 80, and by the individual in 84:

80.5 – יהוה אלהים צבאות עד מתי עשנת בתפלת עמך

84.9a – יהוה אלהים צבאות שמעה תפלתי

This is only one of numerous close links between Psalms 80 and 84, surpassing perhaps even those between 84 and 83. Reasons for this can be found in the nature of Psalms 81–83. These latter three psalms describe repeatedly the 'walk' of the wicked (81.13, 14; 82.5; 83.5) without mentioning this righteous Davidide once. Only at either end (Pss. 80.16, 18 and 84.9, 10, 13) is he mentioned or heard. Consequently, after extensive descriptions of the wicked in 81–83, Psalm 84 picks up again where 80 left off in portraying this one individual who stands out from the rest.[5] As noted above, beginning in Ps. 84.8, 12 is described the 'walk' of the faithful, followed by righteousness personified 'walking' in 85.14, and then the David of 86.11 promising to 'walk' in Yahweh's truth. Consequently, three consecutive psalms describe the walk of the wicked (81–83), followed by three portraying the walk of the righteous (84–86). The verb הלך ceases in Psalms 87–88 before reappearing in the final 89.

Another example of extended parallels, not just individual forms, can be found between 84 and 80:

80.15 – אלהים...הבט משמים וראה...גפן זאת

84.10 – ראה אלהים והבט פני משיחך

Here are found the same pair of synonymous imperatives in either verse. Psalm 84.10 is clearly a request for God to regard the condition of his anointed one. The same can be said for 80.15, which is a request for the deity to regard not only the vine (v. 15) but also the son strengthened for himself (80.16b). In both cases, the community takes part in the petition for its promised anointed king. Psalm 80 is entirely spoken in the first person plural, and 84.10 is one rare example (מגננו) among predominantly first person singular verbs and pronominal

---

4.   Used only four times in the entire Psalter: 59.6; 80.5, 12; 84.9; see Tate, *Psalms 51–100*, p. 305.

5.   Note, for example, how the imperative האזינה ('hearken') of 84.9b repeats the same request of 80.2 (and 77.1; 78.1) without any intervening examples in Pss. 81–83.

suffixes.[6] Perhaps the anomaly of grammatical number in 84.10a is a deliberate attempt to link with the similar communal prayer of 80.16.

Connections between Psalms 84 and 80 continue. Psalm 80 is generally a plea for the nation's restoration, while 84 expresses the prayers of the righteous individual. Nonetheless, included in Psalm 80 is a request that the same chosen man be strengthened in the task of redemption (80.18). Reference to a man by parallel forms אֵישׁ and בֶּן־אָדָם in 80.18, constitute a parallel to the twice-mentioned blessed man (אַשְׁרֵי אָדָם) of 84.6, 13. As a result, both of these psalms can be linked back to the beginning of the Psalter. Psalm 1.1 (opening the Psalter's introduction of Psalms 1, 2) describes a blessed man (אַשְׁרֵי הָאִישׁ) who does not walk (לֹא הָלַךְ, 1.1) in the way of the wicked. That description matches that of the individuals in Ps. 84.8 and 12 who walk with integrity (יֵלְכוּ...לַהֹלְכִים בְּתָמִים). The walk of integrity is also associated with Zion in 84.8 (יֵלְכוּ...בְּצִיּוֹן). In similar fashion, the individual of Psalm 1 becomes, by canonical juxtaposition, the ruler enthroned in Zion of Ps. 2.6 (עַל־צִיּוֹן).[7] The same themes of Zion, the king and integrity are found in Ps. 78.68, 72, discussed earlier.[8] There God chose Zion (הַר צִיּוֹן, 78.68) and installed David, a man of integrity (כְּתֹם לְבָבוֹ, 78.72).[9] So Psalm 84 continues echoing that theme of restoring in Zion a king who walks in faithfulness.

The two manners of walking are especially contrastive between Psalms 82 and 84. Yahweh becomes a 'sun' (שֶׁמֶשׁ) to 'those who walk in integrity' (הֹלְכִים בְּתָמִים), according to 84.12. Psalm 82 condemned those judges who failed to walk in integrity but chose rather the path of darkness (בַּחֲשֵׁכָה יִתְהַלָּכוּ, v. 5). Consequently, a contrast is formed between walking in divine light (Psalm 84) and darkness (Psalm 82). This walk of 84.8 results in increasing strength (מֵחַיִל אֶל חָיִל), a response perhaps to the complaint of the individual in 73.12 that the

6. Note how 84.9, 10b, 11, 12 are all expressed in the first person singular and only v. 10a is plural.

7. This point is apparently recognized as well by Miller, 'The Beginning of the Psalter', p. 91, and by G.T. Sheppard, *Wisdom as a Hermeneutical Construct: A Study in the Sapientializing of the Old Testament* (New York: W. de Gruyter, 1980), p. 142.

8. Cf. the description of those who are eligible for dwelling in Zion of Pss. 15.1-2; 24.3-4. The David of Ps. 72 qualifies under the conditions of Pss. 15 and 24.

9. Note how the speaker of Ps. 84.3 claims a faithful heart (לִבִּי), as does the poet in 73.1, 13, 26.

wicked seem to ever increase power (השׁגוּ חיל).

Above, it was observed that those who walk (הלך) in rebellion are found in Psalms 81, 82 and 83, before the faithful ones appear in Psalms 84, 85 and 86. A similar sequence is found by examining the repetition of 'adam' (אדם) from Psalm 80 to 84. God's chosen 'son of man' appears in 80.18 (בן־אדם), to be followed by judged men in 82.7 (כאדם), 'Edom' and others who become dung on the 'adamah' in 83.7-11 (אדום...לאדמה), and finally in 84.6, 13 a faithful man appears again (אשׁרי אדם). This individual of 84.6 finds strength in Yahweh, notwithstanding a spent condition (84.3). Note the twin descriptions of the blessed man who trusts in God (vv. 6, 13), surrounding the confession in vv. 9-11 of the Davidic heir:

$$\text{אשׁרי אדם עוז לו בך} - \text{v. 6}$$
$$\text{אשׁרי אדם בטח בך} - \text{v. 13}$$

Similarily, in the introduction to the Psalter the blessed man (אשׁרי האישׁ, Ps. 1.1) is joined by all those who trust (אשׁרי כל חוסי בו, Ps. 2.12).[10] The single individual of 84.2-4 who dwells in Yahweh's courts

---

10. The blessed man of Ps. 1.1 is not simply 'generic man' when read in the light of Ps. 2. In fact, Ps. 2 is a further discussion of the same individuals presented in Ps. 1. There is a deliberate attempt on the canonical level to further describe, contrast and identify the individuals of Ps. 1 in the following Ps. 2. The blessed man of 1.2 *meditates* (יהגה) in the Torah, and so stands apart from the *counsel* of the wicked. Likewise, the anointed king of Ps. 2 is resisted by the wicked, who are those *meditating* (יהגו) rebellion in their *councils* (semantic, not formal contrast). The wicked of Ps. 1 are thus identified as the rulers of Ps. 2, and standing apart from them in both psalms is the blessed man, also identified as the anointed one, king in Zion and son of God. Other parallels supporting such a reading include the *stand* of the kings in 2.2, versus the blessed man not *standing* with them in 1.1 (semantic, not formal contrast). The *way* (דרך) of the wicked in 1.1, 6 is the *way* (דרך) destroyed in 2.11, the latter belonging to the kings warned in 2.10. The tree of Ps. 1.3 is *planted* and *gives* (יתן) fruit in its time and so the annointed king of 2.6 is *established* on Mt. Zion and to him God *gives* (ואתנה) an inheritance of the nations. If the blessed man does not *sit* (ישׁב) with the scorners in 1.1, he apparently does *sit* (יושׁב) in the heavens and laughs back (2.4) at the scheming rulers, who are none other than the scorners of 1.2. Note here that the 'Adonay' (אדני) who *sits* in the heavens and laughs in 2.4, is also found *sitting* (שׁב, imperative) in the same heavenly realm in Ps. 110.1 (אדני), there vocalized by the Masoretes as 'Adoni'. The 'sitting one' of 2.4 has been given his seat as a result of the command of 110.1. His establishment on the throne in the royal city is also declared in 2.6, as it is in 110.2. The deliberately ambiguous antecedent to the 'sitting one' (יושׁב) of 2.4

is blessed (אשרי, v. 5) for it, and that blessing is offered to whomever
will trust (אשרי, vv. 5, 6, 13). Between two declarations of blessedness
in the introduction to the Psalter (1.1 and 2.12), Yahweh's anointed
(משיחו, 2.2) suffers opposition from opposing rulers and nations. They
are classed among the wicked (רשעים) of 1.1, 5, whom the blessed man
does not join. Here in 84.10 there is a prayer for the anointed one
(משיחך), who prefers the house of God to tents of the wicked (רשע,
84.11). The divine dwelling so desired by the speaker is called 'Zion' in
84.8, the same place the anointed one is established in 2.6. To these
parallels can be added the images of watery abundance in 1.3 (פלגי מים)
and 84.7 (ברכות, מעין,[11] מורה).[12] Psalm 84 is clearly a resumption of the
ideas found in Psalms 1–2, and confirms the unified reading of the latter
two. Much of what Psalms 1–2 convey when read together is expressed
by the one Psalm 84.

As noted above, the individual quoted and described in 84.9 is
equated with the speaker in 86.6. This is further confirmed by comparing the final statement of 84, assuring the blessedness of the man who
'trusts in you' (בטח בך, 84.13), and that of 86.2 asking for salvation for
the servant, 'the one who trusts in you' (הבוטח אליך). Just as canonical
juxtaposition of Psalms 1 and 2 identifies the blessed man (אשרי האיש)
of 1.1 as the anointed one and king of 2.2, so the juxtaposition of

allows for both Yahweh and his anointed one of 2.2 as referent. Psalm 110 further
clarifies this ambiguity. It turns out that the chosen king is sitting at Yahweh's right
hand and so can laugh and deride the scoffing and rebellious kings from heaven. In
fact, the closest antecedent to יושב in 2.4 is משיחו in 2.2. Without a doubt, the
canonical redaction equates the king of Ps. 2 with that of 110 by close verbal and
thematic parallels, as it does the king of Ps. 2 with the blessed man of Ps. 1.

11. Assuming this refers to 'pools' (cf. Eccl. 2.6), as *BHS* proposes along with
Gunkel, *Die Psalmen*, p. 371, and Dahood, *Psalms* II, p. 281. If one prefers
'blessings', the image of water is still present through the remaining 'spring' and
'rain'.

12. Note how the city of God in Ps. 46.5 is described as having a river whose
channels (פלגיו) gladden the city and its dwelling places (משכני). This matches the
coupling of watery abundance and Zion in 84.8. Also the dwelling places
(משכנותיך) of 84.2 are those of 46.5. Furthermore, the two themes of water channels
and Zion in the one psalm (Ps. 46), repeats what the uniting of Pss. 1 and 2 has
already stated. The blessed man of Ps. 1.3 is compared to a tree planted by channels
of water (פלגי מים), and he is divinely established in the Zion of Ps. 2. Verbal parallels confirm the connection. He is planted 'on' (על) channels of water in 1.3, and
established 'on' (על) Zion in 2.6. As a tree he 'gives' (יתן) fruit in his season, and
so will God 'give' (ואתנה) him the inheritance of nations, as mentioned previously.

Psalms 84–86 identifies the blessed man (אשרי אדם) of 84.13 as the David of 86.2.

In direct contrast to the faithful one(s) of Psalm 84 are the enemies of God in 83, who proudly raise their heads (v. 3), and find strength in the arm of Assyria (זרוע, v. 9). While the enemies unite their hearts (לב, 83.6) in covenant against God, shame and destruction (ויחפרו ויאבדו, 83.18) is the fate requested for them. In contrast, the faithful speaker's heart (לבי, 83.3) finds its strength in God (עוז, 84.6), and is rewarded with favor and glory (חן וכבוד, 84.12). Note as well that the international counsels of 83.4 and 6 (ויתיעצו...נועצו) against God's people end in destruction (ויאבדו, 83.18), just as the counsel (עצת) of the wicked in Ps. 1.1 against God and his anointed (2.1-2), being also international, ends in destruction (ותאבדו, תאבד, 1.6 and 2.12). Note close similarities in descriptions of the enemy plot against Yahweh, his anointed, and his people between Psalms 2 and 83:

יתיצבו...נוסדו יחד על יהוה – 2.2
סוד ויתיעצו על...נועצו...יחדו עליך – 83.4, 6

Not only does Psalm 84 on its own reiterate much of what is stated in the conjunction of Psalms 1–2, but Psalm 83 also recalls themes from the Psalter's introduction. Psalm 83 resonates most closely with Psalm 2, while 84 is most similar to Psalm 1. Even if the order is reversed, the overall message and effect of their juxtaposition is the same.

Psalm 84 resonates with Psalm 73 at the outset of Book III as well. There the distressed speaker whose flesh and heart are spent finds strength in God, as does the individual of 84.3:

כלה שארי ולבבי צור לבבי – 73.26
וגם כלתה נפשי...לבי ובשרי ירננו – 84.3

Since Psalm 73, the innocent and righteous speaker has expressed agony and suffering. That agony is due first to the apparent collapse of divine justice in 73, and as expressed in 77 (נפשי...לבבי, 77.3, 7), the national disgrace which saddens not only the nation (Psalms 74, 79, 80), but also this individual. Here in Psalm 84 this righteous one seeks earnestly the presence and dwelling of God, to the point that his soul is spent as it was in 73. This suggests separation from the divine presence. That separation will be described in Psalm 86 as death (vv. 13, 14), and opposition from those who hate him (v. 17). Psalm 88 will also continue to lament the same separation caused by death, before 89 bursts out in thankful song for deliverance from it. The loneliness and apparent separation from God begin in 73 and continue through 88, but even after apparent salvation out of death (Psalm 89), the restoration of the monarchy to this Davidide is still delayed.

The poet in 84.3 longs for (נכספה) the courts of Yahweh, an expression close, even if not formally identical, to that of 73.25. There the poet desired (חפצתי) nothing on earth except God. If God is his rock (צור) in 73.26, the speaker in 84.6 declares that blessedness comes from making Yahweh one's strength (עוז־לו). He goes on to conclude that closeness to God is his good (לי־טוב) in 73.28. The statement of 84.11, concluding that a day in the courts of Yahweh is good (טוב), better than a thousand elsewhere, coincides with 73.28. The speaker in 84 has also concluded that being close to Yahweh is far better (טוב) than dwelling in the tents of the wicked (באהלי־רשע, 84.11). The identical choice was made by the individual in Psalm 73, who was tempted to throw in his lot with the same (רשעים, vv. 3, 12), but resisted and finally realized that it was better (טוב) to be in God's company.[13] Based on these numerous parallels, one can see that the speaker of Psalm 84 is the same righteous individual heard in Psalm 73, and numerous times since then. He is in fact portrayed as the Davidic scion, as argued previously, and the final psalms in Book III will further confirm this (משיחך, 84.10; 89.21, 39, 52).

Turning to the structure of 84 itself, Auffret notes little unanimity among scholars concerning this.[14] Nonetheless, formal and thematic criteria allow a division between two strophes, the first from vv. 2-8 and the second vv. 9-13. Among formal features, the prominent divine epithet יהוה צבאות (or a lengthened form of it, as in vv. 4, 9) is found twice in each strophe, once at the beginning of each (vv. 2, 9), and then again in places (vv. 4, 13) where it is followed immediately by one or two beatitudes (אשרי, vv. 5, 6 and v. 13). The same divine name (יהוה צבאות) provides inclusio around the whole of the poem (vv. 2, 13):

I.

יהוה צבאות – v. 2
יהוה צבאות...אלהי אשרי...אשרי – vv. 4-6

---

13. It is similarily stated of the blessed man in Ps. 1 that he is not part of the wicked (רשעים), and so Pss. 1, 73 and 84 all repeat the same idea. Book III clearly continues themes already presented in the introduction to the Psalter.

14. P. Auffret, 'Qu'elles sont aimables, tes demeures! Etude structurelle du Psaume 84', *BZ* 38 (1994), pp. 29-33 (29).

II.

יהוה אלהים צבאות – v. 9

יהוה צבאות אשרי – v. 13

A variety of divine epithets are used in Psalm 84, and so the reference to God's name in 83.19, accompanied by a statement of its exaltedness, is a perfect introduction to the next psalm. The speaker of 84.3 exults in the 'living God' (אל חי), the 'Lord of armies, my king and my God' in 84.4 (יהוה צבאות מלכי ואלהי), and declares the Lord God to be a 'sun and shield' in 84.12 (שמש ומגן יהוה אלהים).

Both strophes can be divided into verse paragraphs that parallel each other in content. The first paragraph of strophe I and first two of strophe II (vv. 2-5, 9-10, 11) describe the pleasantness of the divine dwelling, the desire of the poet to dwell within it and attendant blessings. By contrast, in the first paragraph of strophe I praise takes place (vv. 3, 5), while in the first of strophe II petitions are directed to God (vv. 9, 10). Instead of 'dwelling', the second paragraph of strophe I and third of strophe II (vv. 6-8, 12-13) use the image of walking with, and trusting Yahweh, along with the attendant blessings:

> Strophe I – vv. 1-8
>   A. vv. 2-5 – pleasant dwelling, desire, blessing, praise
>   B. vv. 6-8 – blessing, trust, walking
> Strophe II – vv. 9-13
>   A. vv. 9-10 – petition
>   B. v. 11 – pleasant dwelling, desire
>   C. vv. 12-13 – walking, blessing, trust

The theme of Zion in 84.8 reiterates what previous psalms in Book III have already portrayed. The original Zion is in ruins (Ps. 74.2-7), but some future Zion will see the end of war and universal fear of God (76.3, 4, 13). Within 84.8, the same preposition אל is repeated in cola A and B, so that God (אלהים) and strength (חיל) are paralleled across the bicolon. God is thus characterized as dwelling in Zion and possessing strength, repeating a theme found in Psalm 76. In Zion (76.3) God is fearsome (76.8, 12, 13) and defeats armies (76.4-7). Zion appears again in 78.68-69 and is eternally established by God as a dwelling. Later Ps. 87 describes the same Zion, which now includes some of the same enemy nations of 83 as part of its citizenry.

Psalm 84 could be classified as a 'Zion song', based on v. 8 and multiple references to the divine dwelling across the poem. However, vv. 9-10 include a prayer for God to fulfill his promise towards the anointed one. The identical two themes of individual prayer (תפלתי) by the righteous Davidide and appearance of eschatological Zion are found in consecutive Pss. 86.6 (individual prayer) and 87 (Zion), the latter being another example of the Zion songs.[15] Consequently, Psalm 84 parallels within itself what the contiguous 86 and 87 express together.

In summary, Psalm 84 expresses the words of the pious individual who seeks to dwell and walk in the presence of God, not as the wicked Gentiles of 83 and Israelites of 81 and 82. He is the same righteous and suffering Davidide portrayed in Psalm 73, and then periodically throughout Book III. He is also portrayed in Psalm 84 in a manner that identifies him as the anointed king and blessed man of the Psalter's introduction. Links are especially close between 84 and 80, the latter expressing a community request for the appearance of this individual. Following the three consecutive Psalms 81–83 portraying the walk of the wicked in both Israel and the nations, Psalms 84–86 will describe the walk of the righteous. The change from descriptions of disobedience in 81–83 to righteousness in 84–86 occurs precisely at the change from Asaphite to Qorahite psalms.

15. Cf. Gunkel, *Die Psalmen*, p. 378.

Chapter 13

PSALM 85

Except for the rare form על הגתית in Psalm 85, both 84 and 85 have identical superscriptions. This pair of Qorahite psalms is surrounded on both sides by psalms ascribed to different authors, Asaph before (Psalms 73–83) and David after (Psalm 86). Following Psalm 86 are two more consecutive Qorahite psalms (87–88), for a total of four in Book III. The lack of common elements between 86 and its surrounding psalms is overcome by the same Qorahite ascriptions of those on either side. This contrasts with the break in author ascriptions of Psalms 72–73. Preceding 72 bearing Solomon's name are Davidic ascriptions, and following are those ascribed to Asaph, emphasizing the divide between Books II and III. Likewise the Ezrahite Psalm 89 is followed at the transition to Book IV by a Mosaic psalm in 90, followed by superscriptions lacking authorial ascriptions in Psalm 91 and following. Consequently, an editorial easing of the transition from 85 to 88 has been accomplished, as was done between Psalms 83–84 (there using genre instead of author ascriptions) and in contrast to the superscriptions found at the borders on either end of Book III.

The only reference to the nation in Psalm 84 appears in v. 9, where 'Jacob' is used, and there it is in the context of an individual's prayer. In fact, Psalm 84 is the prayer of an individual (except for v.10a as explained above), while 85.2-8 expresses the supplication of a community. Psalm 85 opens with the same name 'Jacob' in v. 2, providing transition from 84, and from that point on the designation is 'people' (עם, vv. 3, 7, 9).

Part of the plea in Psalm 85 is for God to again bring life to the nation (תחינו, v. 7), a request that only the living God (אל־חי, 84.3) is capable of answering. Lifelessness has been expressed already by the individual in 84.3, whose soul is spent, but found strength in Yahweh (בך, 84.6), and trusted in him (בך, 84.13). Likewise, the nation will rejoice in God (ישמחו בך), after being revived (85.7).

Although Ps. 85.2-7 is prayed in the first person plural, the reply is awaited by one individual (v. 9). It is possible that the individual who prayed on his own behalf in Psalm 84 now intercedes for the entire nation in 85. If 85.2-8 are to be heard as words spoken by the entire community, they are the only ones in the stretch of Psalms 84–89, excepting perhaps 89.18-19. On the other hand, this individual has acted as mediator for the lamenting community before, as in Psalms 77 and 78. In spite of his complaint in Psalm 73 about Israel's participation with the wicked, he did not forget them. In Psalm 77 he is praying on their behalf to God, and represents the divine voice in 78 responding to the previous lament. In 84, a psalm of an individual, as the pronominal and verbal forms demonstrate, the speaker at one point in his prayer uses the first person plural (מָגִנֵּנוּ, 84.10a). Here he represents the nation as a whole at one single point in what could be characterized as antici-pation of the following psalm. The first seven verses of Psalm 85 begin in the first person plural (vv. 2-8), including a series of interrogatives (vv. 6-7). It was in Ps. 77.8-10 that the individual also uttered a series of questions to God in the midst of what was otherwise an individual lament. In both psalms the questions are of the continued (הַלְעוֹלָם, 77.8; 85.6) divine anger (אַף, 77.10; 85.6) against the nation. Consequently, it is very probable that this individual voices Israel's prayer in 85.

The appeal to God in Psalm 85, which constitutes the first half of the psalm, ends in v. 8 with an imperative essentially equivalent to one in the previous psalm. God is asked to 'make visible' (הַרְאֵנוּ) covenant faithfulness and 84.10 asks him to 'look at' (רְאֵה) their shield and anointed one. Both voice the desire of the community for salvation out of the present distress through the anointed one. The requested 'covenant faithfulness' (חֶסֶד) of 85.8 is that sworn to David (89.2-5, 50). Parallel to faithfulness in 85.8 is 'your salvation' (יֶשְׁעֲךָ), requested four times previously (80.3, 4, 8, 20), through the empowering of the chosen son (80.16, 18), and promised in 72.4, 12 and 13. Likewise, the anointed one (מְשִׁיחַ) of 84.10 is the divinely chosen Davidic king, expected since the Psalter's introduction (מְשִׁיחוֹ, 2.2). In other words, the petition of 85.8 asks again for the revelation of the promised eschatological kingdom under a Davidide.

The pleas of Ps. 84.9, 10 (with supporting reasons in vv. 11-13) and 85.5-8, including the interrogatives of the latter, all find responses in the second half of 85. In other words, the last half of 85 (vv. 9-14) answers not only the first half but the previous psalm as well. An imperative in

84.9 (שמעה, 'listen to') is followed by two instances in vv. 11 and 12 of the same particle כי. This imperative becomes an imperfect form (אשמעה, 'I will listen') of the same root in 85.9, followed by the identical particle. Between these two parallels are forms of the root 'to see/look' (ראה) in first person plural contexts, 'look at our shield' and 'cause us to see':

$$
\begin{array}{rl}
\text{שמעה...כי...כי} & -\ 84.9\text{-}12 \\
\text{מגננו ראה} & -\ 84.10 \\
\text{הראנו} & -\ 85.8 \\
\text{אשמעה...כי} & -\ 85.9
\end{array}
$$

One could postulate that these verbal parallels create an inclusio around this series of petitions, notwithstanding the fact that they include the second and first halves of two consecutive psalms.

The illustration just given brackets the overt imperatives between 84.9 and 85.9. However, it must be said that the first half of Psalm 84, even if lacking explicit imperatival forms, is likewise a request for the habitations of God. The speaker's stated longings in 84.2-8 are meant to move Yahweh into granting them. Therefore, the entire Psalm 84 and following 85.2-8 are petitionary, and likewise receive answers in 85.9-14.

Introducing Psalm 84 was the exclamatory particle מה (v. 2) in an outburst of desire for the dwellings of God (משכנותיך). In the petition of 84.9-13 the supplicant believes that 'glory' (כבוד, v. 12) and 'good' (טוב, v. 12) are given to those who walk in integrity. Identical in form, if not in grammatical function is the same particle מה used as an indefinite pronoun in 85.9 to introduce Yahweh's answer.[1] That answer expresses assurance that 'glory' will 'dwell' (לשכן כבוד, v. 10) in the land, and that Yahweh will give 'the good' (הטוב, v. 13). One instance of מה begins the prayer of longing and request (84.1) for divine dwelling and glory, while the other introduces as an indefinite pronoun[2] the affirmative answer about to be given (85.9) concerning those same two manifestations of God's presence. Furthermore, the answer of 85.10, assuring that glory will dwell (לשכן כבוד) in the land, takes concepts from the beginning (משכנותיך, 84.2) and end (כבוד, 84.12) of Psalm 84, and

---

1.   Admittedly, the particle מה is a common Hebrew form and so would not otherwise indicate important parallels. However, it is not found in either the three preceding nor succeeding psalms at either end of Pss. 84–85, and its position at decisive points in either psalm argue for intentional correspondence.

2.   GKC, §137c.

unites them in one phrase. The petitions of 84 are thus given an affirmative answer.

Double use of the preposition אֶל ('to/toward') in 84.8 and 85.9
confirms the correspondence between requests of 84 and answers of
85.9-14. The faithful of 84.8 are walking toward God in Zion. A single
occurrence in 84.3 of the same form is part of a cry directed towards
God. If praise in 84.3 and movement in 84.8 is towards God, the direction in 85.9 is now reversed:

84.3 – אֶל אֵל־חָי

84.8 – אֶל...אֶל אֱלֹהִים

85.9 – הָאֵל...אֶל עַמּוֹ וְאֶל חֲסִידָיו

The editors of *BHS* suggest an emendation in 85.9 of הָאֵל to הֲלֹא, missing the parallel alliteration between divine name and preposition that
links both psalms. Tate states that the combination of הָאֵל יהוה 'is
strange'.[3] Perhaps within the syntax of 85.9 itself this form of the divine
name is peculiar, but within Book III it functions as an indication of
linkage between adjacent dialoguing psalms.

The divine answer begins officially in 85.10 in response not only to
the previous psalm, but more directly the interrogatives of 85.6, 7 and
imperatives of 85.5, 8. Verse 6 asks if divine anger will endure forever,
and in response v. 9 affirms that Yahweh will speak peace. Verse 7 asks
if God will not return, revive and thus make 'your people' (עַמֶּךָ) rejoice.
Again, v. 9 answers directly that peace will be spoken to 'his people'
(עַמּוֹ).

Salvation (יִשְׁעֶךָ/יֶשְׁעֵנוּ), seemingly so distant from the speakers of vv.
5-8, is close for those that fear him in v. 10 (יִשְׁעוֹ). However, this salvation is further described as the dwelling of glory (לִשְׁכֹּן כָּבוֹד) in the land
(10b), resuming as noted earlier, the reference to dwellings from 84.2
(מִשְׁכְּנוֹתֶיךָ) and glory from 84.12 (כָּבוֹד). The psalmist had expressed
admiration and desire for the dwellings of Yahweh in 84.2-3, and
seeking that dwelling was synonymous with trust in him (84.5-6, 11,
13). Those who trusted in him and walked in integrity were promised
grace and glory in 84.12 (כָּבוֹד). Such individuals of Psalm 84 are
assured of goodness and will see the ultimate dwelling and glory of
85.10b. The desire for the divine dwelling of 84 is fulfilled by the
eschatological salvation of 85.10, where God's glory takes up residence
in the land.

3. Tate, *Psalms 51–100*, p. 365.

Psalm 85.13 and 14 are remarkable in their resonance with the previous Psalm 84:

84.12 – חן וכבוד יהוה יתן לא ימנע־טוב לַהֹלְכִים בתמים
85.13a-14a – יהוה יתן הטוב...תַתֵן יבולה:...צדק לפניו יְהַלֵך

'Goodness' is equated with 'grace and glory' in 84.12, and the surrounding context of 85.13 reveals that these are eschatological terms (cf. כבוד of 85.10b). If Ps. 84.12 names the beneficiaries of God's ultimate goodness (לַהֹלְכִים בתמים, 'to those who walk with integrity'), 85 reveals the place (בארצנו, 'in our land'), and time (קרוב, 'close'), as well as the beneficiaries (ליראיו, 'to those who fear him') in v. 10. The speaker of 84 and those of an upright walk accompanying him will experience this desired eschatological goodness. Longing for the courts and attention of God in 84 will eventually be rewarded. In the next Psalm 86 the speaker includes himself in this eschatological reward as one who fears the name of God (לבבי לִיראה שמך).

Embodied righteousness (צדק) walks in 85.14a, kisses peace in v. 11, and peers down from heaven in v. 12. The personifications of righteousness begun in vv. 11-12 continue in v. 14 (יהלך). Righteousness personified of 85.14 is among those of Psalm 84 who walk in integrity (לַהֹלְכִים בתמים, v.12) toward Zion (ילכו, v. 8). In 86.11 it will become clear that Yahweh possesses that roadway (called 'truth', אמת, in 86.11, but parallel to 'righteousness', צדק, in 85.11, 12), and that personified righteousness is identified as the speaker:

85.14 – צדק לפניו יְהַלֵך וישם לְדֶרֶך פעמיו
86.11 – הורני יהוה דַרְכֶך אַהַלֵך באמתך

The righteous speaker heard in 86.6 (האזינה...תפלתי) is identical to the speaker of 84.9 (תפלתי האזינה), who in turn was shown to voice the words of Psalm 85 as well. Across three psalms describing the righteous walk (84–86), the same individual speaks. He can speak for himself (Psalms 84, 86), or for Israel (85.2-8), or for the deity (85.9-14).

As just noted, the roadway trod by the faithful leads to Zion (ילכו... בציון, 84.8). The individual of 86.11 walks a path (דרכך) of truth and glorifies Adonay's name (86.12). The nations of v. 9 will also come (ויבאו) to bow before Adonay and honor that name. In Ps. 87.4 the nations are within Zion speaking glorious things. Consequently, from Psalms 84 to 87 all roads of righteousness and integrity lead to eschatological Zion. Righteous 'David' of 86 continues the theme of a pious individual seen in previous psalms such as 73, 76, 77, 78, 80, 84, 85, who is now joined by others, including foreign nations.

The conjunction גַם ('also') of 85.13 adds goodness and 'its produce' (יְבוּלָהּ) to the already mentioned kindness, truth, justice and peace of vv. 11-12. The same conjunction in 84.7b joined blessings and rain to the springs of v. 7a. This formal parallel reveals another of conceptual nature between the abundance of rain and water in 84.7 and the resulting bountiful crop in 85.13. The faithful pilgrimage in 84.6-7 is rewarded in the Zion of 84.8 and by the goodness of 84.12 and 85.13, defined in the latter as bountiful harvest.

Appearance before God in Zion (בְּצִיּוֹן, 84.8), or faith in the ultimate reception of his glory (כָּבוֹד, 84.12), are assured by the ultimate habitation of divine glory (כָּבוֹד, 85.10) in the land. This correspondence drawn between 84 and 85 based on כָּבוֹד continues in Psalm 87 with the glorious things (נִכְבָּדוֹת, v. 3) spoken in Zion (צִיּוֹן, v. 2). In other words, of the two concepts 'Zion' and 'glory' named in 84 only glory is repeated in the following 85. However, that glory is united with the Zion of 87.

Going beyond the immediately previous Psalm 84, one finds further parallels to Psalm 85. In this era of salvation and glory anounced by 85.10-14, righteousness (צֶדֶק) abounds in the land, as the threefold repetition intimates (vv. 11, 12, 14). This is in direct contrast to the lack of righteousness on the part of the nation's judges in 82.3 (הַצְדִּיקוּ). Likewise, peace abounds in the land as 85.9, 11 reveal, in conjunction with the righteousness (צֶדֶק וְשָׁלוֹם, v. 11). Such conditions contrast with those portrayed in Psalm 83 of surrounding nations conspiring to do away with Israel. Thus, the abundance of righteousness and peace (85.11) heralds a new era wholly different from that of the injustice in 82 or warmongering in 83,[4] but identical to that promised in 72:

$$\text{שָׁלוֹם...בְּצִדְקָה} \quad – \quad 72.3$$
$$\text{צַדִּיק...שָׁלוֹם} \quad – \quad 72.7$$
$$\text{צֶדֶק וְשָׁלוֹם} \quad – \quad 85.11$$

---

4. According to P. Auffret, 'Justice et paix se sont embrassées: Etude structurelle du Psaume 85', in P. Auffret, *Voyez de vos yeux: Etude structurelle de vingt psaumes, dont le Psaume 119* (VTSup, 48; Leiden: E.J.Brill, 1993), pp. 262-78 (272), these two nouns in v. 11 are the center of the second strophe (vv. 9-14). They are found separated at both extremes (vv. 9, 14) and they embrace at the center (v. 11). The effect when read from a canonical perspective is to highlight the two which most clearly recall the promises of Ps. 72.

The promises of righteousness in Psalm 72 are reiterated in 85, and assure rectification of the injustices perpetrated in 82:

72.1 – וּצְדָקָתְךָ
72.2 – בְּצֶדֶק
82.3 – הַצְדִּיקוּ
85.11-14 – צֶדֶק...וּצְדֶק...צֶדֶק

One could add that the oft-repeated root ישׁע in noun form of 85.5, 8, 10 corresponds to the same in verb form in 72.4, 13 (יושׁיע). Furthermore, the agricultural prosperity announced in 85.13 for 'our land' (אַרְצֵנוּ) confirms the promise in a similar description in 72.16 (בָאָרֶץ). As a result, the divine answer of 85.10-14 assures the faithful of a long-awaited universal reign of prosperity, peace and righteousness, such as described in 72.

The restoration of peace and righteousness in Psalm 85 reaffirms what 72 promised (צַדִּיק/צֶדֶק...שָׁלוֹם, 72. 2-3, 7), and also contrasts sharply with 73. In 73 there was peace (שָׁלוֹם, v. 3), but the wicked (רְשָׁעִים) were enjoying it, not the righteous. This situation had almost driven the speaker of Psalm 73 to falter. Now in 85.11, assurance is given of the eventual unity between peace and righteousness (צֶדֶק וְשָׁלוֹם).

Time and again in Book III, interrogatives directed toward God ask how long wrath against the nation will endure (Pss. 74.1, 9-10; 77.8-10; 79.5; 80.5), and 88.15 and 89.47 will repeat it again (82.5 is the same interrogative thrown back at Israel by God).[5] Here in 85.6 another instance is found in unmistakable terms: 'Will you be angry at us for-ever? Will you draw out your anger from generation to generation?'

85.6 – הַלְעוֹלָם תֶּאֱנַף בָּנוּ תִּמְשֹׁךְ אַפְּךָ לְדֹר וָדֹר

Verbal correspondences are found in the interrogatives of 74.1 (אַפְּךָ), 77.8 (הַלְעוֹלָמִים), 77.9 (לְדֹר וָדֹר)[6] and 79.5 (תֶּאֱנַף). The interrogative heh opening v. 6 (and v. 7) repeats the same heh found three times in 77.8-

---

5.   Cf. the shorter list of Zenger, 'Zur redaktionsgeschichtlichen', p. 194, who notes the relation of the interrogative in 89.47 to those of 77.8; 79.5; 88.15 in discussing the origin of the collection from Pss. 2–89.

6.   The question of God's enduring anger, i.e., from generation to generation, is answered in Ps. 90.1, stating that he has actually been their refuge from generation to generation (בְּדֹר וָדֹר), in spite of his anger (אַף, 90.7, 11). The repetition of this phrase in 77.9 and 85.6 is a legitimate query after the promised eternal and univer-sal fear of God from generation to generation in 72.5 (דּוֹר דּוֹרִים).

10. So the questioning of God continues unabated through Book III, and here in 85.6 it precedes further answers given immediately following in vv. 10-14.

The imperative of v. 5 (שׁוּבֵנוּ) resembles the request repeated four times in Psalm 80, using the same root (הֲשִׁיבֵנוּ, vv. 4, 8, 15, 20). In addition, the root ישׁע appears here in 85.5, 8 as it does in three of the same verses of Psalm 80 (נוָשֵׁעָה, vv. 4, 8, 20). When 85.10 answers that salvation (יֶשַׁע) is close, it responds to the immediately preceding calls of 85.5-8 and to those repeated in Psalm 80.

Within the interrogative of 85.7 is found another pair of terms that essentially repeats requests of 80:

תְּחַיֵּנוּ...הֲשִׁיבֵנוּ – 80.19b-20a

תָּשׁוּב תְּחַיֵּנוּ – 85.7a

We read then in Psalm 85 petitions that resemble closely those of 80, except that the answers given to each are quite different. Psalm 81 answered 80 with an accusation of disobedience, while here in 85 the reply is of future restoration. The immediate answer to Psalm 80 came in the following 81.9 (שְׁמַע עַמִּי), introduced by the imperfect form אֶשְׁמַע of 81.6b. Similarily, the imperatives and interrogatives of 85.5-8 are answered in v. 9, being introduced again by the practically identical אֶשְׁמְעָה. In fact, 81.9 as a whole addresses God's people with words similar to that of 85.9:

שְׁמַע עַמִּי – 81.9

אֶשְׁמְעָה מַה יְדַבֵּר אֵל אֶל עַמּוֹ – 85.9

In 85.9 the single speaker is the sole listener, although the message is for the nation as a whole. In both cases (81.9; 85.9) Yahweh speaks, but according to 81.12 the nation does not listen (לֹא שָׁמַע עַמִּי). Here in 85.9 at least one individual is attentive to the divine message. Not surprisingly, in the same breath the wayward nation is warned against returning to folly (וְאַל יָשׁוּבוּ לְכִסְלָה).

Just as the human appeal ends at 85.8 and the divine response begins at 85.9, so these two verses mark a division between two major strophes, the first from vv. 2-8 and the second from vv. 9-14. J. Trublet and J.N. Aletti label vv. 2-8 as 'actions divines' and vv. 9-14 as 'attributs divins'.[7] P. Auffret notes that on the extremes of strophe I (vv. 2, 8) the

---

7. J. Trublet and J.N. Aletti, *Approche poétique et théologique des Psaumes* (Paris: Cerf, 1983), p. 85.

two different terms, שַׁבְתָּ ('you returned') and יֵשַׁע ('salvation'), meet at
the center in v. 5, and likewise שָׁלוֹם ('peace') of v. 9 and צֶדֶק ('righteousness') in v. 14 at either end of strophe II meet together ('kiss') in
the center at v. 11.[8] Hakham divides between prayer (vv. 2-8) and
Yahweh's answer to prayer (vv. 9-14).[9] Supporting such evidence for
the strophic division is the fact that the Tetragrammaton occurs at the
beginning and end of strophe I (vv. 2, 8), and then the opening (v. 9)
and near the end (v. 13) of strophe II. This means that the divine name
creates inclusio around the entire psalm and each of the two strophes as
well.[10] Added to the divine name is the noun אֶרֶץ ('land') found in vv. 2
and 13 as well, and thus the inclusio consists of at least two identical
formal elements. His favor shown to the land in times past (v. 2a) is
paralleled by that same land in the future yielding its produce by way of
Yahweh's goodness (v. 13). Meynet notes that Yahweh's land in v. 2
becomes 'our land' in v. 13 (and v. 10).[11] Redemption of the nation
returns it to them.

Redemption is of course dependent on obedience to the warning of v.
9. There the nation is warned not to 'return' (יָשׁובו) to folly, in answer
to the repeated requests in strophe I (and recollections) that God return
and deliver them (שַׁבְתָּ, v. 2; הֵשִׁיבוֹתָ, v. 4; שׁובֵנוּ, v. 5; תָּשׁוּב, v. 7). Psalm
80 also requested repeatedly that they be returned (הֲשִׁיבֵנוּ, 80.4, 8, 20),
only to receive in Psalms 81–82 a divine indictment for disobedience.
Actually, Psalm 80 was a continuation of the community's appeal seen
in 79, which also resembles that seen in the first strophe of 85:

עָזְרֵנוּ אֱלֹהֵי יִשְׁעֵנוּ – 79.9
שׁובֵנוּ אֱלֹהֵי יִשְׁעֵנוּ – 85.5

Although parallels between the laments of 79–80 and 85.2-8 reveal a
basic similarity, responses to each differ. Psalm 85.9-14 (except for the
brief warning of the final colon of v. 9) is a positive response to the
previous lament, in contrast to the divine condemnations expressed by
81–82. Such affirmations of promises have not been seen in Book III

---

8.   Auffret, 'Justice et paix', pp. 268, 272, 278. Both שַׁבְתָּ of v. 2 and שׁובֵנוּ of
v. 5 derive from the same root שׁוב.

9.   Hakham, *Sefer tehillim*, p. 109 (קם).

10.   Cf. Youngblood, 'Divine Names', p. 174, who divides the psalm into four
stanzas (vv. 2-4, 5-8, 9-10, 11-14), noting the appearance of YHWH in each.

11.   R. Meynet, 'L'enfant de l'amour (Ps 85)', *NRT* 112 (1990), pp. 843-58
(855).

since Psalms 75 and 76. As may be recalled, these also answered in the affirmative previous laments (73–74) over the nonfulfillment of Psalm 72. Here again, the coming of the long-awaited kingdom of peace and righteousness described in Psalm 72 is reaffirmed. It is in fact 'near' (קרוב, 85.10) to those that fear Yahweh.

Chapter 14

PSALM 86

The unique character of Psalm 86's superscription in Book III was mentioned in the previous chapter, including a description of the technique utilized to create cohesion with surrounding Qorahite psalms. Unlike author changes at the borders of Book III (72–73, 89–90), the change from Qorah to David (85–86) was achieved without the harsh division of the former. This was accomplished by placing two Qorahite psalms on either side of 86 (84, Qorahites; 85, Qorahites; 86, David; 87, Qorahites; 88, Qorahites), in contrast to 70–74 (David, Solomon, Asaph, Asaph) or 88–92 (Heman the Ezrahite, Ethan the Ezrahite, Moses, authorless, authorless). In addition, the catchwords between 85 and 86 (of different authorial ascriptions) are numerous,[1] in contrast to the scarcity of such between 85 and 87 (of identical authors). On the other hand, while catchwords are not quite as numerous between 86 and 87, 86 and 88 are extremely similar both at the level of content and genre.[2] As a result, the network of interlocking factors both formal and thematic across this string of psalms lessens the effect of division caused by different authorial ascriptions.

While Psalm 86 is well integrated into the context of surrounding psalms, the name 'David' still stands as unique in the titles of Book III. No doubt there existed a desire to maintain in the forefront the eschatological and messianic emphasis that is evident across the canonical Psalter. It reinforces the centrality of the Davidic covenant as commented on by the numerous Asaphite and Qorahite psalms up to this point in Book III.

---

1. P. Auffret, 'Essai sur la structure littéraire du Psaume 85', in *idem, La sagesse a bâti sa maison: Etudes de structures littéraires dans l'Ancien Testament et spécialment dans les Psaumes* (Göttingen: Vandenhoeck & Ruprecht, 1982), pp. 287-300 (297), counts 19 terms common to Pss. 85 and 86.

2. Both are clearly laments of an individual, and designated as prayers (תפלתי, 86.6; 88.3, 14) by the speaker.

Other explanations for the position of Psalm 86 have been offered.
Wilson, in examining the sequence of superscriptions, sees a 'binding/
locking' function for Psalm 86, whereby the Qorahite group of 84–85
and 87–88 with 89 is bound to the whole of Books II and III (42–89,
including the Davidic 51–71 with 72), by this Davidic Psalm 86.[3]
Likewise, the lone Asaphite Psalm 50 performs the identical function
with the other Asaphite Psalms 73-83 by putting a frame around the
Davidic Psalms 51–71 with 72 within Books II and III. As noted many
times already, similar binding functions are evident within Book III for
these authorial ascriptions. Therefore, to find the same in the Psalter at
large would not be surprising.

Zenger suggests that Psalm 86 is part of the final stage in the forma-
tion of Psalms 1–89, stamped with a strong 'theology of the poor',
found also in Psalms 9–10.[4] He notes correctly parallels of this theology
between Psalms 86 and 72.[5] Observing contacts between Psalms 85 and
86, he suggests that 86 may have been composed principally for the
'literary-compositional connection'.[6] The speaker of Psalm 86 does
include himself among the afflicted and poor (עָנִי וְאֶבְיוֹן, 86.1) who are
the object of attention in 72 (vv. 2, 4, 12, 13). However, Psalm 86 also
contributes to a strong 'royal theology', as the repeated noun עַבְדְּךָ
('your servant') in vv. 2, 4, 16 reveals when compared with the same in
Pss. 78.70 and 89.4, 21, 40. Furthermore, the worship of Gentiles
described in closely parallel terms by 72.11 and 86.9 shows that the
petitions of 86.1-7 are answered in a restatement of the promises of
Psalm 72. In fact, Psalm 72 itself is a petition for the royal prince, and
the following psalms of Book III lament the nonfulfillment of the conditions described therein. Psalm 86 continues that theme of lament and
includes an answer. Once again, the righteous Davidic speaker across
Book III is assured realization of that kingdom, described extensively in
72 and more briefly in 86.

3.   G.H. Wilson, 'Shaping the Psalter: A Consideration of Editorial Linkage in
the Book of Psalms', in McCann (ed.), *The Shape and Shaping of the Psalter*,
pp. 72-82 (76-77).

4.   Zenger, 'Zur redaktionsgeschichtlichen Bedeutung', pp. 189-90 n. 42, 192-
93, 195-96.

5.   He does not mention the presence of this same theology in Pss. 74.19, 21
and 82.3, 4.

6.   '[L]iterarisch-kompositionellen Zusammenhang'; in 'Zur redaktionsgeschichtlichen Bedeutung', p. 190 n. 42.

Psalm 86 is a prayer attributed to David according to the superscription and contains clear links to 72, a psalm also attributed to David by the final verse. Therefore, in the canonical Psalter, 72 is important for the correct interpretation of 86. However, Ps. 72.20 purportedly states that the prayers of David, the son of Jesse 'are ended' (כלו, pual perfect). How then did Psalm 86 and many others attributed to David in Books IV and V come to be included in the Psalter? It appears quite obvious that if the final compiler of the Psalter had interpreted this statement as indicating 72 was the final Davidic psalm in the collection, it would have been deleted or placed in another position. The mastery of detail demonstrated in the redaction of Book III obviates any supposed accidents of editing.[7] Furthermore, given the close links between 86 and 72 and the attribution of the former to David, the statement at the end of 72 must have been interpreted otherwise in the final editing of the Psalter. A solution is offered here.[8]

Not only are there close parallels between 86 and 72, but as shown in previous chapters, the fulfillment of Psalm 72's promises is a constant theme through Book III. Psalm 72 is evoked repeatedly when laments and prayers for restoration are made. Furthermore, divine answers given in these psalms reiterate the promises of Psalm 72. It would appear then that the verb in question of 72.20 should be rendered 'are perfected', in the sense that the previous description represented the perfection, culmination and fullest outworking of the promise to David. 'Prayers' (תפלות) are to be understood here as 'prophecies', since 72 itself functions as prophecy, and as will be seen, so does the prayer of 86.[9] Furthermore, the term 'prayers' here in 72.20 undoubtedly covers all utterances of David, regardless of the generic title. Psalm 72 at the

---

7. Manuscript evidence supports the MT of 72.20. The absence of כלו in a few manuscripts and the Syriac is undoubtedly an attempt to harmonize the text.

8. See Mitchell, *The Message of the Psalter*, pp. 66-73, for a review of interpretation.

9. Childs, *Introduction to the Old Testament as Scripture*, p. 513, says, regarding the prayers of the Psalter, 'Because Israel continues to hear God's word through the voice of the psalmist's response, these prayers now function as the divine word itself'. The 'prayer' of Hannah in 1 Sam. 2.1-10 is also included in the book as prophetic of the future anointed king, and serves with David's words in 2 Sam. 22–23 as a bracket around the entire work. In 2 Sam. 23.1-2 it is stated of David, as the 'psalmist of Israel' (זמרות ישראל) that 'the spirit of Yahweh spoke through him', and Yahweh's words were 'on his tongue'. David's words are to be read as prophecy.

end of Book II is the last word on the subject of the promised eschatological kingdom to David's house, surpassing any previous or subsequent descriptions within the Psalter. The 'prayers/prophecies of David
are perfected', and what follows can only repeat what has already been
said or plead for its institution.[10] Here at the center of the book is found
the high point of promises to David.

The latter half of Psalm 85 functioned as an answer to laments in the
first verses, and also evoked and reiterated themes given in Psalm 72.
Repeated references to 'righteousness' (צדק, vv. 11, 12, 14), 'peace'
(שלום, vv. 9, 11) and 'salvation' (ישע, vv. 5, 8, 10) recalled and reaffirmed the conditions promised in 72 (vv. 1, 2, 3, 4, 7, 13). Now the
following Psalm 86 will continue along the same lines and at the same
time focus on the Davidic speaker who is closely linked to the realization of the universal kingdom of righteousness.

The masculine singular adjective חסיד ('pious one') is a self-given
description by the speaker in 86.2. Consequently, the request for
preservation of v. 2 is a logical petition following the statement of 85.9
that the pious ones of Yahweh (חסידיו) will indeed be recipients of
peace (שלום). Just as God's covenant faithfulness (חסד) in 85.8, 11 is
appropriately directed toward his pious ones (חסידיו) in 85.9, so his
kindness (חסד) of 86.5, 13, 15 should be directed to the pious one of
86.2 (חסיד). He is in fact the ideal of piety in Book III.

A portrait of the same individual was encountered in 78.70. There
David is called God's servant (עבדו), and possessed of a heart of
integrity (כתם לבבו) in 78.72 (accomplishing as a leader what Moses
failed to do). Likewise in 86.2, 4, 16 the speaker identifies himself in
first person as God's servant (עבדך) and possessed of an honest heart
(לבבי, vv. 11-12). He prays that God would unite his heart (יחד לבבי,
86.11), and so is like the David of 78.72. Previously in 78.68-72 the
reference to David was in conjunction with the choice of 'Zion that God

---

10. The other example of pual for the root כלה is Gen. 2.1 (see BDB, p. 478b)
which could be read 'be perfected'. The creative work was not only finished, but
perfectly completed. Note how in Gen. 1.31, the completed work is called 'very
good', טוב מאד (in contrast to the simple 'good' of 1.4, 10, 12, 21, 25), which complements the following ויכלו (Gen. 2.1) if it is read as 'perfected' or perhaps
'completed to perfection'. Note as well the noun forms מכלה and תכלה (from the
same root כלל), rendered 'completeness, perfection' by BDB, p. 479. The latter
form תכלה appears in Ps. 119.96a parallel to 119.96b, where the same adjective
מאד is found.

loved' (צִיּוֹן אֲשֶׁר אָהֵב, 78.68b), and so Psalm 86 is followed by reference to the same Zion in 87.2 (אֹהֵב יהוה שַׁעֲרֵי צִיּוֹן). All Gentiles will
come to worship Adonay in 86.9, which 87 reveals takes place in Zion,
a city now composed of many nationalities. There is clearly a renewal
of the promise seen in Psalm 78 of a righteous David, and also of the
universal kingdom portrayed in 72.

Returning to 86.2, the imperative 'save!' (הוֹשַׁע) on the part of the
individual (also v. 16, הוֹשִׁיעָה) again takes up a theme from 85.5, 8, 10.
The community pled for salvation in 85.5, 8 (יֵשַׁע), and the divine
response in 85.10 promised his salvation (יֵשַׁע) to those who feared him
(לִירֵאָיו), another designation for the pious ones (v. 9). The speaker in
86.2a has already proclaimed his piety as a basis for the requested salvation in 86.2b, and then in 86.11 asks that Yahweh unite his heart to
fear (לְיִרְאָה) his name. Thus, the David of 86 on a canonical level is
unambiguously asking for the salvation promised in 85.10-13, and testi-
fying of his moral qualification to receive it.

When this David implores God to save him in 86.2, vocabulary is
resumed from the implorations in 85.5 and 7 as follows:

$$\text{שׁוּבֵנוּ אֱלֹהֵי יִשְׁעֵנוּ...הֲלֹא אַתָּה} - 85.5, 7$$
$$\text{הוֹשַׁע עַבְדְּךָ אַתָּה אֱלֹהַי} - 86.2$$

In this manner, the speaker of 86 identifies himself as an individual
serving the same God of the community in 85.5, 7. The 'God of our
salvation' in 85.5 becomes 'my God' in 86.2. Psalm 85 restricted the
promise of peace and salvation to those who were pious (v. 9) and
feared God (v. 10), which characteristics the David of Psalm 86 applies
to himself.

Not only does the individual of 86 identify himself with the recipients
of salvation in 85, he coincides in various ways with the figure of Psalm
84. If the blessed man of 84.13 trusts in Yahweh (בֹּטֵחַ בָּךְ), the speaker
of 86.2 does the same (הַבּוֹטֵחַ אֵלֶיךָ). He was described in 84.6 as finding
his strength in Yahweh (עוֹז־לוֹ בָךְ), an identical attitude found by the
supplicant in 86.16 (תְּנָה־עֻזְּךָ). These two verses (84. 6, 13) identify this
individual as the blessed man (אַשְׁרֵי אָדָם), while the two verses in Psalm
86 (2, 16) refer to him as God's servant (עַבְדֶּךָ). David, servant of God
in 86, is thus likened to the blessed one of 84.

Further parallels confirming this identification between 84 and 86
include the spent 'soul/life' (נֶפֶשׁ) of 84.3 and the needy 'soul/life' of
86.2, 4, 13, 14 (נֶפֶשׁ), the individual's prayer for a hearing in 84.9 and
the same in 86.6:

84.9 – יהוה...תפלתי האזינה
86.6 – האזינה יהוה תפלתי

If the psalmist in 84.3 rejoices in God with his heart (לבי...אל אל חי), so the individual in 86.12 praises his God in like manner (אלהי...לבבי).

Between the two adjacent psalms 85 and 86 is the parallel use of the root שׂמח ('rejoice', 85.7 and 86.4). If God would again revive his people (85.7), they would rejoice in him, and likewise the individual in 86.4 asks that God make his soul joyful, presumably by responding to his plea for help. In 86.4, the lifting (אשׂא) of his soul to the Lord serves as a basis for divine help. In 85.3 the past forgiveness or lifting (נשׂאת) of sin also serves as a reason for doing the same in the present. Both roots שׂמח and נשׂא of 86.4 are parallel in the bicolon by their collocation at either end, and by grammatical relation to the twice used נפשׁי ('my soul'). These same two roots are joined in 85.3a and 7b by their grammatical relation to the suffixed noun עמך. Lifting the nation's sin in the past (85.3a) and present will result in their joy (85.7b). Likewise, the individual lifts his soul to Adonay (86.4b) so that it may experience rejoicing (86.4a). Both individual and nation experience suffering and pray for relief, but confession of sin is conspicuously absent in the words of the former. He maintains integrity and piety in 86 (as in Psalms 73, 77, 84), while in 85.3 the sin of Israel is stated explicitly, as it has been throughout Book III. If Israel can only appeal to God's mercy in order to assuage divine anger (Ps. 85.4-6), the speaker of 86 can cite his own faithfulness as deserving of favor and kindness.

Another reason given to elicit favor on David's behalf is the stated goodness (כי אתה...טוב) of Adonay in 86.5. This declaration of his goodness only reiterates what the previous two psalms have already stated. Yahweh will give good (הטוב, 85.13) to his people and pious ones, or as in 84.12, good is not withheld (לא ימנע טוב) to everyone who walks in integrity. This would include the 'one who trusts' (בטח) in God of 84.13. The servant of 86 has already declared his integrity in several ways (vv.1-4), including trust (הבטח) in God, and therefore should be a recipient of that goodness. For this reason he asks for a good (טובה, 86.17) sign. The word 'sign' in 86.17 (cf. 74.9; 78.43) implies a supernatural intervention, as the phonetic resonance with 'wonderous things' in v. 10 confirms (נפלאות...אות).[11] It has already been shown in the previous chapter that the 'good' of 85.13 is found in

---

11. See BDB, s.v. אוה, p. 16b.

a context of eschatological promises resembling Psalm 72. This Davidide is asking for a miraculous intervention to usher in the eschatological kingdom, which includes personal deliverance from Sheol itself (v.
13). Kingdom restoration promised in 86.9 and rescue out of death in
86.13 are closely paired in the middle strophe (vv. 8-13), as will be discussed shortly.

The issue of goodness was raised already in 73.1. There the claim
that God was 'good' (טוב) to Israel, specifically to those pure in heart,
was doubted temporarily before being reaffirmed in v. 28.[12] The pure
heart (לבב) of the speaker in Psalm 73 (vv. 1, 13, 26) resembles the
whole heart of 86.11, 12 (לבב). These convergences confirm again that
the pious individual of 73 and 86 (also portrayed in 75, 77, 78, 80, 84,
85) are one and the same. Just as the Davidide of 86 is asking for the
restoration of his kingdom along the lines of promises in Psalm 72, so
did the speaker of 73.

Psalm 86.5 goes on to declare the abundance of 'covenant faithfulness' (חסד) of Yahweh to those who call to him, another divine quality
mentioned previously in 85.8, 11. Indeed, those who called on him in
85.5-8 were assured of its eventual appearance in 85.11 (חסד), and so
the individual in 86 has a right to claim it for himself. His calling (קרא)
on Yahweh is constant (vv. 3, 7) as is that of the nation in 80.19 (נקרא),
but unlike that of the kings of 79.6 (לא קראו). The result is a full
measure of the covenant promises upon him (חסדך גדול עלי), even
rescue out of death (86.13).

An example of calling on Yahweh is that given in 86.6, where the
speaker asks for a hearing (האזינה). This apparently identifies him with
the individual of 84.9 (האזינה), as observed above, and with the faithful
community of 80.2 (האזינה). Previous to these two psalms, the same
lengthened imperative was found in 78.1, put in the mouth of an individual. Moreover, inclusio around the first strophe of 86 (vv. 1-7) is
found in the single bicolon of 78.1:

78.1 – האזינה עמי תורתי הטו אזנכם
86.1, 6 – הטה יהוה אזנך...האזינה יהוה תפלתי

As can be seen, the order of the two imperatives is reversed. A reversal
of direction is also evident, since one is directed to the nation as a divine

---

12. In the comments on Ps. 73.1 (Chapter 2), it was shown that this verse
acknowledged the promises of the previous Ps. 72 before launching a complaint
over its nonfulfillment.

message uttered by the pious individual (78), and the other to Yahweh
on his own behalf (86). The latter not only petitions for himself, but
has also become a mediator between God and the nation. As may be
recalled, Psalm 78 is a narration of the past history by one who
remembered it (as opposed to the forgetful nation described therein), as
testified by the same individual of Psalm 77 (זכר, vv. 4, 7, 12). Supporting evidence for this parallel drawn between Psalms 78 and 86 include
reference to a servant of God (78.70; 86.2, 4, 16), named David (78.70;
86.1), who is of a sincere heart (78.72; 86.12).

Direct links from Psalm 86 to Psalm 77 are equally strong. The
speakers of Psalms 77 and 86 use the identical prepositional phrase to
describe their state of affliction (ביום צרתי, 77.3; 86.7). Just as in 77.2
his voice (קולי) is raised to God, so it is in 86.6 (בקול). Assurance of a
hearing as expressed in 77.2 (והאזין אלי) is of identical verbal root and
pattern (hiphil) used to petition in 86.6 (האזינה). The insistent pursuit
for answers by the speaker's soul in 77.3 matches that of 86.2, 4, 13, 14
(נפש). The bulk of these parallels between 86 and 77 occur within the
opening verses of each (86.1, 6, 7 and 77.2, 3).

As mentioned numerous times, the voice of a single distressed individual is heard speaking across numerous psalms in Book III. His
affliction and need is expressed here in 86.1 (עני ואביון אני) by a phrase
repeated across Book III. That condition identifies him with those in the
preceding Psalm 72:

72.4 – עני עם...לבני אביון
72.12 – כי יציל אביון...ועני
72.13 – דל ואביון...אביונים

He not only partakes of the oppression that identifies those to be
rescued in the coming eschatological kingdom, but becomes the one
who will rescue those suffering the same injustices (72.12). These were
promised deliverance by Psalm 72 and so Book III asks on their behalf
in 74.19, 21:

74.19, 21 – ענייך...עני ואביון

The promises of Psalm 76 assured eventual deliverance for these
oppressed ones:

76.10 – בקום־למשפט אלהים להושיע כל־ענוי־ארץ

Psalm 82 accused Israel's own leaders of ignoring this group:

82.3-4a – שפטו...עני ורש...דל ואביון

The afflicted individual of Psalm 86 seeks salvation for himself (הושע,
vv. 2, 16) in consonance with the promise of salvation in 72.4, 13
(יושיע) for such afflicted ones (the aforementioned 76.10 uses the same
root in infinitive form). Finally, another example occurs in 88.16 (עני
אני), in a similar context to 86.1 of appeal for God to deliver the individual. The continued appeals in Book III hearken back to the words of
72 and are essentially asking that God establish the kingdom of justice
and peace promised to David.

Parallels to both Psalms 72 and 82 continue in 86.9-10. If the first
seven verses ask that God fulfill the promise of 72, the following vv. 8-
13 offer statements of confidence in the reality of that kingdom.
According to v. 9 all the nations (כל גוים) will come to worship and
glorify God, precisely what had been declared in Psalm 72:

$$\text{72.11} - \underline{\text{כל גוים}} \ \text{יעבדוהו...וישתחוו}$$
$$\text{72.17} - \underline{\text{כל גוים}} \ \text{יאשרוהו}$$
$$\text{86.9} - \underline{\text{כל גוים}} \ \text{יבואו וישתחוו}$$

An explicit request for this anticipated universal rule of God had been
made in 82.8:

$$\text{קומה אלהים שפטה הארץ כי אתה תנחל } \underline{\text{בכל־הגוים}}$$

This command to arise and judge the earth in the first colon of 82.8
repeated what 76.10a declared to be certain in the future (בקום למשפט),
which 75.3 also assured (אשפט), and which 74.22 had previously
requested (קומה אלהים). Psalm 73 had also lamented the nonfulfillment
of 72. So the hope given in Psalm 72 of a universal rule of peace and
justice (especially for the afflicted) has been recalled throughout Book
III, and Psalm 86 again assures its eventual fulfillment.

In stark contrast to Ps. 86.9, where all nations worship God, is the
complaint about them in Psalm 79 (גוים, vv. 1, 6, 10). There they had
destroyed Jerusalem (v. 1), shed the blood of God's servants (vv. 2-3),
and did not call on God's name (בשמך, v. 6). Based on appeal to the
honor of God's name (כבוד־בשמך...למען שמך, 79. 9), the faithful
community asked for intervention on their behalf. The same concern for
God's name had been used in Psalm 74 (שמך, vv. 7, 10, 18, 21) as a
motivation for divine judgment upon them. Now in 86.9 it is predicted
that the nations (כל־גוים) will indeed honor his name (ויכבדו לשמך), an
explicit answer to the complaints of Psalm 79. The words of the individual Davidide (Psalm 86) are again the means by which divine
answers to the national complaint are mediated. This also may help

explain the phenomenon seen in Psalm 75 (also an answer to 73 and 74), where God's voice (v. 3), and that of the righteous human individual (vv. 10-11) are hard to distinguish.

Psalm 83 had petitioned God to avenge Israel for the plot against its existence by foreign nations (vv. 3-9). The speaker was certain that through intervention (vv. 14-17a) those nations would finally come to know Yahweh's name and sovereignty over all the earth (v. 19). Foreign enemies in 83.3 are those who hate God (וּמְשַׂנְאֶיךָ), but the prayer is that they will be ashamed in v. 18 (יֵבֹשׁוּ). The speaker of 86.17 prays that these same ones will be ashamed (שֹׂנְאַי וְיֵבֹשׁוּ) after seeing the sign done on his behalf. Certainty of the declaration of 83.19 is confirmed in 86.9, 10:

וְיֵדְעוּ כִּי אַתָּה שִׁמְךָ יהוה לְבַדְּךָ עַל־כָּל־הָאָרֶץ – 83.19
כָל־גּוֹיִם...וִיכַבְּדוּ לִשְׁמֶךָ: כִּי־גָדוֹל אַתָּה...אַתָּה אֱלֹהִים לְבַדֶּךָ – 86.9-10

Formerly plotting nations of 83.7-9 assuredly will recognize Yahweh's name and universal sovereignty as predicted in 83.19, and echoed by 86.[13] Psalm 87.4 reiterates the same promise in words also echoing Psalm 83, as will be seen. However, the time of this eschatological victory, promised since Psalm 72 remains unknown.

Parallels with Psalm 72 mentioned above continue in the central section of Psalm 86:

שְׁמוֹ לְעוֹלָם...שְׁמוּ...שֵׁם כְּבוֹדוֹ לְעוֹלָם...כְּבוֹדוֹ – 72.17, 19[14]
וִיכַבְּדוּ לִשְׁמֶךָ...וַאֲכַבְּדָה שִׁמְךָ לְעוֹלָם – 86.9, 12

In 86.9 the nations will glorify Yahweh's name forever, and in v. 12 the individual poet promises to do the same, repeating the same predicted for the nations and declared by the doxology in Psalm 72. Verse 10 also expresses praise to God using terminology reminiscent of the doxology in Psalm72:

אֱלֹהִים...עֹשֵׂה נִפְלָאוֹת לְבַדּוֹ – 72.18
וְעֹשֵׂה נִפְלָאוֹת...אֱלֹהִים לְבַדֶּךָ – 86.10[15]

---

13. Note the rhetorical flourish created by consonance between וִיכַבְּדוּ of 86.9 and לְבַדֶּךָ of 86.10, one of numerous examples in this psalm.

14. As noted previously, the doxology of Ps. 72 has been well integrated into the psalm as a whole. Here the links between vv. 17 and 19 reaffirm that integrity. Parallels with Ps. 86 reveal that this doxology is not only integral to 72, but also continues the eschatological prayer of the latter's previous verses.

15. As can be seen, from 86.9 to 12 are found numerous explicit correspondences to Ps. 72.

As can be seen, the promised eschatological kingdom, ruled by the Davidic scion in Psalm 72, is evoked repeatedly in 86. This prayer of Psalm 86 attributed to David, as well as those ascribed to Asaph, sons of Qorah and 'Ezrahites', is interpreted as prophetic of the eventual restoration of the monarchy.

Parallels between 86.11 and the previous psalm support the theme of an innocent and righteous Davidide portrayed across Book III. In Psalm 85 righteousness (צדק) had taken on personal characteristics, including the walk on a path before Yahweh—upon which the speaker of 86.11 chooses to walk:

$$\text{85.14 } - \text{ צדק לפניו יהלך...לדרך}$$
$$\text{86.11 } - \text{ הורני יהוה דרכך אהלך באמתך}$$

Righteousness thus becomes embodied in the speaker of 86. The path belongs to Yahweh himself and this David walks before him upon it, asking to be taught his way. The path of 86.11 is called 'truth' (באמתך), a term parallel to righteousness (צדק) in 85.12ab. In 72.1 David prayed that the royal son be given God's righteousness (וצדקתך לבן־מלך), a request similar to what this son (cf. 86.16, לבן־אמתך)[16] affirms for himself in 86.11. He asks also in 86.11 that his heart be united to fear (ליראה) Yahweh's name, since salvation is near to those that fear him (אך קרוב ליראיו ישעו, 85.10). Consequently, the salvation of 85.10, another reference to the eschatological kingdom of 72, is close to the God-fearing and teachable servant of 86.11.

In the same Ps. 85.10, not only was salvation at hand for those that feared Yahweh (ליראיו), but also the establishment of glory (כבוד) in the land. Likewise, in two consecutive verses of Psalm 86, the speaker wishes to fear (ליראה) the divine name (v. 11) and then promises to glorify (ואכבדה) that name forever (v. 12). Again, the Davidic servant is an example and even initiator of the eschatological salvation to be revealed.

The second verse paragraph (vv. 11-13) of strophe II (vv. 8-13) begins and ends with terms that are found together in 85.11a (חסד ואמת). In 86.11 the speaker is walking in the way of truth (באמתך) and then confesses that Yahweh's kindness (חסדך) is great upon him (86.13). Apparently the servant of 86 is experiencing a considerable measure of the salvation promised to those who fear God in 85. In other words, the nearness of the salvation in 85.10 is borne out by these statements of

---

16. Note the polyvalency of אמתך in 86.16, meaning either 'truth' or 'handmaid'.

86.11, 13. A more pointed parallel to 85.11 is found in 86.15, where the same pair (וחסד ואמת) appears. Such a striking repetition again shows that the salvation of 85.10-14, with its eschatological overtones, is sought and obtained by the speaker of 86. Psalm 86 emphasizes the abundance of covenant faithfulness accessible to all (v. 5), and specifically to the servant in v. 13:

$$
\begin{array}{rl}
86.5 & - \text{ורב־חסד} \\
86.13 & - \text{חסדך גדול} \\
86.15 & - \text{ורב־חסד ואמת}
\end{array}
$$

Between the question of 85.6 and affirmation of 86.12 a contrast can be discerned by the parallel use of 'forever' (לעולם). In 85.6 the community wonders if God's anger will be against them forever (הלעולם). Expressing a more faithful attitude, the individual of 86 vows to glorify the name of Yahweh forever (לעולם). If in previous parallels the servant's cries of 86 echoed those of the community in 85, now a contrast is evident.

Similar contrast can be shown between 85.6b and 86.15, where the subject addressed is God's anger. The community in 85.6 wonders if that wrath will be drawn out (תמשך אפך) forever, while 86.15, using the well known text of Exod. 34.6, recalls that God is actually slow to anger (ארך אפים). This contrast in reference to anger resembles closely that seen between the questions of 77.8-10, asking if God would ever again be gracious and kind, and the answer given by the description of how Israel was ever again sinning in the following Ps. 78.17, 32, 40. Now the nation wonders anew how long divine anger will endure (85.6), while the servant (86.15) recognizes Yahweh's enormous patience demonstrated before it is expressed.

Psalm 85.8 expressed a direct request of Yahweh to make visible his covenant faithfulness (חסדך) and salvation to the community. While the latter verses of Psalm 85 assured the eventual appearance of that salvation and faithfulness (vv.10-11), the Davidic servant of 86.13 declares that covenantal faithfulness (חסדך) is great upon him. Psalm 86.13 is the last in the second strophe (vv. 8-13), which includes in vv. 8-10 a reiteration of the promises of Psalm 72, and salvation shown to the righteous individual speaker (86.11-13). Thus, this individual of 86 is the one through whom the requested salvation of Psalm 85 and the universal kingdom of 72 are wrought.

A contrast is formed between the personified figure of righteousness in 85.14 who 'put' (וישׂם לדרך) his steps to the path, and the violent of

86.14 who failed to 'put' God (ולא שמוך לנגדם) before themselves (שים being the common root to both verb forms). The personified righteousness in 85 turns out to be the servant of 86, as seen previously in the comparison of 86.11 and 85.14. Moreover, the same root שים is linked to פנה within both 85 and 86. Righteousness in 85.14 put (וישם) its feet to the path and walked 'before him' (לפניו). In 86.14 the wicked do not put (לא שמוך) God before themselves, while the righteous servant in 86.16 asks that God 'turn' (פנה) toward him.

The abbreviated divine name 'God' (אל) reveals another facet of the relation between Psalms 85 and 86. In 86.15, 16 the speaker calls on God (אל) to turn toward him (אלי) and be gracious. His request is valid, being based on the statement in 85.9 that 'the God' (האל) Yahweh will speak peace to (אל) his people and to (ואל) his pious ones (חסידיו), among whom the speaker of 86.2 (חסיד אני) has already identified himself. Included in the 'peace' (שלום) spoken to his people of 85.9 are the twin qualities of 'covenant faithfulness and truth' (חסד ואמת, 85.11a, parallel to צדק ושלום, 'righteousness and peace', in 11b), and thus the speaker of 86.15b can appeal to the same pair חסד ואמת.

Two more requests in Ps. 86.16-17 are also based on statements made in Psalm 85. The servant asks God to 'give' (תנה, v. 16) strength to him, a legitimate petition, since 85.13 states that Yahweh 'will give' and so the land 'will give' (יתן...תתן) good to his people. The promise of 'goodness' (הטוב) in the same 85.13 serves as a basis for the request in 86.17 that God perform for the servant a sign 'for good' (טובה).

The servant of Psalm 86 (עבדך, vv. 2, 4, 16) is identified previously as David by the superscription, being canonically consistent with Ps. 78.70, where David is also designated the servant of Yahweh. Parallel to the servant designation in 86.16 is the name בן־אמתך, a designation meaning 'son of your handmaid'. The formal similarities of this feminine noun in its construct form[17] to the term 'truth' (אמת), repeated in vv. 11 and 15, produce an example of paronomasia.[18] As a result, 'son of your handmaid' can be read also as 'son of your truth'. Such a pun is consistent with the identification in 86.11 of this speaker as the personified righteousness of 85.14. Both 'righteousness' and 'truth' are parallel terms in 85.11 and 12. This servant of Psalm 86 becomes the

---

17. The absolute form is אמה.

18. W.G.E. Watson, *Classical Hebrew Poetry: A Guide to its Techniques* (JSOTSup, 26; Sheffield: JSOT Press, 1984), p. 242.

personification of both 'righteousness' (צדק) from 85.11, 12, 14 and its
twin noun 'truth' (אמת) from 85.11, 12:

וְאמת...צדק – 85.11
אמת...צדק – 85.12
צדק...יהלך...לדרך – 85.14
דרכך אהלך באמתך...לבן־אמתך – 86.11, 16

This collocation of Psalms 85 and 86 suggests that the Davidic servant
of the latter is the trailblazer of righteousness/truth along the path to
salvation described in the former.

The 'son of your handmaid/truth' in 86.16 recalls references to a son
in a previous psalm of Book III. Two examples of the single noun 'son'
(בן) occurred in Ps. 80.16, 18, in forms that also reveal consonance with
that of 86.16:

בן אמצתה – 80.16
בן אדם אמצת – 80.18
בן אמתך – 86.16

In both psalms the son is associated with strength. He is called the 'son
(of man) whom you strengthened for yourself' in these two examples
from Psalm 80, and the 'son of your handmaid' for whom strength is
requested in 86.16 (תנה עזך).

What both Psalms 80 and 86 seek is the fulfillment of that which was
promised to the 'son of the king' in Ps. 72.1 (לבן־מלך). This prince of
Psalm 72 is to be granted universal power and authority (vv. 8-11), and
so these two psalms of Book III (80, 86) make petition based on a
former promise. When this poor and afflicted (עני ואביון, v. 1) son of
Psalm 86 has been saved by Yahweh (והצלת, v. 13), and helped by him
(עזרתני, v. 17), he can do the same for others who are in like situation:

כי יציל אביון משוע ועני ואין־עזר לו – 72.12

Further parallels to Psalm 72 noted previously include the nations
kneeling before this royal scion in v. 11:

וישתחוו לו כל־מלכים כל־גוים יעבדוהו – 72.11
כל־גוים אשר עשית יבואו וישתחוו לפניך – 86.9

While the correspondence is unmistakeable, and not the first time references are made to Psalm 72 in Book III, the worship of Yahweh in 86 is
directed to the son in 72. The latter apparently functions as the representative of Yahweh on the throne. This close identification between

the deity and the human king continues to surface in these psalms and will be seen again before the end of Book III.[19]

A major component of Psalm 86 is the repeated second person singular masculine independent pronoun אתה (vv. 2, 5, 10-twice, 15, 17). Surrounding these six pronouns are four instances of the first person singular pronoun on either end of the psalm, twice in independent form and twice as pronominal suffixes. An unmistakeable inclusio is thereby created:

אני...אָנִי – vv. 1, 2
אתה – v. 2
אתה – v. 5
אתה...אתה – v. 10
אתה – v. 15
אתה – v. 17
-נִי...-נִי – v. 17

The independent pronouns at the beginning are among a series of requests to God, while the two pronominal suffixes at the end are similarily included in petitions. However, the suffixes at the conclusion belong to a clause expressing confidence that help and comfort are forthcoming. By isolating the four first person pronouns at either end, the move from anguished requests (vv. 1, 2) to help and comfort (v. 17) is highlighted. Verse 17, in fact, reaffirms the positive divine response as already given in the middle strophe of vv. 8-13.

Both pairs of pronouns at either extreme are introduced by the particle כִּי, twice in vv. 1, 2 before each, and once for both in v. 17:

כי...אני – v. 1
כי...אני – v. 2
כי...עזרתני ונחמתני – v. 17

In the first two verses the particle gives reasons why Yahweh should intervene on the speaker's behalf, while in the final v. 17 the same particle gives reasons why his enemies will be ashamed.

This individual is afflicted (כי עָנִי..., v. 1), but becomes confident of help at the psalm's end (כי...עזרתני, v. 17), the initial consonant 'ayin adding strength to the cluster of parallel forms. (Compare the repetition of the same consonant bringing together in one colon of 72.12b the same two terms, וְעָנִי ואין־עֹזֵר לו.) If the first members of these two pairs

---

19. As far back as the introduction to the Psalter (Ps. 2.2c), there is evidence of this close relation between the deity and the human king (עַל יהוה ועל מְשִׁחו).

at either end display consonance, the second two do likewise. The consonant ḥeth adds to the formal correspondence:

86.2 – כִּי־חָסִיד אָנִי
86.17 – כִּי...וְנִחַמְתָּנִי

He is afflicted yet pious, and so is afforded help and comfort in the end. This inclusio only serves to reiterate the fact that this individual speaker stands out from the suffering nation of previous psalms by his piety. His wholeheartedness (לבבי) expressed in 86.11, 12 recalls one of the dominant terms of Psalm 73. There purity of heart (לבב) is mentioned right from v. 1, and then repeated in vv. 13, 26 (twice) in contrast to the wicked of v. 7, which group includes Israel. Their rebellion is then repeated throughout Book III, including the immediately previous Ps. 85.3, 4.

The sixfold repetition of 'you' (אתה), the independent second person masculine pronoun, across Psalm 86 is reminiscent of previous psalms in Book III. The lamenting Psalm 74 repeated this same pronoun seven times in the middle strophe (vv. 12-17), a paean to divine power. The hope was that God would again demonstrate that power and judge the enemy. In Psalm 76 his power is revealed in eschatological judgment on the nations and again the second person pronoun is repeated (vv. 5, 8 twice). In Ps. 77.15 the same pronoun appears when the speaker remembers past divine exploits in the midst of desolation. In 82.8 and 83.19 it is utilized again in pleas for judgment on the nations, and then in the immediately previous 85.7 in a request for salvation. The direct requests in Psalm 86 appear to be mainly for the individual speaker's salvation. However, an answer to those requests is found in strophe II (vv. 8-13), which includes universal subjugation and resultant worship of Adonay by the nations. All those nations will come before him and honor his name (v. 9), as requested in 82.8. In the following verse (86.10) the same independent pronoun is repeated twice and resembles closely the aforementioned reference of 77.15 to divine exploits in the exodus:

77.14b-15 – מִי אֵל גָּדוֹל כֵּאלֹהִים אַתָּה הָאֵל עֹשֵׂה פֶלֶא הוֹדַעְתָּ בָעַמִּים עֻזֶּךָ
86.9-10 – כָּל גּוֹיִם...כִּי גָדוֹל אַתָּה וְעֹשֵׂה נִפְלָאוֹת אַתָּה אֱלֹהִים לְבַדֶּךָ

The future subjugation of the nations will resemble that of a previous deliverance from Egypt. Furthermore, the double use of the masculine singular pronoun in this one verse of Psalm 86 serves to emphasize its role as an answer to the previous requests in Book III for judgment. It also parallels the twofold use of the same pronoun in 76.8, where the eschatological battle is also described.

In addition to the use of first person singular pronouns at either extreme, there are other means used to create inclusio around Psalm 86. One of these is the Tetragrammaton in the opening clause of v. 1, and second clause of the final v. 17. Both are preceded by consonantally (voiceless dental stops), if not grammatically, similar forms:

$$\text{הטה יהוה} - \text{v. 1a}$$
$$\text{אתה יהוה} - \text{v. 17b}$$

The first example is imperative and the final is vocative, reflecting the change from desperation to confidence. Not only does v. 17 wrap up vv. 1, 2b, but v. 2b's use of the second person pronoun adds another example of inclusio:

$$\text{אתה אלהי} - \text{v. 2b}$$
$$\text{אתה יהוה} - \text{v. 17b}$$

Immediately previous to this example of v. 2 is a request for salvation of the servant, utilizing a pair of forms found at the midpoint of v. 16bc:

$$\text{הושע עבדך} - \text{v. 2}$$
$$\text{לעבדך והושיעה} - \text{v. 16bc}$$

In this case, both are part of imperatival clauses that dominate both strophe I (vv. 1-7) and III (vv. 14-17). Each of these two strophes is similar in wording and certainly spoken to the same desperate plight of the speaker. The life (נפש) of the individual servant is in danger in both strophes (vv. 2, 4, 14), but in v. 13, the end of strophe II (vv. 8-13), is a reference to the saving of that same life (נפשי) from Sheol. The purpose of the following strophe III (vv. 14-17) is to explain the speaker's (נפש) descent to death's realm.

Although both strophes I and III reflect a situation of affliction and opposition, the final statements of each assure God's help (vv. 7b, 17c). Sandwiched between the desperate pleas of strophes I (vv. 1-7) and III (vv. 14-17), is the more confident strophe II. Not by coincidence, it contains the most parallels with Psalm 72 and its description of the eschatological kingdom. It is also from this middle strophe (vv. 8-13) that most lexical parallels to the likewise eschatological Zion song of Psalm 87 are to be found.

Across Psalm 86 are found repeated forms of divine names. We find Yahweh (four times), Elohim (four times), Adonay (seven times) and El (once). Each of the three strophes includes an example of the first three names. It is not by coincidence that Adonay ('Lord') is the dominant name in a psalm that promises the obedience of all nations. As already stated, the concern expressed for the honor due God's name (שמך) in previous psalms (74.7, 10, 18; 79.6; 83.17, 19) is answered here in 86. In Psalm 79.6 the request for help and salvation on behalf of Israel was based on concern for honor due to God's name (כבוד שמך). In 86.9 the nations finally honor that name (כל גוים...ויכבדו לשמך). This fulfills the promise expressed in the doxology of Psalm 72 where his glorious name is blessed forever and his glory fills all the earth (v. 19). In addition to this universal worship, the individual speaker also is honoring and fearing that name (שמך, 86.11, 12). Psalms 74 and 79 also express lament over the disrepute given to God's name because of his inaction on behalf of the nation. That nation was of course suffering because of its wickedness. By contrast, here in 86 we read of divine action on behalf of this pious Davidic speaker (vv. 11-13), resulting in honor for the name.

The threefold strophic division of this psalm is not difficult to discern. Strophe I (vv. 1-7) is dominated by imperatives and כי ('because') clauses giving reasons for Yahweh to respond. Verses 1-4 begin with requests, followed immediately by reasons in their כי clauses. The entire v. 5 introduces reasons (כי) before expressing the petition in v. 6. As a result, there is a lengthening of content and reversal of the syntax seen in the previous four verses. The concluding verse 7 also gives a reason clause introduced by כי, but following an indicative, not imperative statement.

Strophe I begins and ends with forms of the root ענה ('answer') in vv. 1 and 7. The first is an imperative seeking an answer (ענני), and the second is confident of constant divine answers (תענני). In addition, the noun אזנך ('your ear') of v. 1 finds its counterpart in the imperative of identical root האזינה ('give ear!') in v. 6 and the superscription's use of תפלה ('a prayer') is balanced by תפלתי ('my prayer') in v. 6. This demonstrates how superscriptions were included with close attention to the poem's content.

This string of requests to God of strophe I is bounded on either end of the strophe by the root ענה ('to answer'). In v. 1a an answer is requested (imperative), and in v. 7b answers are assured (indicative). Verse 8 obviously begins a new strophe expressing adoration to God who performs matchless deeds. The change in mood and vocabulary of vv. 8-13

is self-evident, and the juxtaposition immediately following v. 7b (תענני
כי) implies its role as the divine answer to strophe I.

Strophe I can be divided into two verse paragraphs. The first (vv. 1-
2) is dominated by repetition of the first person singular pronoun אני.
The second (vv. 3-7) begins and ends with the same form אקרא ('I
call'), and at v. 5 between them is the participial form of the same root
קראיך ('those who call upon you'). Accompanying the two forms at
beginning and end is a form of the same noun יום ('day'):

$$
\begin{array}{ll}
\text{אקרא כל היום} & - \text{86.3bb} \\
\text{לכל קראיך} & - \text{86.5bb} \\
\text{ביום צרתי אקראך} & - \text{86.7a}
\end{array}
$$

The divine epithet 'Adonay' dominates the second verse paragraph
(vv. 3-7), being found once in each of vv. 3-5. Furthermore, the
suffixed imperative חנני ('show favor to me'), opening the second verse
paragraph in v. 3, resonates with v. 6b where a suffixed noun form of
the same root is used, תחנונותי ('my request for favor'). The same root is
found in successive vv. 15, 16 of strophe III, first in adjective form
(חנון) and then as a suffixed imperative (חנני) identical to that found in
v. 3.

Strophe III is similar in vocabulary and mood to strophe I, revealing
the suffering of this individual speaker. However, as noted previously,
both the first and third strophes conclude on a note of confidence and
faith (vv. 7, 17) and are wrapped around the eschatological deliverance
of strophe II. Further details of this suffering will be given in Psalm 88,
another individual lament quite like 86. It (Psalm 88) is most similar to
the lamenting strophes I and III of 86 and further expounds the reference
to Sheol in 86.13. By way of contrast, Psalm 88 lacks any positive note
such as seen in the middle strophe of 86. Answers to the laments of
Psalm 88 will be revealed in Psalm 89. Psalm 87 will continue discussion of promises given in 86.8-10.

Strophe II (vv. 8-13) brings together the universal worship of God
(vv. 8-9) and its reason (v. 10) under one paragraph, with the individual's wholehearted worship (vv. 11-12) and its reason (v. 13) as
paragraph two. Both verse paragraphs conclude with references to the
greatness of God, either as worker of wonders or in kindness to the
speaker:

$$
\begin{array}{ll}
\text{כי גדול אתה} & - \text{86.10} \\
\text{כי חסדך גדול עלי} & - \text{86.13}
\end{array}
$$

The close formal relationship here between these two clauses implies a connection at the conceptual level. God's greatness in v. 10 is due to performance of wondrous deeds (ועשׂה נפלאות). The latter half of v. 13 speaks of rescue from lower Sheol of the speaker's life. It appears that one of the miraculous deeds included in v. 10 is that very rescue of this Davidide from the realm of death in v. 13. This will be confirmed again in the discussion of Psalms 88 and 89. Consequently, the aforementioned parallels between 86.10 and 13 are complemented and confirmed by the canonical juxtaposition of 88 and 89.

The rescue of this individual's life in v. 13 is an answer to the request in v. 2 that his life be kept. That request was based on the 'piety' of the speaker, a term related by root to 'covenant faithfulness':

86.2 – שׁמרה נפשׁי כי חסיד אני
86.13 – כי חסדך גדול עלי והצלת נפשׁי

Apparently the piety of the speaker explained the greatness of divine kindness upon him, and as a result, his life was saved out of the recesses of death.

The third strophe begins (v. 14) with exact repetition of two forms seen in the previous v. 13. Just as God's kindness was great 'upon me' so that 'my life' (עלי...נפשׁי, v. 13) was saved, so in v. 14 we read that insolent ones have risen 'up against me' and a congregation of formidable ones sought 'my life' (עלי...נפשׁ). This correspondence of preposition and suffixed noun reveals that the situation in v. 13 was caused by the conspiracy described in the following v. 14. Out of those threats and conspiracy against his life, the speaker asks in v. 17a for a sign. The term 'sign' suggests a supernatural intervention and the request resonates closely with the statement in v. 10 where God performs wondrous deeds:

86.10 – ועשׂה נפלאות
86.17a – עשׂה עמי אות

Consequently, the rescue from death of v. 13, which came about through the attack described in v. 14, resulted in a request for a miraculous sign in v. 17a. The miraculous sign was clearly given, since a close verbal connection between vv. 10 (כי גדול) and 13 (גדול...כי) implied it. The just-mentioned lexical and phonological parallels between vv. 10 and 17a confirm the idea. To state it another way, the rescue from death in v. 13 was due to the work of miraculous power described in v. 10, and requested in v. 17a.

The unity of strophe III can be seen by the reference to adversaries at the beginning (v. 14ab) and the end (v. 17b). The twofold direct address to God using the independent masculine pronoun אתה (vv. 15 and 17) matches the two of strophe I (vv. 2 and 5) and of strophe II (v. 10).

At either end of strophe III are a pair of verbs that resonate phonologically and canonically. Verse 14 states that a congregation of violent ones 'sought' (בקשׁו) his life, but at the other end of the strophe his haters are assured of 'being ashamed' (ויבשׁו). This pair (בקשׁו...ויבשׁו) of verb forms is found at the end of Psalm 83 in a petition for vengeance on Israel's enemies. The speaker asks for them to be filled with ignominy so that they will 'seek' (ויבקשׁו, 83.17) the name of Yahweh. Then in the following 83.18 his desire is that they 'be ashamed' (יבשׁו). It should be noted that prior to this request of 83.17-18, the enemies are called 'those who hate you' (משׂנאיך) in 83.3. Likewise in 86.17, those who will be ashamed are 'my haters' (שׂנאי). However, many of those once plotting nations of Psalm 83 have now become worshippers of Yahweh according to 86.9. Proof of this is found in Ps. 87.4, where Philistia and Tyre, two nations specifically named in 83.8b among the enemies of Israel, are now adopted as citizens of Zion.

A direct contrast is created within Psalm 86 itself between these violent ones who seek the life of the Davidide (86.14), and the nations that have bowed the knee to Adonay (86.9). Obedient nations will come and bow down 'before you' (לפניך, 86.9), as opposed to those who do not set God 'before themselves' (לנגדם, 86.14). Here the prepositional forms and accompanying suffixes ('you' versus 'themselves') highlight the contrast. Between the glorification of 'your name' in v. 9 and rejection of God in v. 14 (לשׁמך...לא שׂמוך) is another antithesis. The semantic contrast is highlighted through the consonance of lamedh, sibilants shin/sin, mem and final kaph. Since v. 9 of the strophe II states that *all* the nations will come and bow before Adonay, these arrogant ones of strophe III (vv. 14-17) are either destroyed or possibly had a change of heart.

Strophe II is to be read as a resolution of the opposition to the servant in strophe III, and also provides the answers of which the final clause of strophe I (v. 7b) is certain are forthcoming. These answers of strophe II which conclude with a reference to deliverance from Sheol (v. 13), then required an explanation of that experience. The immediately following strophe III provides the explanation, and perhaps for this reason it was postponed until after strophe II, in spite of its similarity to strophe I.

Assurance of a divine response to the requests of strophe I is given in the last clause (v. 7b, כי תעני, 'because you answer me'). Implied by the juxtaposition of strophe II immediately following v. 7 is that it expresses the answer to the individual's lament. Several verbal links between strophes I and II prove the latter's role as response to the former. In v. 2 the individual sought protection for his 'life' (נפש) and we read in v. 13 that his 'life' (נפש) was saved. (Verse 4 also refers twice to the poet's life, נפש/נפשי, in the cry to God.) In v. 5 he appeals to Adonay's abundant 'covenant faithfulness' (חסד), and v. 13 again refers to that 'faithfulness' (חסדך) as great, to the point that it saves him from Sheol.

The repeated pattern of imperative or indicative (once in v. 7) followed by a reason clause (כי) in strophe I (reversed in vv. 5-6) is also followed in strophe II. Two successive verses 8 and 9 describing God's uniqueness and fame are followed in v. 10 (כי) with the principal reason for that fame. He is the only one who does wondrous deeds. All three verses are united by the common use of the verbal root עשה ('to do'). It begins with a declaration that there is none like God among deities (v. 8), and concludes on the same note declaring that 'you alone are God' (v. 10). This concludes the first verse paragraph of strophe II.

Following in v. 11 is a request for God to teach him and unite his heart. The following v. 12 promises wholehearted and eternal praise to God. The reason for that praise is given in v. 13, and it is again introduced by the same particle כי. This second verse paragraph (vv. 11-13) is united by its emphasis on the heart (vv. 11, 12) and life (v. 13) of the individual speaker who praises and fears God. In paragraph one the focus was on the worship of the nations, and that is narrowed in the second to this afflicted Davidide.

Numerous parallels also unite the two paragraphs of strophe II into one. Both the nations and the speaker will glorify the name of Adonay:

86.9 – כל גוים...ויכבדו לשמך
86. 11-12 – שמך ...בכל לבבי ואכבדה שמך

'All' the nations will glorify the name, and this corresponds to the individual who promises to glorify the name with 'all' his heart. The nations will 'come' (יבואו) to worship before Adonay in v. 9, while the individual of v. 11 'walks' (אהלך) in his truth. One could infer from the differing verbs that the nations must come to the place of worship, a place where the pious servant of God has always been. Finally, the Lord is 'great' (גדול) in v. 10 for his wondrous deeds and 'great' (גדול) in kindness to the individual servant of v. 13 by rescuing him out of Sheol.

As noted above, this miraculous deliverance of v. 13 is included among the wondrous deeds of v. 10.

Strophe II of 86 as an answer to the pleas of strophe I resembles the answer to the prayers of 85.1-8 (first strophe) given in 85.9-14 (second strophe). Both the servant (86.12) and the nations (86.9) 'honor' (כבד) the name of God. In 85.10 'honor' (כבוד) resides in the land as a response to laments over its apparent absence in 85.2-8. The nation speaking in 85.8 pled for Yahweh's 'faithfulness' (חסד) to be revealed, and so it was promised in 85.11 in conjunction with 'truth' (חסד ואמת). In the same manner, the individual in 86.5 appeals to divine 'faithfulness' (חסד), and v. 13 assures its appearance (חסדך) to the servant. The same individual servant seeks to walk in 'your truth' (באמתך, 86.11). As noted previously, the eschatological conditions of Psalm 85's second strophe are personified by the individual speaker in Psalm 86's second strophe. Furthermore, the second strophe of 86 assures a universal glorification (ויכבדו) of Adonay, while the second and final strophe of 85 assures residence of glory (כבוד) in Israel's own land.

The answer in each psalm is given through the mouth of the individual poet. Note that 85.9 cites the words of an individual who 'listens' (אשמעה) to the words of Yahweh, having previously asked God in 84.9 to 'listen' (שמעה) to his prayer. A comparison noted before between 86.6 (האזינה יהוה תפלתי, 86.6) and 84.9 (יהוה...תפלתי האזינה, 84.9) confirms that the same righteous speaker is heard across this stretch of three psalms. He not only cries in petition to God, but becomes the mediating voice for divine answers to the nation and himself. In 84.9 he requests a hearing from God and in 85.9 listens to the answer, after apparently being the voice of the nation in previous verses. Then in 86.1-7 he cries to God on his own behalf and immediately becomes the voice of reply in 86.8-10. This would explain why his voice becomes indistinguishable from God's in psalms such as 75 and from the nation's in 85. He expresses the laments and questions of the nation and himself, while also serving as the spokesman for divine responses.

A common theme seen across the sequence of Psalms 84–86 is that of 'walking' (הלך). In 84.8 the righteous 'walk' (ילכו) from strength to strength on their journey to Zion, and in 84.12, 'to those who walk' (להלכים) in integrity no good will be withheld. It is righteousness itself that 'walks' (יהלך) in 85.14 and, as shown previously, the Davidic servant of 86.11 'walks' (אהלך) in truth, becoming its very embodiment.

Psalms 84 to 86 portray the walk of the righteous, while the previous three Psalms 81–83 describe that of the wicked (81.13, 14; 82.5; 83.5). In addition, a contrast between the first in this series (Psalm 81) and the last (Psalm 86) can be discerned. Israel is accused in 81.14 of not 'walking in my paths' (לו...בדרכי יהלכו), in comparison with the pious servant of 86.11 who requests to be taught 'your path, I will walk...' (דרכך אהלך). The same type of contrast can be seen between the nation of 81.12, 14 that did not 'listen' (שמע) to the voice of Yahweh and the righteous individual of 85.9 who 'listens' (אשמעה) to what Yahweh will speak to his people and his pious ones. Once again, the righteous individual Davidide stands out from the rest of the nation.

The following Psalm 87 will portray the habitation of all nations in Zion, the city from where this Davidic individual presumably will reign.[20] A list of their names in 87.4 gives specificity to the general 'all nations' (כל־גוים) of 86.9. Then in the subsequent Psalm 88 the situation from which this individual was rescued (86.13) is elaborated.

20. Cf. Ps. 2.6.

Chapter 15

PSALM 87

In spite of its brevity, Psalm 87 plays an important role in the dialogue of Book III. After a description of the disaster that came upon Zion in 74.1-8, the city was mentioned again in 76.3, 78.68 and 84.8, all in contexts indicating its restoration. Now in 87 that restoration is described more explicitly and serves as a perfect complement to the eschatological promises in the immediately previous 86.

Psalm 87's superscription ties it closely to Psalms 84–85 and the subsequent 88. Each of these four is ascribed to the sons of Qorah as a מזמור. The titles of Pss. 87.1 and 88.1a (the first third of 88's superscription) form a neat concentric structure:

$$
\begin{array}{ll}
\text{לבני קרח} & - \text{ A (87.1)} \\
\text{מזמור} & - \text{ B} \\
\text{שׁיר} & - \text{ C} \\
\text{שׁיר} & - \text{ C'} \\
\text{מזמור} & - \text{ B'} \\
\text{לבני קרח'} & - \text{ A' (88.1a)}
\end{array}
$$

The designation 'song' is lacking from the two previous Qorahite Psalms 84–85, and so its use here is a deliberate attempt to bind both superscriptions of 87 and 88 together. Such linking devices are conspicuously absent between the titles of Psalms 86 and 87 (or between 85 and 86), as discussed in the previous Chapter, and as a result the name David of 86.1 stands out from all others in Book III.

It was in 86.9 that the promise of an eventual universal worship of Yahweh was given (כל־גוים), and now in 87 some of those many nations are named specifically (87.4). The correspondence is not formal, but rather conceptual. A formal correspondence of 87.4 to a previous list of enemy nations in Psalm 83 is quite transparent:

$$
\begin{array}{ll}
\text{פלשׁת עם־ישׁבי צור} & - \text{ 83.8b} \\
\text{פלשׁת וצור עם־כושׁ} & - \text{ 87.4b}
\end{array}
$$

The conspiracy of Psalm 83 (note the twofold use of the preposition 'with' עם in 83.8, 9) of enemy nations has now become a unity of citizenship within Zion. Just as the writer of 83 had desired that these nations 'know' (וידעו, v. 19) Yahweh as the highest one over all the earth, so in 87.4 they are listed among those who 'know me' (לידעי).[1] Likewise, the writer of 83 had asked that God 'do' (עשה, v. 10) to these enemies as he had to former foes, and so in 86.8-10 his deeds (the same root עשה used three times) had brought them to their knees. Thus, the collocation of 86 and 87 repeats a theme found within 83 itself.[2] All these nations in 86.9 (כל־גוים) who submit are only following the prediction of 82.8 (בכל־גוים) and corresponding 83.19 (כל־ארץ).

The same can be said of 86–87 when compared with Psalm 78. Psalm 86 is a prayer of David (דוד, v. 1; cf. 78.70), the servant of Yahweh (עבדך, vv. 2, 4, 16; cf. 78.70), whose heart (לבבי, vv. 11, 12; cf. 78.72) was whole, while 87 is the description of his royal seat Zion, a mountain loved and established by Yahweh. In like manner, Psalm 78 shows Zion to be the mountain loved and established by Yahweh:

87.1b-2a – יסודתו בהררי־קדש: אהב...ציון
78.68b, 69. – הר ציון...אהב...מקדשו...יסדה

His love for Zion surpassed that of any other locale in Jacob (87.2b). The same preference of Zion (and Judah) is expressed in 78.67, while Joseph and Ephraim are rejected within Israel. In spite of the quite different genre of Psalms 86 (individual lament) and 87 (song of Zion), together they repeat a promise made previously within a single psalm of Book III regarding the future Zion and its king.

This restored eschatological Zion is described in terms reminiscent of the previously destroyed one in Psalm 74. There Zion was the mountain where God had dwelled and here it is also his preferred habitation:

74.2, 3, 7 – הר־ציון...שכנת...בקדש...משכן
87.1, 2 – הררי־קדש...ציון...משכנות

However, in contrast to Psalm 74, the Zion of 87 is populated by formerly enemy nationalities, including those presumably responsible for

1.   Within the one verse of 87.4 are correspondences relating to both 83.8 and 19.

2.   Note similar comments of E. Zenger in 'Zion als Mutter der Völker in Psalm 87', in N. Lohfink and E. Zenger (eds.), *Der Gott Israels und die Völker: Untersuchungen zum Jesajabuch und zu den Psalmen* (Stuttgart: Katholisches Bibelwerk, 1994), pp. 117-50 (139).

its destruction ('Babylon', בבל in 87.4). The war that brought about this catastrophe will be terminated 'there' (שמה) in Zion according to Ps. 76.4, and consequently all kings will bring tribute to Yahweh (vv. 12-13). Correspondences with Psalm 87 are again visible, where 'there' (שם) is also Zion:

$$76.3, 4, 5 \quad - \quad בציון: שמה...מהררי$$
$$87.1, 2, 4, 5, 6 \quad - \quad בהררי-...ציון...שם...ולציון...שם$$

The destruction of weapons and warfare with its resulting tribute from all the kings of the earth in 76 (v. 13) is perfectly congruent with the Zion of 87, where foreigners are now part of its citizenry. The renown (נודע, 76.2) of God in Judah (and by extension his dwelling: Salem and Zion of 76.3) corresponds well with the knowledge of him (לידעי) in 87.4 by a varied Gentile populace. Both Psalms 76 and 87 promise a restored Zion living in peace at the center of world power, in response to the lament over ruined Zion in 74.

The affection for Zion held by Yahweh in 87.2 recalls the same sentiment expressed in 84.2. If Yahweh loves Zion most of all dwelling places (משכנות, 87.2b) in Jacob, so the speaker of 84.2a desires Yahweh's dwelling places (משכנותיך). Here the sentiments of the righteous individual and Yahweh merge. Provision of water also characterizes both descriptions of Zion. The blessed man of 84.5, 6 travels along the highway to Zion (בציון, v. 7) and is refreshed there by a spring (מעין, v. 7), just as the Zion of 87.2, 5 contains springs (מעיני, v. 7).

Reaching from the first Qorahite psalm of Book III (84), up to and including 87, is the repeated theme of 'glory' (כבוד). One of the benefits of habitation in the dwellings of Yahweh (משכנותיך, 84.2) was the reception of grace and 'glory' (כבוד, 84.12) from him. So in 87.3 'glorious things' (נכבדות) are spoken in the 'dwellings' (משכנות, v. 2b in parallel to 2a) of Zion. In 85.10 glory is said to take up residence (לשכן כבוד) in the land, using the same two roots again of 87.2b, 3b. Subsequently in Psalm 86 the nations give glory (ויכבדו, v. 9) to Adonay, as does the servant himself (ואכבדה, v. 12). The righteous individual of 84 (and 86), joined by a restored people in 85 (cf. v. 13), and the nations in 86 and 87, will all experience glory in a restored Zion.

Hakham notes that the form נכבדות ('glorious things') of 87.3 belongs to the same noun pattern as נפלאות ('wondrous things'), without noting that it appears in the previous Ps. 86.10.[3] By combining

---

3. Hakham, *Sefer tehillim*, p. 124 (קכד).

these two nouns, given their similar context and form, one may conclude that the glorious things spoken by these nations within Zion (87.3) are the very wonders done by God (86.10). Indeed, the reason (כי) given in 86.10 for the glorification of the nations in 86.9 is the performance of these extraordinary works. The motivation to glorify based on wondrous deeds was already made obvious in 72.18 (נפלאות) and 19 (כבודו) in a similar context of eschatological and universal worship. Thus, the repetition of this term 'glory' from Psalms 84 to 87 reiterates the promise of its appearance given in 72 and reaffirms participation of the nations in worship of Yahweh for the performance of marvelous deeds.[4]

If the glorious things (נכבדות) spoken are the divine wonders done in 86.10 (נפלאות), the prepositional phrase בך of 87.3a should be rendered 'in you'.[5] This would be consistent with the following two parallel prepositional phrases of v. 5 (בה, 'in her') and v. 7 (בך, 'in you'), both used in a spatial sense. In other words, the nations gathered in Zion (Psalm 87) would be speaking of the glorious things performed by Yahweh, thereby giving glory to his name (Psalm 86). A comparison with Ps. 48.2 (another Qorahite Zion song) supports this interpretation:

48.2 – גדול יהוה ומהלל מאד בעיר אלהינו
87.3[6] – נכבדות מדבר בך עיר אלהים

In both psalms the citizenry within Zion laud Yahweh. Attribution of 'greatness' (גדול) to God in 48.2 also recalls the 'greatness' (גדול) of his name in 76.2 in Judah, Israel and Zion (76.2-3).

If Psalm 87's role in the dialogue of Book III seems reasonably clear, details of its content and structure is more difficult. The opening clause of the psalm (v. 1b) includes a masculine singular pronoun that apparently lacks any parallel or antecedent. The most logical parallel to v. 1b appears in v. 5b, and so Gunkel combines 1b and 5b.[7] Another difficulty is v. 7, whose interpretation Tate calls 'problematic at best'.[8]

From vv. 3 to 5 Smith has postulated a 'concentric pentacolon', constituting an 'integral whole'.[9]

---

4. Universal worship under the Davidic king on Mt Zion is a stated theme already in the Psalter's introduction (Ps. 2.6-12).

5. BDB, s.v. דבר, p. 181.

6. Besides the underlined parallels, both texts express the attributed laudation by means of pual participles (מדבר, מהלל).

7. Gunkel, *Die Psalmen*, p. 378.

8. Tate, *Psalms 51–100*, p. 387.

בְּךָ – A (v. 3)
שָׁם – B (v. 4)
בה – C (v. 5)
שָׁם – B' (v. 6)
בְּךָ – A' (v. 7)

From this he concludes that the first two verses of the psalm 'function as a thematic preface to what follows'.[10] However, if one includes the first two verses (which include the superscription), another concentric pattern emerges:

שִׁיר...בְּ- – A (v. 1)
יהוה – B (v. 2)
צִיוֹן...בְּךָ...עִיר הָאלֹהִים – C (vv. 2-3)
צִיוֹן...בה...יְכוֹנְנֶה עליון – C' (v. 5)
יהוה – B' (v. 6)
שִׁיר...בְּ- – A' (v. 7)

As this illustration demonstrates, the superscription and first clause fit into the warp and woof of the psalm's structure. Furthermore, use of the roots שׁכן and כבד in the contiguous vv. 2b and 3a demonstrates how vv. 1-2 are consistent with the canonical structure and message, given the combination of these two in 85.10 (cf. also 84.2, 12). If a 'preface' were added it would have probably included v. 3 as well. However, it is more probable that the psalm is an integrated unity in its present shape. Another noteworthy feature of this outline is the even placement of the preposition beth (-בְּ) four times across the psalm (vv. 1, 3, 5, 7). In every case it is locative in function and each noun complement refers to Zion, the central theme of the psalm.[11]

The above illustration suggests a unity between the superscription (1a) and opening clause (1b) of the psalm. The MT also considers v. 1 to be whole, including the superscription. Rashi takes the masculine noun מזמור of the superscription as antecedent for the pronominal suffix of the noun, 'his/its foundation' (יסודתו).[12] While it is unlikely that this suffix refers to the previous noun, 'psalm', it is correct not to overlook

---

9.   M.S. Smith, 'The Structure of Psalm LXXXVII', *VT* 38 (1988), pp. 357-58 (357).

10.   Smith, 'The Structure', p. 357.

11.   In the case of בכתוב (v. 6), the preposition beth functions temporally, being attached to an infinitive in contrast to nominal forms in the other examples.

12.   Rashi, *Miqraot gedolot* (New York: Shulsinger Bros., 1945), p. 55 (overleaf of p. נה).

superscriptions and their contribution to individual psalm structures (or
to the entire Psalter). This was seen previously in Psalm 75, where the
root זמר functioned as an inclusio between the superscription (v. 1) and
penultimate v. 10. Likewise in Psalms 75 and 80, the form למנצח of the
superscription followed the repeated use of לנצח in the previous psalms
74 and 79.

This third masculine singular pronominal suffix (יסודתו, 'his foundation') without an overt antecedent was perhaps originally proleptic in
function to the clause now found in v. 5c. There, the only independent
personal pronoun in the whole psalm appears (הוא), and is of the same
number and gender. Supporting this is the fact that the two roots כון and
יסד of these two separated cola are paired in Ps. 24.2 and Prov. 3.19.

In its present position the pronominal suffix of יסודתו remains proleptic in function (anticipating formerly the pronoun הוא), now being
resumed by the Tetragrammaton of v. 2a.[13] The feminine pronominal
suffix of יכוננה ('he established her', v. 5c) would have originally
referred to the opening noun, 'foundation' (יסודתו), but now resumes
the proper noun, 'Zion' of v. 5a. In its present location, v. 5b serves to
designate quite specifically the builder of this new Zion. The city is
constructed of people from all nations brought together and declared
citizens by the 'Highest One' (עליון). Verses 4, 5a and 6, on all sides of
5b, also declare that individuals of many nations, even former enemies,
are being registered by Yahweh as citizens. Immediately following in v.
6a, the recording of these foreigners is stated most emphatically to have
been done by Yahweh. So the clause of v. 5b functions where it is now
to identify Israel's own god as the one responsible for this surprising
adoption of Gentiles into eschatological Zion. Furthermore, Yahweh
even 'loves' (אהב, v. 2a) the gates of Zion, another way to designate its
citizenry.[14]

It is, however, necessary to mention that the antecedent of the pronoun 'he' (הוא) in clause initial position of v. 5b is not unambiguous,
since the preceding v. 5a contains a possible antecedent, 'each one'
(איש ואיש). To avoid confusion, the divine epithet 'Highest One' (עליון)
appears awkwardly in final position of v. 5b to identify the 'he' placed
clause initially. Another effect of its final position in the clause of 5b is

---

13. The LXX and Syriac, as noted by *BHS*, have plural pronominal suffixes anticipating the plural noun 'gates' of v. 2a.

14. Both Ruth 3.11 and Isa. 14.31 demonstrate that 'gate' (שער) is a metonymi-
cal designation for the inhabitants of a city.

that following immediately is the divine name 'Yahweh' of v. 6a (יהוה
יספר), and so Israel's own god is recording these nations into Zion. In
an astonishing reversal, people from those nations which attacked and
sought Zion's destruction (Psalms 74, 83) now form an integral part of
its citizenry and so partake of the promised eschatological kingdom.

The description given to the incorporation of these foreign individuals into the new Zion is quite similar to that used to describe the establishment of the same city's king in Ps. 2.7. Both king and foreigner are
established in their present position by using the language of birth
(ילדתיך, 2.7, ילד; 87.4, 5, 6). The king's coronation in Psalm 2 is
accomplished by decree (אספרה, 2.7) and in like manner the declaration
of citizenship is decreed (יספר, 87.6). Within the first decree, God
speaks to his son (אמר אלי, 2.7), and speaks of Zion's citizenry in the
second (ולציון יאמר, 87.5).

Psalm 87 expounds upon the previous 86.9, 10, which verses themselves were a reiteration of the promises of Psalm 72. It also repeats
descriptions of Zion seen as far back as 74 within Book III, and complements descriptions of the city seen in Psalm 2 of the Psalter's introduction. Psalm 86 also spoke of the rescue of the Davidic servant from
death (v. 13), an event to be investigated in Psalm 88, and a figure to be
further discussed in 89. In fact, the glorious situation of 87 is in stark
contrast to the lament of 88, both psalms corresponding to themes
found at the heart (strophe II) of 86.

Chapter 16

PSALM 88

The lengthy superscription of this psalm has been partially discussed before, especially in relation to that of the previous Psalm 87. As noted there, between the first third of 88's title and that of 87 is formed a concentric pattern of ABCC'B'A'. The last third corresponds closely to the superscription of the following Psalm 89, differing only by the ascribed authors Heman and Ethan:

$$88.1c - \text{משכיל להימן האזרחי}$$
$$89.1^1 - \text{משכיל לאיתן האזרחי}$$

The middle third of the superscription (למנצח על מחלת לענות) is difficult to interpret, but contains elements creating unity around the immediate group of four Qorahite psalms (84, 85, 87, 88) that surround the Davidic 86. Specifically, both the formations למנצח and על plus noun complement occur in 84 and 88, the first and last of the Qorahite group:

$$84.1a - \text{למנצח על הגתית}$$
$$88.1b - \text{למנצח על מחלת}$$

The remaining element לענות of 88.1b fits well with the theme of affliction in Psalm 88 itself (vv. 8, עניתי; 10, עני; 16, עני).[2] Consequently, the first third of the superscription is a direct link to the previous 87, the second third to the body of 88 itself (and to the title of 84), while the final third corresponds closely to the subsequent 89.

While the superscription of Psalm 88 resembles surrounding Qorahite

---

1. Without discussing the difficulties of identifying these two individuals, suffice it to say that their names are likewise linked in texts such as 1 Chron. 2.6; 6.18, 29; 15.17, 19; 1 Kgs. 5.11. Hakham, *Sefer tehillim*, p. 128 (קכח), notes that according to 1 Chron. 6.18 Heman is a Qorahite, and so the first third of this superscription of Ps. 88 (שיר מזמור לבני קרח) and final third (משכיל להימן האזרחי) are consistent.

2. Reading לענות from the root ענה, 'be afflicted'.

psalms, its content and form show remarkable parallels with Psalm 86, a psalm attributed to David. Trublet and Aletti have noted similarities between these two 'prayers of supplication with concentric parallelism', where each central portion (86.8-13; 88.10b-13) consists of propositions about God.[3] Nonetheless, their study is a form-critical one, not taking into consideration the message created by their canonical collocation. It becomes plain when the canonical dialogue is considered that the lament of 88 is an extended description of the affliction in 86. Both psalms open in remarkably similar ways, asking God to incline his ear to the individual's prayer:

$$86.1 - \text{תפלה...הטה יהוה אזנך}$$
$$88.2, 3 - \text{יהוה...תפלתי הטה אזנך}$$

In Ps. 86.6 essentially the same vocabulary is repeated again (הַאֲזִינָה יהוה תפלתי), creating further resonance with Psalm 88. In 88.14 the same noun, 'my prayer' (תִּפְלָתִי), is repeated, resulting in its twofold repetition by both psalms. This prayer is directed toward God in each psalm (אליך), the identical prepositional phrase used three times in 86 (vv. 2, 3, 4) and twice in 88 (vv. 10, 13). The individual describes himself as 'afflicted' in each psalm using the same terminology:

$$86.1 - \text{עני...אני}$$
$$88.16 - \text{עני אני}$$

He pleads for his own 'life' (נֶפֶשׁ) in both psalms (86.2, 4 twice, 13, 14; 88.4, 15), because it has descended to 'Sheol', place of the dead:

$$86.13 - \text{נפשי משאול}$$
$$88.4 - \text{נפשי...לשאול}$$

In 86 he is thankful for being saved out of Sheol, but 88 is spoken while still there. It is the very 'lowest Sheol' or 'pit' in which he finds himself in each psalm:

$$86.13 - \text{משאול תחתיה}$$
$$88.7 - \text{בבור תחתיות}$$

God's wrath comes down upon him (עלי) like waves of water in 88.8, 17, 18, while in 86.14 the distress is described as enemies coming against him (עלי). In a deliberate contrast within Psalm 86, the saving

---

3.   Trublet and Aletti, *Approche poétique*, p. 197, 'Le Ps 86 n'est pas la seule prière de supplication à parallélisme concentrique où l'unité centrale est constituée par des propositions sur Dieu'.

of his life from Sheol of v. 13 results from the greatness of Yahweh's kindness upon him (עלי). Psalm 88 expresses no hope or salvation, but the following 89 serves that purpose. Thus, the collocation of Psalms 88 and 89 express together what is found in the single 86.

Constant (lit. 'all day', כל היום), supplication ('I call', קרא), to Yahweh (lit. 'to you', אליך), is expressed in each psalm, to create unmistakeable correspondence:

אליך אקרא כל־היום – 86.3
קראתיך...בכל־יום...אליך – 88.10
כל־היום – 88.18

By means of such similarities the speaker of each psalm is to be read as one and the same individual. Appeals are made to Yahweh's 'covenant faithfulness' (חסד) in Psalm 86 (v. 5) which then acknowledges when that faithfulness rescued his life from Sheol (חסדך, 86.13). Psalm 88 returns to a time before the rescue and reveals the complaint in Sheol asking whether God's faithfulness (חסדך, 88.12) can be recounted there. Praise to Adonay for faithfulness shown in 86.13 is an anticipatory answer to 88.12. Psalm 88.12 goes back to the experience of death and the complaint then lodged, while 86.13 is an expression of thankfulness following deliverance.

The psalmist also asks if Yahweh will 'perform wondrous deeds' (תעשה פלא, 88.11) for the dead or if they can 'be known' there (היודע...פלאך, 88.13). These questions correspond to Psalm 86 where his deeds performed (עשה נפלאות, 86.10; cf. 72.18) have caused the nations to worship and glorify him. Presumably, these deeds were to bring about the promised kingdom of Psalms 72, 86, 87, over which the Davidic scion was to rule. If that individual speaking in 88 is now in the grave, how can this come about? The answer was given in Psalm 86, where he was rescued from death, as the parallels between 86.10 (כי גדול) and 13 (כי...גדול) already proved in that psalm, and which further statements in Psalm 89 will confirm. That deliverance out of death brought about restoration of this Davidide to his throne and guaranteed the subjugation of all nations to him (86.8-10 and 11-13). In 88.15 he asks why Yahweh hides his face (פניך) from him, repeating essentially the request of 86.16 for the deity to turn (פנה) toward him and have mercy. Again, the prayer of 88 turns out to be essentially the same as that of 86, but without the assurance of an answer. Answers are delayed until the following 89.

These numerous parallels between 88 and 86 (in addition to those between 86, 87, 85, 84, etc.) confirm that the lone Davidic psalm was placed at the heart of a series of four Qorahite poems with good reason. The prayer of the first and last strophes of Psalm 86 resembles that of 88 so much as to be practically the same. The speaker in each prayer is suffering the same affliction. At the heart of 86 (vv. 8-13) is found the answer to questions at the heart of 88 (vv. 11-13), the psalmist being rescued from the very bowels of death. One could say that 88 is temporally previous to 86, but clarifes the miracle of its answer in 86.13. Each prayer is to be interpreted as coming from the same Davidic figure. However, the canonical context of Book III clearly demonstrates that this is a future David. This David is one who actually reached the realm of the dead for a time, but was rescued therefrom. His rescue from death is apparently a permanent one, according to 89.2, 3, 6 where he praises forever the covenant faithfulness and fidelity demonstrated to him. Nonetheless, he laments in 89 the delayed establishment of the promised eternal kingdom to David's house.

If Psalms 88 and 86 are remarkably parallel in form, vocabulary and content, 88 and 87 present a strong contrast. As discussed in the previous Chapter, 87 is a picture of the restored Zion where all nations worship Yahweh. Such a vision of Zion is followed immediately in 88 with the picture of its Davidic king being consigned to the realm of death. Such a contrast is not unlike that between the peaceful conditions of 72 and the opposite cruel reality of 73. His hope of ever inheriting the promise of a universal kingdom extending from Zion appears to be lost. In this eschatological Zion, Yahweh 'loves' (אהב, 87.2) its inhabitants and they are 'those who know me' (לידעי, 87.4). By deliberate contrast, the individual of 88 is separated from 'loved ones' (אהב, 88.19) and 'those who know me' (מידע, 88.9, 19). Here the nominal form of the root ידע is found in 87.4 referring to close acquaintances and is repeated twice (88.9, 19) in the following psalm, as if to emphasize the contrast. The same root is found in 88 in verbal form, where he wonders if divine miracles will ever 'be known' (היודע, 88.13) in the grave. In other words, how can glorious things (87) or those wondrous divine deeds, including rescue from death (86), be spoken of (87) or known (88) in the darkness of the grave?

According to the canonical juxtaposition and explicit verbal links just cited, the strong bond of relationship between Yahweh and the citizens of Zion in Psalm 87 is severed in the following 88. However, the speaker of 87 describes Yahweh's loving relationship with Zion's citi-

zens in 87.2 (אהב יהוה), and Yahweh himself speaks in 87.4 (לידעי)
referring to those of his acquaintances. The following 88 expresses the
voice of a human cry to Yahweh decrying the separation from those
same beloved ones. Therefore, the voice of Yahweh in 87 and that of
the afflicted unto death Davidide in 88 become one and the same. At the
same time, the Davidide's prayer in 88 is to the same Yahweh (vv. 2,
10, 15) who speaks in 87. Thus the sufferer and Yahweh maintain an
independent identity. Nonetheless, their voices and roles are almost
indistinguishable at the canonical level.

This blending of voices between Yahweh and the speaker of Psalm
88 through the juxtaposition of 87 and 88, is accompanied by the
equally surprising statement in 88 of his descent into death. What kind
of divine representative is this who suffers affliction and abandonment
to the point of death? The difficulties of this reading of these two
psalms was perhaps foreseen by the compiler, and so the extraordinary
efforts to link them at the point of 88's superscription. A deliberate
attempt has been made to fuse together into one the voice of each
speaker. Not only are 87 and 88 welded together by this lengthy title,
but as already shown, 89 becomes inextricably connected as well. Not
surprisingly, the latter psalm continues with the amalgamation of
Davidic and divine prerogatives.

Further verbal connections between the juxtaposed and editorially
bound Psalms 87 and 88 can be found. The citizens of eschatological
Zion live together 'with' (עם, 87.4) members of many nations, while in
88.5 the lonely individual descends 'with' (עם) those consigned to the
pit. In that place 'you do not remember them' (לא זכרתם, 88.6), but
those many residents of Zion in 87.4 are specially 'remembered' for
citizenship (אזכיר). They are recalled and 'recorded' (יספר) by Yahweh
as members of Zion in 87.6, while in the grave this afflicted one wonders if God's faithfulness can ever 'be recounted' (היספר, 88.12). As a
result of eschatological restoration, Zion is singing and 'dancing'
(כחללים, 87.7), but its Davidic king lies lifeless in the grave like 'slain
ones' (כמו חללים, 88.6). Zion is the place where the speaker finds 'all'
(כל) his refreshing springs of water (87.7), and in 87.2 it is preferred
over 'all' (כל) other dwellings in Jacob. On the other hand, the individual of 88 suffers 'all' (כל, vv. 8, 18) the pounding of Yahweh's watery
breakers and spends 'all' (כל, v. 10) the day crying out for mercy.
Waters of refreshment in 87 are the antithesis of the watery death
pictured in 88.

The contrast between eschatological promise (Psalm 87) and its opposite (Psalm 88) characterized the contrasts between 72 and 73 as well. There the glorious kingdom promised to the king's son in 72 did not correspond to the reality of the afflicted individual in 73. Here the glorious Zion promised in 87 does not correspond to the reality of the deathly afflicted and isolated Davidic king of 88. At the same time, 86.13 has already foretold the eventual redemption of this Davidide out of Sheol. There he attributes it to Yahweh's faithfulness (חסדך). Not coincidentally, 89.1, 2 sing of faithfulness (חסד) as an answer to the doubt cast on that same faithfulness from Sheol in 88.12. In 89 it is faithfulness to the Davidic covenant (cf. 89.29, חסדי ובריתי) being praised. Consequently, the faithfulness (חסד) which delivered him from death in 86.13 is the same covenant faithfulness praised in 89 for the deliverance from death described in the previous 88.

The two contrasting images between Psalms 87 and 88 repeat the same found in the single 84, creating another inclusio of sorts around this group of Qorahite psalms (84–88). Zion is the desired dwelling place of the speaker in 84.2-8 (cf. משכנות and ציון in 84.2, 8 and 87.2). Following in 84.9 is the prayer of this speaker using terminology close to that of 88.3:

$$\text{תפלתי האזינה} \quad - \quad 84.9$$
$$\text{תפלתי...אזנך} \quad - \quad 88.3$$

In fact, all five psalms from 84 to 88 are punctuated at each end (84, 88) and in the middle (86) by requests for a hearing to this individual's prayer:

$$\text{תפלתי האזינה} \quad - \quad 84.9 \text{ (A)}$$
$$\text{תפלה...הטה אזנך} \quad - \quad 86.1 \text{ (B)}$$
$$\text{האזינה...תפלתי} \quad - \quad 86.6 \text{ (A')}$$
$$\text{תפלתי הטה אזנך...תפלתי} \quad - \quad 88.3, 14 \text{ (B')}$$

The reference of 86.1 corresponds to 88.3, 14, where the imperative הטה is added, while 86.6 corresponds to 84.9, where the imperative 'hearken' (denominative of the same root אזן, 'ear', used in 86.1 and 88.3 in noun form) is found. Psalm 86 here becomes the center and this only repeats what the superscriptions reveal, being the lone Davidic title at the midpoint of four surrounding Qorahite ascriptions. 'David' stands out not only from this Qorahite group, but also from Book III as a whole, and again reinforces the idea of a 'Davidide' as the dominant speaker across these seventeen psalms.[4]

While Psalm 88 is rightly labelled an individual lament,[5] it contains elements that resemble the preceding community laments of Book III. Psalm 74 opens with a question quite similar to 88.15:

74.1 – למה אלהים זנחת
88.15 – למה יהוה תזנח

Just as the nation was rejected in 74, so the individual suffered the same in 88. In 88.11-13 are found three consecutive questions (using heh interrogative) directed toward Yahweh by the individual. The same pattern was found in 77.8-10 (heh interrogative) but with temporal references ('forever', לעולמים, לנצח). In either case, the following psalms (89, 78) answer those questions directly.

Having examined the role of Psalm 88 in the design of Book III, it remains to trace the rhetorical devices used in its own composition. As is true of Psalm 86, it can be divided into three strophes (vv. 2-10a; 10b-13; 14-19). The central strophe (vv. 10b-13) is primarily a series of rhetorical questions that are finally answered in the subsequent 89, just as the central strophe of 86 (vv. 8-13) was further expounded in 87.[6]

Each strophe opens with a direct address to Yahweh, sharing common elements. The first address covers vv. 2-3, while the third is a combination of the indicative v. 14 and interrogative v. 15. At the beginning of strophe II is a single bicolon (v. 10bc) functioning as the opening address before the three following interrogatives. All three addresses are characterized by pleas to Yahweh (צעקתי, v. 2; קראתיך, v. 10b; שועתי, v. 14), expressing the desperate situation of the supplicant. In addition to the common divine name 'Yahweh' (יהוה) in all three addresses (vv. 2, 10b, 14-15), a reference to one of the twenty-four hour day's divisions is also present. In v. 2 the psalmist cries out 'by day' (יום) and 'by night' (בלילה), that is, constantly to God. The same idea is

---

4.   A unity around the larger group of 84 through 89 is formed by repetition of 'your anointed one' (משיחך) at either end (84.10 and 89.21, 39, 52).

5.   Cf. Gunkel, *Die Psalmen*, p. 382.

6.   The three central rhetorical questions of Ps. 77.8-10 were likewise answered in the subsequent psalm. The two similar Pss. 79 and 80 contained a pair of interrogatives (79.5, 10; 80.5, 13) that were finally answered in the following Ps. 81.9-17. Then God in 82.2 ironically questioned the nation using the same interrogative form עד-מתי. The questions raised in Ps. 74 by the nation were likewise answered in the subsequent 75–76. This pattern of interrogative–response is an essential part of the dialogue continued throughout Book III.

expressed by the form 'every day' (בכל־יום) in v. 10b. The one division
of a day not stated explicitly, even if assumed in the first two strophe-
openings, appears in the third address of v. 14 – 'in the morning' (בבקר).
Each of these temporal references functions as a complement of the
preposition beth:

$$
\begin{array}{rl}
\text{v. 2} & - \quad \text{בלילה נגדך} \\
\text{v. 10bc} & - \quad \text{בכל־היום...אליך} \\
\text{v. 14b} & - \quad \text{בבקר...תקדמך}
\end{array}
$$

The destination of this plea is clearly reiterated by the identical second
person singular masculine suffix (ך-).

Further parallels have been created between the beginning of the last
two strophes. In v. 10c direction is expressed by the prepositional form
אליך, seen again in v. 14a. This phrase is accompanied in both 10c and
14a by first person singular perfect verb forms, formed from shin–initial
and laryngeal–final roots:

$$
\begin{array}{rl}
\text{v. 10c} & - \quad \text{שטחתי אליך} \\
\text{v. 14a} & - \quad \text{אליך...שועתי}
\end{array}
$$

The latter verb form of v. 14a ('I cried for help') also exhibits deliberate
consonance with the suffixed noun of v. 2a ('my salvation') at the
opening of strophe I (יֵשׁוּעָתִי...שִׁוַּעְתִּי). In fact, these two forms may
derive from an original root שׁוע.[7] Their use in 72.12 (מְשַׁוֵּעַ, 'crying for
help') and 13 (יוֹשִׁיעַ, 'he will save') is clearly based on their consonantal resemblance. Moreover, in the same 72.12, 13 it is the cry of the
'humble (אֶבְיוֹן) and 'afflicted' (עָנִי) that receives a response of salvation. The individual of Psalms 86 and 86 identifies himself as afflicted
and humble (86.1; 88.8, 10, 16), and so again in Book III there is a
request that the promises of Psalm 72 be kept.

The reference to 'morning' (בקר) in v. 14 serves as an inclusio
around strophe III in conjunction with 'all the day' (כל־היום) of v. 18.
'Day and night' of v. 2 (strophe I) become 'morning and day' in vv. 14,
18 (strophe III) respectively. The placement of 'day' close to the end of
the psalm creates inclusio around the whole (היום/יום, vv. 2, 18).
Parallel to the night of v. 2 (בלילה) is the darkness (מחשך) of v. 19,
forming another bracket. These temporal references create a pattern of
ABA'B'A" across the psalm:

---

7.   See BDB, s.v. שׁוע, p. 1002.

יוֹם – A (v. 2)
בְלַיְלָה – B (v. 2)
בְכָל־הַיּוֹם – A' (v. 10b)
וּבַבֹּקֶר – B' (v. 14)
כָל־הַיּוֹם – A" (v. 18)

The constancy of cries to God are emphasized at the opening and close of the entire poem and at the outset of each strophe.

The double reference to the speaker's prayer (תְפִלָּתִי) in vv. 3 and 14 is accompanied by further parallels. In each case the suffixed noun is the subject of an imperfect verb predicating direction toward God:

תָבוֹא לְפָנֶיךָ תְפִלָּתִי – v. 3
תְפִלָּתִי תְקַדְּמֶךָ...פָנֶיךָ – vv. 14, 15

While the form פָנֶיךָ is repeated in vv. 3 and 15, the first describes a desire for the prayer to come before the very presence of Yahweh, while the second complains that he conceals his presence from the supplicant. Without the confident confessions of 86.13 and 89.2-6, it would appear that the supplicant was never answered.

Although the general context of suffering in Psalm 88 does not suggest a watery grave, there are interesting parallels with Jonah 2. Two references to the waters in 88.7b ('in the depths') and 88.8ab ('upon me...all your breakers') recall the 'breakers' and 'depths' of Jon. 2.4:

בִמְצֹלוֹת...עָלַי...וְכָל־מִשְׁבָּרֶיךָ – Ps. 88.7b-8b
מְצוּלָה...כָל־מִשְׁבָּרֶיךָ...עָלַי – Jon. 2.4

The parallels do not end here. Both find themselves in Sheol (Jon. 2.3; Ps. 88.4). Their cries to God are described twice with identical verbs 'to call' and 'to cry': קָרָאתִי, Jon. 2.3; קְרָאתִיךָ, Ps. 88.10b; שִׁוַּעְתִּי, Jon. 2.3 and Ps. 88.14. Jonah 2.4 is further paralleled in Ps. 88.17-18, and again by use of water imagery. Divine anger 'has passed over me...it surrounded me like water' in Ps. 88.17-18. In Jon. 2.4, 6 a current of water and the deep 'surrounded me', and the breakers and waves 'passed over me':

עָלַי עָבָרוּ...סַבּוּנִי כַמָּיִם – Ps. 88.17-18
יְסֹבְבֵנִי...עָלַי עָבָרוּ – Jon. 2.4, 6

Other correspondences are the idea of 'descent', both in Jon. 2.7 (יָרַדְתִּי) and Ps. 88.5 (יוֹרְדֵי), the desire to be seen or heard 'before you' in Jon. 2.5 (מִנֶּגֶד עֵינֶיךָ) and Ps. 88.2 (נֶגְדֶּךָ), the confession of Yahweh as his 'salvation' in Jon. 2.10 (יְשׁוּעָתָה) and Ps. 88.2 (יְשׁוּעָתִי), the 'life' of the individual in Jon. 2.7 and Ps. 88.4 (חיי) and the twofold use of the first person singular independent pronoun (אני) in Jon. 2.5, 10 and Ps. 88.14, 16. In both cases the supplicant's 'soul/life' (נפש) is in danger (Jon. 2.6, 8; Ps. 88.4, 15). Last but not least is the expressed desire for his prayer to come before God by both individuals, in practically identical terminology:

תבוא אליך תפלתי – Jon. 2.8c
תבוא לפניך תפלתי – Ps. 88.3

The fact that both references to water in Psalm 88 (vv. 7-8, 17-18) are closely parallel to Jon. 2.4, and that the supplication vocabulary at each strophe opening (Ps. 88.2-3, 10bc, 14) likewise corresponds to the same in Jonah 2, suggests that both individuals are being deliberately paralleled through intertextuality.[8] Here the text is informed beyond the immediate Book III, or the Psalter itself, by the larger Hebrew canon. This borrowing is not fortuitous, since the predicament of Jonah helps explain that of the individual in Psalm 88. Both are as good as dead and nothing short of divine intervention will save them. Such help is stated explicitly in the text of Jonah and clearly implied in the context of Psalms 86–89.

Psalm 88 ends pessimistically, the speaker still isolated in the dark depths of Sheol. However, the immediately following Psalm 89 opens with a burst of song, spoken in direct answer to the questions raised in 88.11-13, and confirming the deliverance from Sheol stated briefly in 86.13. That deliverance was due to Yahweh's 'covenant faithfulness' (חסדך) upon the speaker in 86.13, but questioned while in the very depths of Sheol by 88.12 (חסדך), and finally confirmed in 89.2 (חסדי יהוה).

---

8.   See R. de Beaugrande and W. Dressler, *Introduction to Text Linguistics* (New York: Longman, 1981), p. 10, for whom intertextuality is defined as concerning 'the factors which make the utilization of one text dependent upon the knowledge of one or more previously encountered texts'. The word for word use of Jonah 2.4c by Ps. 42.8b is another example of intertextuality between these two books.

Chapter 17

PSALM 89

As illustrated in the previous chapter, the final third of Psalm 88's superscription and that of 89 are identical except for the proper names (אֵיתָן, 89; הֵימָן, 88). Hakham has noted that the three levitical singers appointed by David were Asaph, Heman and Ethan according to 1 Chron. 6.18, 24, 29; 15.17, 19.[1] The first of these (Asaph) opens Book III of the Psalter (Psalms 73–83) while the second two (Heman, Ethan) close it (Psalms 88–89). In addition, the David who appointed this trio (1 Chron. 15.16) is ascribed the authorship of Psalm 86, also in Book III.

The proper name 'Ethan' (אֵיתָן) of this superscription is found in adjectival form in Ps. 74.15. These are the only two uses in the whole of the Psalter and therefore contribute to the unity of Book III. As the adjective 'permanent', it corresponds to the temporal theme found throughout Book III. In 74.15 the form in question simply refers to 'permanent streams' (נַהֲרוֹת אֵיתָן), which God dried up. The seemingly perpetual desolation described in Psalm 74 could be reversed, just as had occurred with perpetual phenomena of nature. Here in Psalm 89 the eternal faithfulness of God's covenant with David is a central theme. The operative term is 'forever' (עוֹלָם), which opens (vv. 2, 3, 5) and closes the psalm (v. 53), and is found repeatedly between (vv. 29, 37, 38). Consequently, this proper name אֵיתָן fits well in the superscription as an introduction to a psalm recalling the eternal nature of God's covenant with David.

The following Psalm 90 (vv. 1-4) responds by giving the divine perspective on time to repeated questions in Book III, and to Psalm 89 in particular. At the conclusion of Book II the promises to David's house were followed immediately by the questions and complaints of Psalm

---

1. Hakham, *Sefer tehillim*, p. 159 (קנט). In 1 Chron. 25.1; 2 Chron. 5.12; 35.15; the three appointed are Asaph, Heman and Jeduthun.

73. Here the hard questions that conclude Psalm 89 (and Book III) are followed by divine answers and another temporal question in 90.

Hakham notes rightly that 89 and 73 are both laments, so that the book ends and begins in the same mood. He also sees the 'particular intention' (כוונה מיוחדת) behind the Psalter's present canonical order of Psalm 2 at the beginning, 72 at the end of Book II and 89 concluding Book III, all discussing the Davidic covenant.[2] Psalm 2 describes the victory of the anointed Davidic king over the rebellious rulers, 72 describes the picture of an ideal Davidic king, and 89 laments the apparent failure of the promise to this royal house. He does not, however, document the laments over this failure of 72's promises begun already in 73, continuing through Book III, and yet interspersed with further promises of eschatological restoration. McCann analyzes the inner structure of Book III form-critically, characterizing its composition as alternating expressions between lament and hope.[3] Nonetheless, he too overlooks the fact that references to 72 abound throughout Book III, beginning right at 73.[4]

At this point it would be appropriate to compare the promise to David's house in 72 and the complaint regarding its apparent failure in 89. Their common position at the end of contiguous books in the Psalter is the first indication of possible parallels. Within the first four verses of 72, the word pair 'righteousness' (צדק or צדקה) and 'judgment/just judging' (משפט or ישפט) is found three times. The kingdom therein described thus matches Yahweh's in 89.15 (צדק ומשפט), suggesting that they are one and the same (cf. also צדקתך in 89.17b). This is consistent to the situation within 89 itself, where the reign of Yahweh in 89.6-19 is described in ways identical to the one promised to the Davidic house of 89.20-38.

A picture emerges from this psalm of a David who rules as Yahweh's very representative. Dumortier, in explaining this phenomenon in 89, designates the Davidic servant of that psalm as Yahweh's 'véritable lieu-tenant' on the earth.[5] However, after the canonical reading of Psalms 87 and 88 of the previous chapter, it becomes evident that the roles and voices of the Davidide and Yahweh are merging close enough

---

2. Hakham, *Sefer tehillim*, p. 159 (קנג).
3. McCann, 'Books I–III', pp. 96-97.
4. McCann, 'Books I–III', p. 96.
5. J.-B. Dumortier, 'Un rituel d'intronisation, le Ps. LXXXIX, 2-38', *VT* 22 (1972), pp. 176-96 (187, 193).

as to be indistinguishable. The same occurs in Psalm 72, where the blessing (ברך) on the royal prince (vv. 15d, 17c) coincides with the doxological blessing on Yahweh (vv. 18, 19). If the prince's name will endure and be blessed forever (שמו לעולם, 72.17a), the same is said of Yahweh's name immediately following (שֵׁם...לעולם, 72.19a).

Further parallels can be shown between Psalms 72 and 89. The prince of 72.4 will crush (וידכא) the oppressor, as does Yahweh Rahab in 89.11 (דכאת). Just as they will fear the prince of 72.5 (ייראוך), so Yahweh is fearsome (נורא) to all those around him in 89.8. In each case, the kingdom is eternal and so necessarily one and the same. That of 72 endures as the sun and moon (שמש...ירח) according to v. 5, and even beyond the moon's existence in v. 7. It continues from 'generation to generation' in the same 72. 5 (דור דורים), and in v. 17b his name will endure as long as the sun. Parallel to the sun reference in 72.17b is the 'forever' (לעולם) of v. 17a. All these find parallels in Psalm 89. The throne of David will be established for all generations (לדר ודור, v. 5). Between vv. 37b and 38a that same throne endures as the sun and moon (כשמש...כירח). The noun (לְ)עולם is repeated sevenfold (vv. 2, 3, 5, 29, 37, 38, 53) across 89 to describe this kingdom's endurance and the consequent praise of Yahweh.

The dominion exercised by the prince in Psalm 72 stretches from sea to sea and from the river to the ends of the earth (מים עד־ים...ומנהר, v. 8), while that of Psalm 89 likewise includes the sea and rivers (בים...ובנהרות, v. 26). His enemies (אויביו) lick the dust in 72.9 and their subjugation is equally complete in the kingdom of 89.11, 23 (אויב, אויביך).[6] The latter promises then motivate questions regarding ignominy and enemy (89.43, 52) victories in the present. If the kings of the earth in 72.10-11 (מלכי, מלכים) are forced into subservience under the Davidic prince, so the Davidide in 89.28 is promised dominion over the same (מלכי). Destined to rule these vanquished kings in 72 is the royal heir of v. 1 (למלך...לבן־למלך) and likewise 'our king' (מלכנו) of 89.19. Sarna notes that מלכנו in 89.19b (at the end of an oracle concerning the divine kingdom) serves as a transition to the oracle of the immediately following (vv. 20-38), in which the Davidic covenant is

---

6. The subjugation of enemies described in 89.11, 23 is a characteristic of the kingdom of Yahweh, which is equated with David's kingdom in this psalm. Verse 11 is from an oracle regarding divine rule, while v. 23 comes within a rehearsal of the Davidic covenant.

discussed.[7] In fact, 'our king' of v. 19 is the Davidic descendant who rules over the kingdom of God on an eternal throne (vv. 5, 29, 37, 38).

The blessed nation of 89.17 exults in Yahweh's name throughout the day (כל־היום), and so subservient kings of 72 also bless that prince all day long (כל־היום, v. 15). As noted before, the perpetuity of the prince's name in 72.17 is a description matching that of Yahweh's name in 72.19. Psalm 89.37a states that David's descendant will continue forever:

$$72.17a - יהי שמו לעולם$$
$$72.19 - שם...לעולם$$
$$89.37a - זרעו לעולם יהיה$$

As the eternal name of the Davidic prince in 72.17a endures forever, so will he be blessed, or the source of blessing continually. Immediately following in the doxology of 72.18-19, blessings are called for on Yahweh and his name. Psalm 89 ends in the same manner:

$$72.15 - יברכנהו$$
$$72.17b - יתברכו בו$$
$$72.18a - ברוך יהוה$$
$$72.19a - וברוך שם...לעולם$$
$$89.53 - ברוך יהוה לעולם$$

This comparison of 72.15, 17, 19 demonstrates how the same eternal blessing is called upon the names of both the Davidic prince and Yahweh. The final doxology of 89 resembles closely that of 72:

$$72.18-19 - ברוך יהוה...לעולם...אמן ואמן$$
$$89.53 - ברוך יהוה לעולם אמן ואמן$$

This final blessing of 72 follows immediately the blessings heaped upon the royal prince in the preceding vv. 15-17, as noted above. However, a contrast consonant with the mood of Book III can be seen between the concluding comments of these two royal psalms. The final blessing of 89 is immediately preceded by reproach (חרף) heaped upon the anointed Davidide (v. 52b), Yahweh (52a) and fellow servants (v. 51). Nonetheless, the speaker steadfastly chooses to bless Yahweh, having believed that the promises to David are trustworthy.

The reproaches against God, his anointed king and servants at the

7. N. Sarna, 'Psalm 89: A Study in Inner Biblical Exegesis', in A. Altmann (ed.), *Biblical and Other Studies* (Cambridge, MA: Harvard University Press, 1963), pp. 29-46 (31).

conclusion of Psalm 89 (חרף, vv. 51-52) continue a theme expressed by the same root since the complaints of 74.10, 18, 22. There the enemy was despising God's name, instead of uttering blessings as promised in 72. In Ps. 78.66 the enemies of Adonay were to suffer eternal reproach, but 79.4, 12 laments again the reproach suffered by Adonay and his servants. Here at the end of Psalm 89 the mood and plight has not really changed, since 72's promises have yet to be realized.

While the blessings called upon the eternal name in the doxology of Psalm 72 continue those called upon the Davidic prince of 72.15, 17, the blessing of 89's doxology contrasts decidedly with the preceding vv. 39-52. On the other hand, there is a note of confidence in Yahweh, expressed by the twofold 'amen' (אמן) of 89.53. 'Amen' is built upon the same root used in describing Yahweh's faithfulness to David (אמונה, נאמנת, נאמן, אמת) throughout 89 (vv. 2, 3, 6, 15, 25, 29, 34, 38, 50). Clearly the root אמן continues and is consistent with the body of 89, being an 'amen' of confidence in divine faithfulness to the Davidic covenant.[8] David himself in 1 Chron. 17.23, 24 uses this root in response to the covenant made with his house. The similarities with the doxology of 89.53 are remarkable:

$$\text{ועל ביתו יאמן עד עולם} - \text{1 Chron. 17.23}^9$$
$$\text{ויאמן ויגדל שמך עד עולם} - \text{1 Chron. 17.24}$$
$$\text{ברוך יהוה לעולם אמן ואמן} - \text{Ps. 89.53}$$

At the conclusion of David's response to the covenant, he blesses God in a form that resembles closely the doxology given at the end of Psalm 89:

$$\text{כי אתה יהוה ברכת ומברך לעולם} - \text{1 Chron. 17.27}^{10}$$
$$\text{ברוך יהוה לעולם אמן ואמן} - \text{Ps. 89.53}$$

Discussion of this covenant with David is concluded in either case with blessings on God. Consequently, doxologies (as well as superscriptions) are appended to the psalms, and to 89 in particular, in a manner that contributes to their individual and canonical message.

---

8. BDB, s.v. אמן, p. 53, suggests the translation 'God of faithfulness' for אלהי אמן in Isa. 65.16.

9. Compare the use of אמת in 2 Sam. 7.28 in the response by David to the covenant.

10. Again, the root ברך is also found in 2 Sam. 7.29 as a response to the covenant.

Psalm 72 is the culmination of David's prayers, according to the final verse (20) of its doxology (כלו תפלות דוד בן ישׁי), thereby interpreting the superscription as 'for', not 'by' Solomon (לשׁלמה). As a result, the son of 72.1 (לבן מלך) would also refer to Solomon. Furthermore, a short genealogy consisting of David (v. 20), his father Jesse (v. 20) and his son Solomon (v. 1) is formed around the psalm with the common term 'son' (בן) repeated at either end. Similar emphasis on David's family in Psalm 89 goes without saying. David himself (דוד) is named directly four times across 89 (vv. 4, 21, 36, 50). Warning to his sons (בניו) is given in v. 31. Thus, the promise to David and his sons is the dominant concept in both Psalms 72 and 89.

As discussed before, the idyllic description of Psalm 72 is followed by the descent into reality of 73. This contrast between promise of 72 and reality of 73 parallels the promise of 89.20-38 and reality of 89.39-52. Injustice and violence had almost brought the speaker of 73 to the point of scepticism (v. 15, אמרתי), a place at which God's people had already arrived (vv. 10-11, ואמרו). However, he considered the effect on succeeding generations (דור בניך, v. 15b), and finally confessed that God was indeed his rock forever (צור...לעולם, v. 26). Similarily, the speaker of 89 declares that God's kindness endures forever (אמרתי עולם, v. 3), after promising to make known his faithfulness to all generations (לדר ודר, v. 2). Then the chosen son in v. 27 calls God his rock (צור) of salvation. Consequently, both psalms express confidence in the face of oppression and defeat. Psalm 73 laments the oppression first (vv. 1-12), before confession of faith (vv. 18-28), while in 89 the order is faithful praise first (vv. 2-19) and complaint following (vv. 39-52). These various resemblances suggest that the complaining individual (אני) of 73.2, 22, 23, 28 is identical canonically with the individual (אני) of 89.48. In fact, that righteous Davidide has lamented repeatedly throughout Book III.

A contrast of mood between the beginning and end of 89 can be demonstrated formally. The speaker begins 89 singing of Yahweh's covenant faithfulnesses in 89.2 (חסדי יהוה), and follows with direct ('You', אתה, vv. 10, 11, 13, 18) expressions of praise to God. That mood suddenly changes in v. 40, where the direct address to God (ואתה, 'But you') opens a protest and complaint, asking where the covenant faithfulness (חסדיך, v. 50) to David has gone. The result is a chiasm of sorts between the first nineteen verses and the final fifteen:

חסד...יהוה חסדי – 89.2-3, A
אתה – 89.10-13, 18, B
ואתה – 89.39, B'
חסדיך – 89.50, A'

Between these two contrasting extremes is the rehearsal of the Davidic covenant, where חסד is recalled repeatedly (vv. 20, 25, 29, 34) as a preparation for the complaint of vv. 39-52. Within that rehearsal is the prediction that the promised Davidic heir would cry to God, 'you are my father' (אבי אתה). This single instance of אתה at the heart of the poem identifies the speaker who repeats this second person pronoun as the Davidic heir and son of God.

The series of interrogatives in Book III directed to God begins in Psalm 74 and continues through 89. Common vocabulary to both includes the interrogative form עד־מה in 74.9 and 89.47, both asking 'how long' the distress will continue. In each psalm, an interrogative clause asks whether the rejection will continue forever, using the same term לנצח (74.1; 89.47). The latter term dominates Psalm 74, even as the semantically close עולם does 89, revealing the similarity of each lament. This discouraging mood in both poems is caused by the continued rejection (זנחת) either of the whole nation (74.1) or its anointed leader (89.39). A similar parallel occurs between the defiled temple in 74.7 (לארץ חללו) and defilement of the anointed servant's crown (לארץ חללת) in 89.40. The final strophe of each psalm also commands God to remember the reproach by Israel's enemies using identical vocabulary:

חרפה...זכר...חרפת...חרפו אויביך...חרפו – 89.42, 51, 52
זכר...אויב חרף...זכר חרפתך – 74.18, 22

Identical vocabulary used to identify the reproaching enemy is found numerous times across each psalm. In 74.3, 10, 18 and 89.11, 23, 43, 52, אויב is used, as is צר in 74.10 and 89.24, 43 (also the similar צרר of 74.4, 23). Remembrance is asked not only of the enemy's calumny in each psalm, but also the plight of the nation (זכר עדתך) in 74.2 and the individual speaker in 89.48 (זכר־אני).

Another common element between 89 and 74 is the repeated second person singular masculine pronoun אתה (74.13-17; 89.10-18). Each series of this pronoun (not including the single instances of 89.27, 39 mentioned above) falls in a strophe that recalls past deeds of Yahweh's power (עז, 74.13; 89.11, 14, 18), including subjugation of the sea (ים, 74.13; 89.10). That power was exerted through his hand (or right hand), as stated in 89.14, although 74.11 asks why it is presently restrained:

74.11 – ‏ידך ימינך‏
89.14 – ‏ידך...ימינך‏

Finally, it bears repeating the two instances of ‏איתן‏, one in 89's superscription (Ethan) and the other in 74.15 ('perpetual'), the latter related to the temporal terms mentioned above (‏עולם‏, ‏נצח‏). Furthermore, the covenant is remembered (‏הבט לברית‏) in 74.20, and throughout Psalm 89 (vv. 4, 29, 35, 40). One could argue that this covenant is remembered in the context of the land then filled with 'violence' (‏חמס‏, 74.20b), and not the monarch. However, it is precisely in the covenant with David, as described in Ps. 72.14, that a promise was made to abolish violence (‏חמס‏). References to the poor and humble of 74.19 (‏ענייך‏) and 74.21 (‏עני ואביון‏) demonstrate that there the poet was pleading for the fulfilment of promises made to these same afflicted ones in Ps. 72.2, 4, 12, 13.

In Psalm 75 a promise was made by God to judge (‏שפט‏, vv. 3, 8) with equity. Part of that judgment was to exalt (‏רום‏, vv. 5, 6, 11) the horns (‏קרן‏, vv. 5, 6, 11) of the righteous (‏צדיק‏, v. 11) and bring down the wicked. In like manner, God's throne described in Psalm 89 is sustained by righteousness and just judgment (‏צדק ומשפט‏, v. 15; see also ‏ובצדקתך‏, v. 17). The work of exalting (‏רום‏) the righteous is found repeatedly (vv. 14, 17, 18, 20, 25) across 89. With good reason then, the speaker complains that the enemy has been exalted (‏רום‏) in 89.43. Just as in 75, the expression 'raising [‏רום‏] of the horn' is used in 89.17-18, 25. The following illustrates how close the wording is between each psalm:

75.11 – ‏תרוממנה קרנות צדיק‏
89.17-18 – ‏ובצדקתך ירומו...תרים קרננו‏
89.25 – ‏תרום קרנו‏

Psalm 75 promised the exaltation of the righteous and debasing of the wicked. The latter are warned and their assured destruction described at length by 75.5-11a in consistently plural references. One would expect reference to the righteous of 75.11b to be in the plural also (as in Ps. 1.5-6, where the same word pair is used), but surprisingly the singular ‏צדיק‏ ('righteous one') is found instead. Apparently, the same royal figure who stands out from the nation across Book III is here in view. Psalm 89 focuses on the singular leader (vv. 20-38), whose horn is to be raised (‏תרום קרנו‏, v. 25). Annihilation of this royal figure's foes as promised in 89 (vv. 23-24) resembles closely the hewing down of the wicked in 75.9, 11 by the speaker himself. Finally, the speaker of Psalm 89 promises to praise the kindness of Yahweh forever (עולם, v. 2), which praise is continued in v. 53 (לעולם). Likewise, the speaker of 75.10 promises to sing continually (לעלם) to the God of Jacob.

The predominant pronoun in Psalm 76 is the second person masculine singular אתה of vv. 5 and 8 (twice). As is often the case, repetition of this particular pronoun occurs in contexts of praise to God for extraordinary deeds. Its repetition in Ps. 74.13-17 occurred in a description of divine dominion over the forces of nature. In Psalm 76 triumph over human enemy forces is celebrated. Twice within that praise God is characterized as fearsome (נורא, vv. 8, 13). Likewise the pronoun אתה is repeated in 89.10, 11, 12, 13, 18 in a hymn to Yahweh, preceded by his designation as נורא in v. 8. Moreover, Yahweh's power over both nature and his enemies is acclaimed in these same verses (89.10-13).

Psalm 76 concludes with assurance of Yahweh's dominion over all the kings of the earth. Using quite similar wording, Ps. 89.28 promises that the Davidic king would reign over these same kings. This fusion of divine and Davidic roles is repeated when the assertion of 83.19 that Yahweh alone was the highest over all the earth is compared with the latter two texts.

$$
\begin{array}{r}
\text{נורא למלכי־ארץ} \quad - \quad 76.13 \\
\text{עליון על כל הארץ} \quad - \quad 83.19 \\
\text{עליון למלכי־ארץ} \quad - \quad 89.28
\end{array}
$$

The description of Yahweh as fearsome to all those kings surrounding him in 76.12-13 is taken up again by 89.8-9. Those kings bring tribute before him in 76.12 in a depiction that resembles closely that of 72.10-12. However, in Psalm 72 the offerings and worship are given directly to the Davidic prince by all the kings and their peoples:

$$
\begin{array}{r}
\text{מלכי...מנחה...מלכי...אשכר...וישתחוו לו כל מלכים כל גוים} \quad - \quad 72.10\text{-}12 \\
\text{כל־סביביו יובילו שי למורא...נורא למלכי הארץ} \quad - \quad 76.12\text{-}13 \\
\text{ונורא על־כל־סביביו...סביבותיך} \quad - \quad 89.8\text{-}9
\end{array}
$$

Once again there is a complete merging of divine and royal Davidic prerogatives. The latter becomes a sovereign in every sense of the word.

When justice (ומשפט) is called the foundation of God's throne in 89.15, it reaffirms the promise of its eventual appearance in 76.10 (למשפט). The latter psalm was continuing the answers of 75.3, 8 (שפט) to the complaints of 73–74. Justice (משפט), mentioned twice in

Ps. 72.1-2, but not yet seen, aroused the complaints of the following two psalms. Just as the promises of Psalms 75–76 are followed by the laments and questions of 77, so the confidence of divine justice asserted in 89.15 precedes the final complaint of 89.39-52.

Consistent with this pattern of divine answers followed by further complaints is another parallel between 76 and 89. War and its imple-ments (וחרב ומלחמה) were to be destroyed in the final victory of 76.4. For good reason 89.44 expresses discouragement at the enemies's vic-tory in battle (חרבו...במלחמה). Since the destruction of enemy weapons and warfare in 76.4 takes place in Salem/Zion, the speaker of Psalm 89 rightly expects the Davidic descendant to have supremacy in his royal city. However, the anointed one of David is defeated and vanquished. The very opposite conditions to those portrayed in Psalm 76 are in effect, and therefore the lament of Psalm 77 follows, as does the lament of 89.39-52 follow promises in 89.1-38.

Psalm 89.47 is an interrogative asking if Yahweh will hide himself forever (לנצח). Using the same prepositional form לנצח, Ps. 77.9a also asks if Yahweh's kindness has ceased forever. Parallel to this expres-sion of 77.9a is the semantically parallel לדר ודר of 77.9b, in a repeti-tion of the same question. In contrast, the twofold use of the identical prepositional phrase in 89.2, 5 is a confession of faith in Yahweh's covenantal faithfulness. That faithfulness, plus the prepositional phrase, create a double correspondence between the two texts:

$$\text{חסדו...לדר ודר} - \text{77.9}$$
$$\text{חסדי יהוה...לדר ודר...לדר ודור} - \text{89.2, 5}$$

The concept of faithfulness (חסד) used in these two psalms and else-where in Book III (such as 85, 86 and 88) is in direct reference to the covenant with David. Parallels illustrated here point up the contrast between bitter questions about Yahweh's promise (77.9) and confident hope in its trustworthiness (89.2, 5). Nonetheless, in 89.47 the same type of despairing question resurfaces, revealing that the covenant has not been fully realized.

The first interrogative (v. 8) of three at the heart of Psalm 77 asks if Adonai 'is rejecting' (יזנח) 'forever' (הלעולמים). Rejection (זנחת) in 89.39 is not only parallel in form but also by its lament context in the final strophe (vv. 39-52). A contrast to זנחת of 89.39 is provided by the repeated singular form 'forever' (עולם), dominating the first two thirds of 89 (vv. 2, 3, 5, 29, 37, 38) and its final doxology (v. 53), demonstrat-ing confidence in Yahweh's promises. In fact, immediately after affirming the eternal (עולם) nature of the Davidic throne in 89.37-38, v. 39 accuses God of rejecting its occupant. Consequently, the root 'rejection' (זנח) is repeated in similar questioning contexts of both 77.8 and 89.39. At the same time, the adverbial 'forever' (לעולמים) used by the despondent questioner of 77.8 contrasts with the sevenfold עולם of confidence across the first two thirds of 89.

A further contrast can be detected between praise for the work of Yahweh's right hand (ימין) in 89.14 (or the same of the Davidide in 89.26), and the doubting question of 77.11. Psalm 77.11 wonders if the Highest One's right hand (ימין עליון) has changed, but in 89.28 the final victory of the עליון is promised. In the latter example, עליון is the son of David (and uniquely 'firstborn' or 'son of God', 89.27-28), the 'highest' of the earth's kings, truly opposite the situation of 77.11.

Both Psalms 89 and 77 express praise of Yahweh's person and wondrous deeds using parallel vocabulary. The speaker of 77 recalled Yahweh's 'deeds' (פלאך) of old in v. 12, and present performance of them (פלא, v. 15; cf. פלאך in 89.6). Psalm 77.15 includes the independent personal pronoun אתה, seen already in 89.10-18 and 74.12-17 within similar contexts. Other terms such as 'strength' (עז) and 'arm' (זרוע) of 77.15-16 are also found in the hymnic context of 89.11, 14, 18. The rhetorical question of 89.9, 'Who is like you?' (מי כמוך), and that of 77.14, 'Who...like God?' (מי...כאלהים) continue parallel patterns between these two hymns to Yahweh's person and power. The same can be said for the 'world' (תבל) of 89.12 and 77.19 under his control. These parallels show a repeated pattern of references to previous divine exploits as an incentive to present intervention.

Just as Psalm 89 is dominated by the root אמן in its various permutations (אמונתך, אמת, נאמן, נאמנת, אמן, vv. 2, 3, 6, 9, 15, 25, 29, 34, 38, 50, 53), so 78 repeats it at important junctures of the psalm (vv. 8, 22, 32, 37). However, in Psalm 78 the root appears only in verbal or participial form (האמינו, נאמנו, נאמנה), as opposed to the mostly nominal forms of 89. The most telling contrast between these two lengthiest psalms of Book III is the fact that 89 reiterates by means of this root the faithfulness of God to the Davidic covenant, while 78 emphasizes Israel's unfaithfulness:

78.37 – ולא נאמנו בבריתו
89.29 – ובריתי נאמנת לו

Divine anger is expressed similarily in Psalms 78 and 89. Whether by noun (חמה, 78.38; 89.47), or verbs (התעבר, 78.21, 59, 62; 89.39), it is present in both. That wrath is directed exclusively against Israel in 78, but in 89.39, 47 against the anointed one. The same pair of verbs describes anger and rejection against either one:

78.59 – ויתעבר וימאס מאד בישראל
89.39 – ותמאס התעברת עם משיחך

In spite of his integrity, the individual Davidide suffers the same ignominy as that of wayward Israel. From the beginning of Book III, the individual Davidide has protested his innocence and integrity, and yet suffers along with the guilty nation. The depth of his suffering is revealed especially in the final psalms of Book III, reaching the point of death itself (Pss. 86.13; 88.4-6; 89.49). Nevertheless, that suffering is interspersed in 85.9-14; 86.8-13; 87; 89.1-38 with promises that his kingdom will be re-established.

One reason for divine anger in Psalm 78 was Israel's prevarication (יכזבו־לו, v. 36) against God. In contrast, Yahweh promised not to deceive David (אם...אכזב, 89.36). A result of divine wrath in 78 was the exile of his power and beauty (עזו ותפארתו, 78.61), a reference to the tabernacle at Shiloh (cf. v. 60). Here in 89 the power and beauty of a nation walking in divine light (v. 16) is God's very person (תפארת עזמו אתה, 89.18). Another reason for God's anger was the lack of trust in his salvation (בישועתו), according to 78.22, in contrast to God's chosen son in 89.27, who does express trust (ישועתי).

References to God's choice of David, servant of God, are found in both Psalms 78 and 89, using identical vocabulary:

78.70 – ויבחר בדוד עבדו
89.4 – לבחירי...לדוד עבדי
89.20d-21a – בחור...דוד עבדי

This choice in 78 of the faithful shepherd David presumably brought about the defeat of God's enemies, to the point that eternal reproach (חרפת עולם, 78.66) was put upon them. In addition, the holy place was established forever (לעולם, 78.69). In light of these statements, the poet in 89 rightly asks God to remember the reproach (חרפת...חרפו...חרפו) now suffered by his servants and his anointed one in 89.51-52. The eternal reproach promised for the enemy in 78.66 would presumably come through establishment of the eternal (עולם) covenant made with David (89.2, 3, 5, 29, 37, 38, 53). Finally, the arousal of Yahweh in 78.65 as a strong man (כגבור) to bring in the Davidic kingdom resembles the ascription of strength (גבורה) to him in 89.14 and the naming of

David as a strong man (גבור) in 89.20c. The choice of David would bring about the defeat of his foes (צריו), according to 78.66 and 89.24, as had happened in the past (78.42). Therefore, with good reason the speaker in 89.43 complains that his foes (צריו) now have the upper hand.

Psalm 79 continues the national lament, noting that Israel still suffers the reproach (חרפה, v. 4) of its neighbors. According to 78.66, David's kingdom was to abolish such shame, and so the fulfilment of God's promise remains to be seen. Repetition of the same noun חרפה (or its verbal form) in 89.42, 51, 52 confirms the delay. Just as reproach against Israel (79.4) is later stated as the same against Adonay (79.12), so in 89 reproach against the anointed one (vv. 42, 52b) and God's servants (v. 51) is also against God (v. 52a). The resemblance extends to the relative pronoun and divine name used in each of these complaints as well:

79.12 – חרפתם אשר חרפוך אדני
89.51-52 – אדני חרפת עבדיך...חרפת...אשר חרפו אויביך יהוה אשר חרפו... משיחך

The position of these correspondences is also noteworthy. Either complaint occurs in the penultimate or, in the case of Psalm 89, both penultimate and antepenultimate verses of the psalm. Both are followed, nonetheless, by a final expression of eternal (לעולם) blessing on Yahweh, in the case of 89.53, or promise to praise him forever (לעולם) in 79.13.

Resemblances between the described reproach against the nation in 79.4 and the individual in 89.42 are also quite striking, becoming even more impressive if the immediately following interrogatives of 79.5 and 89.47 are included in the comparison:

79.4a, 5 – היינו חרפה לשכנינו...עד מה יהוה תאנף לנצח תבער כמו אש קנאתך
89.42b, 47 – היה חרפה לשכניו...עד מה יהוה תסתר לנצח תבער כמו אש חמתך

Undoubtedly a deliberate attempt is being made by the redactor of the Psalter to portray both nation and anointed Davidide in the same predicament. A further link consists of suffered reproach always carried in the bosom of either the individual (בחיקי, 89.51) or enemies (אל־חיקם, 79.12). In spite of these almost identical pessimistic questions, a demonstration of faith is also expressed in both psalms, as noted above. Psalm 79.13 quotes the repentant nation promising to praise God

forever, using vocabulary identical to that found at the beginning and
end of Psalm 89 (vv. 2, 53):

79.13 – נודה לך לעולם לדר ודר

89.2 – עולם אשירה לדר ודר

89.53 – ברוך לעולם

Although these psalms ask serious questions of Yahweh, they do not
abandon hope, and in fact promise eternal adoration.

The condition of God's servants (עבדיך) is similar between Psalms
79 and 89. They are food for the fowl of the air in 79.2, and subject to
reproach (חרפה) in both 79.4 and 89.51. The survivors among those
servants appeal three times to the reputation of God's name (שמך, 79. 6,
9 twice). Concern for that name began in Psalms 74 and 79 continues
the appeal. Its restoration to honor is assured first in 86.9, and then in
89.13, 17 (שמך), in the midst of a hymn to Yahweh (89.6-19). In 89.25
the anointed king's horn will be raised by means of the divine name
(בשמי) when David's covenant is fulfilled. Therefore, Psalm 89 serves
as an answer to concern over the divine name expressed in Psalms 74
and 79, confirming its restoration to prominence.

The interrogative seen so often in Book III, and pointed out in Ps.
79.5, appears again in 80.5 (עד־מתי) in a form similar to that of 89.47
(עד־מה). Likewise, the image of hot anger (עשנת) in 80.5 resembles
89.47 (אש חמתך). This question of 80.5 is directed to God using a
lengthy epithet (יהוה אלהים צבאות, cf. v. 20 also), practically identical
to that of 89.9 (יהוה אלהי צבאות). However, 89.9 is part of a paean to
Yahweh, not a complaint, as 80.5, 20. Psalm 80 appeals to past works
of Yahweh in settling Israel on the land, followed by defeat, as a basis
for action in the present. On the other hand, 89 appeals to past promises
to the king, and the subsequent defeat, as a basis for action in the
present.

Striking formal similarities also exist between the lamented defeat of
Israel in 80 and of the anointed one in 89. Just as Israel's walls were
broken down, resulting in despoliation by passers-by (80.13), so the
protection around the anointed king was penetrated, with the same
results (89.41-42):

80.13 – פרצת גדריה וארוה כל־עברי דרך

89.41-42 – פרצת כל־גדרתיו...שסהו כל־עברי דרך

As was shown in the comparison between 79.3-5 and 89.42, 49, the
opprobrium suffered by the nation is felt by the individual speaker of

Book III as well. In spite of their common predicaments, the nation admits its sin and rebellion (79.8-9, of which it was directly accused in 78.17, 32), in contrast to the innocent individual (72.2, 7; 73.13, 26, 28; 75.11; 84.11; 86.2).

When God first planted Israel in the land, their shoots spread from the sea to the river (נהר...ים, 80.12), and likewise the Davidic covenant promised an equally extensive dominion for the king (בים...ובנהרות, 89.26). For the final compiler of the Psalter there was the expectancy of an eternal and unambiguously universal kingdom under a Davidic descendant. Proof of this can be seen by comparing the descriptions of this 'son' between Psalms 89 and 80. The speaker in 80.16, 18 prays for his establishment in terms ('your hand upon the son/anointed one which you strengthened for yourself') closely parallel to the Davidic covenant in 89.22-23:

אֲשֶׁר...יְמִינֶךָ וְעַל־בֵּן אִמַּצְתָּה לָּךְ – 80.16
יָדְךָ...עַל־בֶּן־אָדָם אִמַּצְתָּ לָּךְ – 80.18
מְשַׁחְתִּיו אֲשֶׁר יָדִי...תְּאַמְּצֶנּוּ...וּבֵן – 89.22-23

An oft-repeated plea in Psalm 80 was for God's face (הָאֵר פָּנִים) to shine upon his people so that they would be delivered (80.4, 8, 20). Such a request is apparently based on the knowledge shown in 89.16 that a nation walking in his light (בְּאוֹר פָּנֶיךָ) would be blessed. This was much preferable to the present destruction by fire (בָאֵשׁ) of 80.17 and continuing in 89.47 (אֵשׁ).

The opening of Psalm 81 quotes a community (first person plural) confession of God being their strength (עוּזֵנוּ, v. 2), which parallels the same thought in 89.18 (עֻזָּמוֹ) in the third person. Each of these references is found in similar contexts of rejoicing before God, and are the emotions of a people that walks (יְהַלֵּכוּן, 89.16) in the divine light. Nevertheless, the joyous note becomes negative in Psalm 81 when Yahweh accuses Israel of walking (יֵלְכוּ, 81.13) in their own counsels and ways (יְהַלְּכוּ, 81.14). If obedience had been forthcoming, Israel's enemies and foes (אוֹיְבֵיהֶם...צָרֵיהֶם, 81.15) would have been quickly defeated. As it stands presently, these enemies of God (אוֹיְבֶיךָ, 89.52) and of his anointed (צָרָיו...אוֹיְבָיו, 89.43) have the upper hand and reason to rejoice. One reason for the lamentable situation of the Davidic house can be found in the unheeded warning of 89.31 to not stray from walking (יֵלֵכוּן) in God's counsels. If obedience had been forthcoming, the enemy (אוֹיֵב, 89.23) would not have arisen, and enemies of the Davidic son (אֹיְבָיו, 72.9) would lick the dust before him.

The negative assessment of Israel, and especially of its rulers, continues in Psalm 82. They do not measure up to the divine ruler, including
the expected Davidide of 72 and 89. Judges in Israel are being judged
by God (יֹשֵׁפֹט, 82.1), asked why they do not judge justly (תִּשְׁפְּטוּ, v. 2),
and then commanded to do so (שְׁפְטוּ...הַצְדִּיקוּ, v. 3). The speaker finally
asks God to arise and judge (שָׁפְטָה, v. 8). Injustice and unrighteousness,
which characterize these magistrates, contrast with Yahweh's rule of
justice and righteousness (צֶדֶק וּמִשְׁפָּט, 89.15) and that of the ideal
Davidide in 72.1, 2, 4. Since the Davidic descendants had not followed
the warning about walking in Yahweh's judgments (מִשְׁפָּטַי, 89.31), their
crown was in the dust. In a similar description, the rulers of Psalm 82
(called 'princes' in 82.7, שָׂרִים) will die for not administering justice
(82.1, 2, 3).

Consequently, the lamented situation of 89.39-52 can be explained
by the previously described corruption of 82. In fact, 89.49 asks who
would be the man not conquered by death (מָוֶת), a direct question to the
verdict of death in 82.7 (תְּמוּתוּן).[11] In addition, God had declared in
89.23 that corrupt individuals (וּבֶן־עַוְלָה) would not oppress the ideal
future Davidic king. In an ironic reversal, the rulers of Israel dispense
injustice (עָוֶל, 82.2) to others.

Unlike most of the rhetorical questions throughout Book III, that of
82.2 (עַד־מָתַי) is directed from God back to Israel's rulers, asking how
long wickedness will prevail. This question responds directly to the
question of the previous 80.5 (עַד־מָתַי), directed towards God from the
chosen nation. Repeated questions to God are answered in return by
another question using the same form. As noted previously, the questioning continues in 89.47 (עַד־מָה). This wickedness of Israel in 82 is
described as ignorance and darkness, in direct contrast to the knowledge and light in which that obedient joyful nation of 89 walks:

82.5 – לֹא יָדְעוּ...בַּחֲשֵׁכָה יִתְהַלָּכוּ
89.16 – יוֹדְעֵי...בְּאוֹר־פָּנֶיךָ יְהַלֵּכוּן

In Psalm 82, the condemned rulers are called 'gods' and 'sons of the
Highest One' (אֱלֹהִים...בְּנֵי עֶלְיוֹן, 82.6). Because of their corruption they
were condemned to die (in the following v. 7) like normal men (כְּאָדָם
תְּמוּתוּן). In Ps. 89.7 we read of the 'sons of God' (מִי...בִּבְנֵי אֵלִים) within
an interrogative asking who is like Yahweh. The latter question resembles that regarding the 'sons of men' in vv. 48-49 (מִי בְנֵי־אָדָם), asking

---

11. Also a direct question to Pss. 89.37 and 88.4-6.

whether there may be a man who will not see death (מות). In other words, the question regarding the sons of God in 89.7 hints at the ability to overcome death, which 89.49 states explicitly. The latter interrogative arises from the promise of v. 37a of an eternal seed (זרעו לעולם יהיה) for David. Supporting this interpretation is the use of the term 'wonder' (פלאך) in 89.6, resuming the questions of 88.11-13 (הלמתים פלא...) from death's realm.

The conclusion of Psalm 82 contains further parallels to 89. Yahweh is said to inherit all the nations (כי־אתה תנחל בכל־הגוים) in 82.8b, utilizing the second person masculine singular pronoun regularily found in hymnic contexts. If God is the owner of all the nations, he is authorized to establish a chosen son (89.27) as the highest over all the kings of the earth (עליון למלכי ארץ, 89.28b). As discussed previously, 82.8 and 83.19 are closely parallel in their promise of universal rule for Yahweh. Therefore, it is not surprising to find parallels between 83.19 and 89.28:

83.19b – לבדך עליון על־כל־הארץ
89.28 – עליון למלכי־ארץ

As noted above repeatedly, the coincidence between God's dominion and that of his anointed Davidic son is quite explicit.

For God to establish universal rule he must respond and defeat the enemies (אויבך) of 83.3a that roar against him. His ability to defeat them is recognized in 89.11 (אויבך), and the same is promised for his Davidic servant in 89.23 (אויב). However, the disgraceful situation of 83.3 continues, as shown by 89.43 (אויביו) and 89.52 (אויבך). Hope is still kept alive by the fact that for those 'haters' of God (משנאיך) of 83.3b, 89.24 (משנאיו) promises destruction. The latter group of 89.24 are actually identified as haters of the anointed Davidide. Because the latter is so closely identified with Yahweh, hatred of one is tantamount to hatred of the other.

Psalm 83 is an extended request for response to enemy threats, among which is the desire that they be consumed by fire (כאש תבער, v. 15). Israel is acquainted with this element, since in the present distress the speaker of 89.47 complains of being its target (תבער כמו־אש). In sum, Psalm 89 promises eventual relief through the promise to David from the disgrace described in 83. Nonetheless, the final verses of 89 demonstrate that that deliverance has not been fully realized yet.

Psalms 89 and 84 both portray a blessed and rejoicing community that walks in the paths of Yahweh and requests favor upon the anointed

one. The individual in 84.3 rejoices in God (ירננו), as the creation does
in 89.14 (ירננו). He recognizes Yahweh as his king (יהוה...מלכי) in 84.4,
just as the community in 89.19 speaks of its monarch (ליהוה...מלכנו).
That community of 89 is called blessed (אשרי, v. 16), as it praises and
finds its strength (עזמו, v. 18) in God. Likewise, those of 84 are blessed
threefold (אשרי, vv. 5, 6, 13) as they praise Yahweh (v. 5), and in him
find their strength (עוז־לו, v. 6). The blessed individuals of 84.8 are
among those who walk (ילכו) in strength and appear before God, just as
those of 89.16 walk (יהלכון) in the light of his presence. The same
group is described in 84.12 by the phrase, 'to those who walk in
integrity' (להלכים בתמים).

Both psalms make reference to the nation's shield (מגננו, 84.10a;
89.19a), one being identified through parallelism to 'our king' (89.19b),
and the other to 'your anointed one' (84.10b). Actually three references
in 89.18b-19, 'our horn', 'our shield' and 'our king', can be identified
as the same individual. 'Our king' found at the end of 89.19b introduces
a recitation of the Davidic covenant in the ensuing verses, and so is a
designation of the expected anointed one. 'Our shield' is in the parallel
colon 89.19a, which in Ps. 84.10 is parallel to 'your anointed one'
(משיחך). The latter is named again in 89 (v. 21, משחתיו; also in vv. 9, 52,
משיחך), all following the reference to 'our king' of v. 19. Later in Psalm
84, the 'shield' of v. 12 is identified clearly as Yahweh (ומגן יהוה), and
thereby demonstrates another example of coincidence between the deity
and anointed regent. The lack of strict delineation between divine and
Davidic roles is a message resulting from the composition of both
individual psalms and Book III. At the same time, the anointed one of
89.39 and 52 (משיחך, at both ends of the final strophe of 89) finds
himself persecuted and rejected, a situation that explains his prayer of
84.10.

The twofold interrogatives of 85.6, 7 ask essentially the same question as that of 89.47, that is, how long will God be angry? For 85.6, the
temporal adverbs are 'forever' (לעולם) and 'generation to generation'
(לדר ודר). On a purely formal level, the first question of 85 corresponds to non-interrogative statements of confidence in 89.2, 5:

$$
\begin{array}{ll}
\text{85.6} & - & \text{הלעולם...לדר ודר} \\
\text{89.2} & - & \text{עולם...לדר ודר} \\
\text{89.5} & - & \text{עד־עולם...לדר־ודור}
\end{array}
$$

If the divine wrath seems endless to the community in 85, the individual of 89 is confident that divine faithfulness to the covenant is eternal.

Nonetheless, pessimism appears again in the final strophe of 89, apparently because the complete fulfillment of the Davidic covenant has not been accomplished.

The request by the community for revelation of Yahweh's covenant faithfulness in 85.8 (חסדך) is repeated in 89.50 by the individual in interrogative form (חסדיך). A divine response in 85.9-14 confirms that kindness, truth and righteousness will be revealed, all characteristics of God's rule within the hymn of 89.6-19:

חסד־ואמת...צדק...צדק...צדק   – 85.11, 12, 14

צדק...חסד ואמת   – 89.15

Taken together, these texts imply that God's throne (כסא, 89.15a) of righteousness, covenant faithfulness and truth will eventually be set up in the land (בארצנו, 85.10). That divine throne (כסא) of 89.15 is the same one established (כון) eternally (עד עולם, לעולם, לעד) for David's descendant, as a comparison of 89.5, 15, 30, 37-38 shows.

The individual in 89.2 singing the covenant faithfulness and fidelity of Yahweh (חסדי...אמונתך) is confident that the promises to David are eternal and that the conditions of Psalm 84 will eventually be ushered in.

The metaphor of righteousness walking before Yahweh in the last verse of 85 is repeated in 89.15:

צדק לפניו יהלך   – 85.14

צדק...יקדמו פניך   – 89.15

This personification of righteousness, along with peace, truth and covenant faithfulness in Psalm 85, is exemplified in the pious David of 86.11.

As the poet listens in 85.9 for the divine answer to his plea, a pattern is used which 89.20 repeats quite closely:

ידבר...אל־עמו ואל־חסידיו   – 85.9

דברת...לחסידיך...מעם   – 89.20

Since both messages of 85.10-14 and 89.20-38 are introduced by the same formula, a correspondence is created between them which is confirmed by further parallels. Psalm 85.10 promised a near salvation (ישעו) to those who fear Yahweh, which is part and parcel of the Davidic covenant (ישועתי, 89.27). The promise of covenant faithfulness and truth in 85.11 (חסד־ואמת) is repeated throughout Psalm 89's comments on the promised Davidic kingdom:

89.15 –	חסד ואמת
89.25 –	ואמונתי וחסדי
89.29 –	חסדי...נאמנת
89.34 –	וחסדי...באמונתי

The kingdoms portrayed by 85.10, 12 and 89.6, 12 both encompassed heaven and earth (אר׳ץ...שׁמים). Similarily, the promise to David was of a dominion over all kings of the earth (אר׳ץ, 89.28), which would endure as the days of heaven (שׁמים, 89.30).

If the conditions of the future kingdom in Psalm 89 match those in 85.10-14, the ruler of that kingdom as described in 86 also matches 89. Psalm 86 is ascribed to 'David' in the superscription (לדוד), and he identifies himself as Yahweh's servant (עבדך) in vv. 2, 4, 16. Yahweh cut a covenant in 89.4 with his servant David:

89.4 –	לדוד עבדי
89.21 –	דוד עבדי
89.36 –	לדוד
89.50 –	לדוד

It can be assumed therefore, that the prayer of 86 is another expression of and plea for the fulfillment of the Davidic covenant, later described in more detail by 89.

David claims to be a pious or faithful one (חסיד) in 86.2, one of the same group in 89.20 (חסידיך) to whom Yahweh spoke regarding the covenant. This David not only claims to be pious, but based on that quality he appeals to the covenant faithfulness (חסדך, 86.5, 13) of Yahweh to deliver him from distress. His appeal to the faithfulness and truth of 86.15 (חסד ואמת) is legitimate, seeing that such characteristics are the foundation of Yahweh's kingdom in 89.15 (חסד ואמת), and what motivate the establishment of the Davidic reign in 89.25, 29, 34 (אמונה, חסד). Even in lament, the individual of 86 recognizes the faithfulness of God upon him in (חסדך...עלי, 86.13) and so praises him for it in 89.2 (חסדי...אמונתך).

In his distress, he calls (אקראך...אקרא) upon Yahweh in 86.3, 7, just as Yahweh in 89.27 said he would (הוא יקראני). David would also call upon Yahweh using the second person singular independent pronoun אתה (89.27), repeated in 86.2, 5, 10, 15, 17. Each instance of this pronoun in 86 is again found in contexts extolling the virtues of Yahweh, corresponding to its use in the hymn of 89.10-19.

The calls (קרא) to 'you' (אתה) of 86.3, 5, 7, and assurance of an answer in 86.7, are followed immediately by details of that promise. All the nations would bow before Adonay as part of the answer to this Davidide's call. In 89.27 we read that the anointed Davidide would call (יקראני) to God, 'you [אתה] are my father', followed by the answer of 89.28. This answer also promises worldwide subservience by all the kings of the earth. The prayers of 'David' in Psalms 86 and 89 and their answers are portrayed as one and the same. The answer supposes a worldwide kingdom under the rule of the righteous Davidide as promised in Psalm 72 and even as far back as Psalm 2.

In three instances in Psalm 86, the name of God (שמך) is either honored or feared (vv. 9, 11, 12) by the nations and the righteous speaker. In Psalm 89 his name is glorified by the mountains (בשמך, v. 13), his people (בשמך, v. 17) and his king (ובשמי, v. 25). Indeed, that name is recognized universally. These examples all represent answers to the laments of 74.7, 10, 18, 21; 79.6, 9 and 80.19 over God's name. The words of 86.9, promising the nations would honor the divine name (ויכבדו לשמך), represent a direct answer to concern in 79.9 (כבוד שמך). Both psalms (79.1, 6, 10; 86.9) mention the nations (גוים) in general, while in 87.4 specific names are given confirming worldwide worship of Yahweh. Through the Davidic covenant all nations and creation itself will recognize his name.

Psalm 86.8 describes the incomparability of God (אין־כמוך) at the outset of the second strophe, which consists of answers to the prayer of vv. 1-7 (cf. כי תענני in v. 7).[12] Likewise, 89.9 asks, 'Who is like you?' (מי־כמוך), in the context of answers to the previous prayer of Psalm 88. Both prayers of 86 and 88 are quite similar, and so the answers of 86.8 and 89.9 do not only magnify God in a corresponding manner, but also correspond in their placement.

If the David of 86 promises to honor Yahweh's name forever (לעולם, 86.12), so the speaker declares intent to sing forever in 89.2 (עולם) to Yahweh, and to bless him in 89.53 (לעולם). When 89.11 extols the strength (עזך) of Yahweh, it follows the appeal to that same strength (עזך) in 86.16 and supposes the speaker had received a portion of it.

After the appeal for strength in 86.16, the poet expresses confidence in v. 17 that Yahweh would help him (עזרתני) in v. 17, which corresponds to 89.20c promising help (עזר) to his servant David.[13] Since 89.20 is the opening comment on the Davidic covenant, 86.17 is con-

---

12. In fact, strophe II answers the prayers of the previous strophe I (vv. 1-7), and the following strophe III (vv. 14-17), as discussed previously.

13. Does this explain the use of עזר here in 89.20c, which *BHS* emends to נזר?

fident of help based on a previous promise. Help is sought for his life
(נפשי, 86.2, 4, 13, 14), because of the enemies' intent to destroy him.
His prayer was answered in 86.13, a close parallel to 89.49. The same
death experience is being described by 86 and 89, and as already shown
in 88 as well:

והצלת נפשי משאול – 86.13
ימלט נפשו מיד־שאול – 89.49

Psalm 86 speaks of a rescue out of lower Sheol, while 89.49 in an
interrogative bicolon wonders who could escape from its clutches. The
previous Psalm 88 in its entirety details the death experience of this
individual, and abundant ties between 86 and 88 imply the same subject
of both. Furthermore, 89.1-6 demonstrates that the individual will be
rescued from death. Why then, is there a question in 89.49 about the
possibility of defying death? First of all, it must be stated that the interrogative of 89.49 is directly commenting on 88.4-6. The latter is spoken
as a complaint from the depths of Sheol, and the former wonders who
can ever escape from its power:

נפשי וחיי לשאול...כגבר...במתים...לא...מידך – 88.4-6
מי גבר יחיה ולא יראה מות ימלט נפשו מיד שאול – 89.49

In spite of the fact that 89.1-6 affirms quite explicitly (as will be seen
below) the deliverance from death of 88's speaker, he has not yet
appeared to the house of David. In fact, 89.49 wonders who can live
forever, a direct question to the promise of 89.37 predicting a Davidide
seated eternally on his throne:

זרעו לעולם יהיה וכסאו כשמש נגדי – 89.37
מי גבר יחיה ולא יראה מות – 89.49

If the Davidic descendant and his throne will continue forever (89.37),
who is the man who will continue living and not experience death
(89.49)? In other words, who is the one described in Psalm 88 who
enters death, but survives and sings of his deliverance in Ps. 89.1-6?
Although his voice is heard throughout these psalms, his identity is
apparently unknown. The psalms of Book III ascribed to Asaph, the
sons of Qorah, David, Heman and Ethan have all voiced the words of
this promised but unknown mediator and anointed one out of the house
of David. In fact, it is deliberately made difficult to distinguish his royal
function from that of king Yahweh himself.

Further evidence of the conflict between promise and fulfillment
within Psalm 89 itself is found by comparing vv. 4 and 50. Praise for

the covenant faithfulness is expressed in 89.2-3, and a statement of the covenant sworn to David is given in v. 4. Such confidence changes to lament in 89.50, which asks the whereabouts of that faithfulness sworn to David. The Davidic crown is in the dust (v. 40), and that situation seems to continue interminably (v. 47). In fact, the entire center strophe (vv. 20-38) is a repetition of the Davidic covenant itself, so that the beginning, middle and end are all intensely concerned with this pact and its fulfillment.

Especially important for the repeated questions of Book III is, of course, the time of his appearance. They begin in Psalm 74 asking, 'why?' and 'how long?' to which must now be added, 'who?' (89.49). Who is this son of David who will be delivered out of death, who will usher in the eschatological kingdom, and how long before he is brought to his throne? Just as Psalm 72's delayed promises of a kingdom are lamented throughout Book III, so is the non-appearance of its king. For example, in Ps. 80.16, 18 the community prays for the appearance of this monarch (according to the promise of 89.22). To complicate matters further, the voice of this promised righteous Davidide is heard throughout the dialogue of Book III speaking on behalf of Yahweh, the people and himself. That dialogue is prophetic and so the voice is indeed heard, but the speaker has not made an appearance.

The foregoing abundance of correspondences between 86 and 89 is not matched with 87, for the simple fact that the latter is a short Zion song and this city is never mentioned specifically by 89. Psalm 78 concluded with references both to a covenant with the Davidic servant king and the choice of Zion (vv. 68-72). Psalm 89 concentrates on the covenant, Zion having been discussed in the preceding 87. One would then expect continuity between a psalm of the royal city (87) and its king (89), and so there is.

The eschatological Zion of 87 includes numerous foreign inhabitants, consistent with the universal kingdom of 89.26, 28. The builder of that Zion is the 'highest one', עליון (87.5). In 89.28 the eschatological Davidic king is designated the 'highest one' (עליון) of the kings of the earth, and it goes without saying that Zion of 87 is the center of his kingdom. Reference to the 'Highest One' in 87.5 specifies Yahweh as builder of the city, and in 89.28 it is the Davidic scion receiving this epithet. Again there is no attempt to sharply distinguish between roles of the two, and undoubtedly the king takes part in the enrollment of Zion's citizens as described in 87.4-6. As noted previously, the voice of

Yahweh in 87 is heard again through the lamenting Davidide of 88.

Those who know Yahweh of 87.4 (לידעי) take part in the singing (שרים) and dancing of v. 7, undoubtedly the same group found again in 89.16 who know (יודעי) the sounds of rejoicing, and including the individual singer of 89.2 (אשירה). Their depiction as the generalized blessed nation (אשרי העם) in 89.16 makes room for Gentiles (such as those of 87.4) within the rejoicing community. Apparently, the citizens of Zion in 87 and the joyful throng in 89.6-19 are one and the same.

The city of Zion is located in the 'hills of holiness' according to 87.1. Such a description suggests a connection with the 'company of holy ones' in 89.6:

$$\text{בהררי־קדש} - 87.1$$
$$\text{בקהל קדשים} - 89.6$$

Given the heavenly (שמים...שחק) context of 89.6, 7, undoubtedly the citizens of the heavenly eschatological Zion in Psalm 87 (cf. Pss. 46.5-6; 48.2-3; Isa. 14.13) are being identified now as 'holy ones'. Further support for this identification comes from the fact that the holy ones are characterized as constituting a council in 89.8, a designation that also resonates phonetically with 87.1:

$$\text{יסודתו בהררי־קדש} - 87.1$$
$$\text{בסוד־קדשים} - 89.8$$

The common consonantal sequence illustrated, here of samekh, long vowel, daleth along with the adjective קדש ('holy'), suggests a link. The use of יסודתו ('his foundation') in 87.1 implies what 87.5 states explicitly, that Yahweh is the builder of this city Zion. By use of the same root in the verb יסדתם ('he established them') of 89.12, he is praised for the founding of heaven, earth and their fulness. The builder of Zion, and the heavens wherein this city is found, is one and the same creator.

A third designation of this congregation in Psalm 89 is 'mighty ones' (בני אלים). Although this is a difficult phrase to understand, the parallel nouns throughout vv. 6-8 referring to the same group provide an interpretive context. They include, 'heavens...congregation of holy ones' (v. 6), 'heavens...mighty ones' (v. 7), 'council of holy ones...those surrounding him' (v. 8). This company of beings surrounds God in the heavens but, because of his incomparability 'praise you' for the 'wondrous work' (ויודו...פלאך, v. 6). That praise is explained by Psalm 88, where it is asked in v. 11 regarding the dead whether Yahweh will perform a 'wondrous work' so that they 'will arise and praise you' (פלא...יקומו יודוך). Psalm 89.6 is a clear affirmative answer to this question, and identifies these formerly dead ones as part of a heavenly congregation surrounding Yahweh. Consequently, a canonical reading of Psalms 87–89 clarifies the picture of this company of people. The multi-national inhabitants of heavenly Zion in 87 are praising Yahweh for his incomparability in 89 (note that in 87.3, 7 they are also speaking/singing glorious things in Zion; cf. also 86.9, 10), after a death experience in 88. The question in 88.11 of whether they will arise (יקומו) is answered in the affirmative by 89.17b (ירומו). Furthermore, the blessed nation of 89.16-17 can be identified with this heavenly group of many nations, resurrected through the righteousness of Yahweh (בצדקתך, 89.17b). Psalm 88.13 had asked whether God's righteousness (צדקתך) could be known in the realm of the dead, and 89.17 (צדקתך) provides an affirmative answer.

The identification of Yahweh as 'my salvation' at the outset of Psalm 88 (ישועתי, v. 2), demonstrates that the same Davidic servant of 89.27 (ישועתי) continues speaking. That speaker's life has reached Sheol itself in 88.4, a verse which resonates closely with the interrogative of 89.49 asking if one can live and escape from the power of Sheol:

88.4 – נפשי וחיי לשאול
89.49 – יחיה...נפשו מיד־שאול

The reader already knows from 86.13 of a rescue from death's realm (נפשי משאול) for a Davidic scion. Psalm 88 details that death more vividly and 89.49 seeks to know the identity (and time in 89.47) of that Davidide's appearance. The following v. 50 continues in the interrogative mood, asking when the Davidic covenant will be kept, assuming eternal life for the descendant who will sit on the eternal throne (cf. vv. 30, 37-38). If the promise to David was of an everlasting throne and seed, who is the individual who can live perpetually to fulfil such a covenant? As discussed above, his descent into death is described in 88.5b as becoming like a man (כגבר) without help. In a direct reference, 89.49 asks who such a man (מי גבר) could be. While the speaker of 88 has entered the realm of the dead (מתים, 88.6a, 11), 89.49a seeks to know the identity of such a one over whom death (מות) has no dominion.

In 88.6 the speaker likens himself to the slain (כמו־חללים), a fate reserved for the enemy in 89.11 (כחלל). Ironically, the faithful individual of 88 has suffered the same fate as God's enemies, and rightly protests. Verse 6 goes on to complain that the dead are forgotten by God (לא זכרתם), which explains the request in 89.48, 51 for Yahweh to remember (זכר). It also presents a contrast with the preceding 87.4, where Zion's inhabitants are kept in remembrance (אזכיר).

The complaint in 88.6 continues, describing the dead as those cut off from God's hand (מידך). The Davidide justly laments this situation, since God's promise was support with his hand (יד, 89.22) as part of the covenant expressed in 89. Numerous other direct answers to the deadly predicament of Psalm 88 occur, especially in the following 89.1-19, and so the praise there of God's powerful hand (עזך...תעז ידך, 89.11, 14) promises eventual deliverance.

In spite of deliverance from death in the first third of Psalm 89, it is apparently only prophesied, and not actually fulfilled. Similarly, the promises of 72 were not yet seen, being a prophecy of an eternal king upon the throne (72.5, 7, 17). Within Psalm 89 itself the rehearsal of the Davidic covenant promised a seed upon the throne that would go on forever, even as the sun and moon (89.37-38). (That promise repeats the same given in 72.5.) An eternal king was expected and his permanent escape from death is predicted (Psalms 86–89), but apparently he had not yet appeared as promised conquering king. His complaints demonstrate that he endures the same affliction as the nation. For this reason, lament over the continued desolation and persecution of the Davidide continues in the final third of 89. Divine wrath (חמתך) upon him in 88.8 is lamented in the sad question of 89.47 (חמתך). Promises to David included eventual freedom from affliction (לא יעננו, 89.23), but in 88.8, 10, 16 a threefold complaint of affliction (עני, עניח) is found. His predicament causes him to call to Yahweh (קראתיך) in 88.10, just as Yahweh predicted he would in 89.27 (הוא יקראני).

Beginning in 88.11 through 12 is a series of desperate questions that appear to be rhetorical only. Surprisingly, the immediately succeeding Psalm 89 provides direct and positive answers.[14] In 88.11 the speaker asks if God will do a 'wondrous deed' for the dead, meaning that they will arise and 'thank' him. An answer comes shortly thereafter in the following psalm where:

---

14. M.D. Goulder, *The Psalms of the Sons of Korah* (JSOTSup, 20; Sheffield: JSOT Press, 1982), p. 220, likewise observes a connection between 88 and 89. Tate, *Psalms 51–100*, p. 418, suggests that, 'the placement of Ps. 89 in the canonical form of the Psalter is worth consideration...[and] needs additional study and reflection (for example, how are Pss 88 and 89 related?).'

פלא...יודוך – 88.11
ויודו...פלאך – 89.6

'The dead' (המתים) and 'shades' (רפאים) of 88.11, who presumably could not laud his works, rise to the heavens (שמים) and join the holy ones (קדשים) of 89.6 in thankful praise for his wondrous deed. A company of heavenly dwellers was raised from a former dead state, and consequently able to praise God for wondrous deeds and faithfulness.

The series of questions continue in 88.12, asking whether Yahweh's covenant faithfulness and fidelity (חסדך אמונתך) will be recounted in the grave. That same company in 89.6 praises his faithfulness (אמונתך) and the individual speaker in 89.2 sings the praises of Yahweh for faithfulness and fidelity (חסדי...אמונתך). Apparently the single speaker, along with the company of Psalm 89, is confident of rescue from death to praise the faithfulness of Yahweh. The word pair 'covenant faithfulness–fidelity' (חסד אמונה), found at the very heart of Psalm 88's threefold questions (v. 12), dominates the following 89, being repeated six times (vv. 2, 3, 25, 29, 34, 50), and singly another three times (vv. 6, 9, 15). This does not even include other instances of the same root אמן (vv. 38, 53). Without question Psalm 89 has been intentionally placed, following the desperate and seemingly hopeless queries of 88 with praise and confidence.

Answers to a threefold series of questions in one psalm by the next has already been seen between Psalm 77 (vv. 8-10 are the questions), and the immediately following 78. The two questions of 74.9-10 are answered directly by 75, and the same can be said for the double questions each in 79 and 80 being answered overtly by 81 and 82. Psalms 88 and 89 are following an established pattern in Book III.

The final question of 88.13 asks if Yahweh's wondrous deed will be known in the darkness of death (הידוע...פלאך). Psalm 89.2 provides the response, in that the speaker will make known (אודיע) God's fidelity (אמונתך). 'Fidelity' is part and parcel of his wondrous deeds (פלאך), as shown by the parallel use of both terms from 88.11-13 and in 89.6.

The final question regarding the dead (88.13) asks concerning 'your righteousness' (צדקתך). Again the answer is 'yes', based on 89.17, where through Yahweh's righteousness a people arises (ובצדקתך ירומו), answering not only the צדקתך of 88.13, but also the יקומו ('will they arise...?') of 88.11. By comparing 88.11, 13 and 89.17, the conclusion is drawn that through Yahweh's righteousness a knowledgeable and rejoicing people will be raised from the dead. Resurrection is also promised to 'our horn' (תרים קרננו) in the immediately following 89.18, a reference to the king and shield mentioned in the following v. 19 (מגננו...מלכנו). A series of the verb רום ('to rise'), beginning in v. 14 where the subject is Yahweh's powerful hand, to v. 17 where it is the nation, and to vv. 18-19 where it is the king, indicates resurrection for the king and his people together. Thus, the surprising answer to each rhetorical question of 88.11-13 is an emphatic 'yes!' Not coincidentally, most answers to the interrogatives of 88 are found immediately in the first 19 verses of 89.

The poet in 88.14 declared that his prayer would come before Yahweh (תקדמך), while lamenting the hidden face (פניך, 88.15). Such a prayer is assured an answer due to the fact that covenant faithfulness marches before Yahweh (יקדמו לפניך) in 89.15. Use of the singular independent pronoun אני in 88.14 and 16 (as in 86.1, 2), apparently designates the same afflicted individual of 89.48 (אני) who has also been heard since 73.2, 22, 23, 28 (אני).

Between the two occurrences of the pronoun in 88.14 and 16 is the interrogative lamenting his rejection (תזנח, v. 15) by Yahweh. Rejection (זנחת) is likewise seen in 89.39 of Yahweh's anointed (משיחך), again proving that the anointed Davidide speaks in Psalm 88. Just as 89.39 opened the first verse paragraph of the final strophe of Psalm 89 (vv. 39-53) by using a verbal root from 88.15 (זנח), so the second paragraph begins in 89.47 with another root (סתר) from the same bicolon of 88.15. The speaker of 88.15 wants to know why Yahweh hides (תסתיר) his face, and in 89.47 the question is how long this hiding (תסתר) will continue.

It is quite remarkable that the root סתר and the final suffixed noun חמתך ('your anger') of 89.47 are the only two elements of this interrogative that do not match the interrogative of 79.5, as illustrated above.[15] The reason can only be that they provide direct links to the divine anger (חמתך) of the immediately previous 88.8 and hiddenness (תסתיר) of 88.15. Here is quite explicit evidence of the final compiler's hand shaping successive psalms into a cohesive chain, while at the same time maintaining unity across Book III.

Rejection of the anointed's soul (נפש) is repeated from 86.2, 4, 13, 14, to 88.4, 15 and finally 89.49, all within contexts of affliction. His affliction has been the subject of pleading since 84.10 at the outset of

15. Page 81 n. 5.

the Qorahite group (משיחך), and even back further to 73 and 77. The references to himself in 88.4 and 89.49 are transparently parallel:

88.4 – נפשי וחיי
89.49 – יחיה...נפשו

Further parallels to the suffering of this individual between both psalms are not necessarily formal, but unmistakable nonetheless. His affliction in 88.16 was causing him to decline in the midst of his youth (גוע מנער), while the complaint in 89.46 is because the days of his youth are cut short (הקצרת ימי עלומיו). Divine wrath is again portrayed by 88.17 using the same root form as that of 89.39 (עבר), even if not semantically equivalent. In both instances, the same individual suffers:

88.17 – עלי עברו חרוניך
89.39 – התעברת עם־משיחך

Thus, the sufferings and even death of this royal individual continue from 86 through 89, with interspersed promises of deliverance in 86.13; 87 (a restored Zion) and 89.1-19. These latter prophecies apparently remain unfulfilled, and so 89.39-53 resumes the now common laments and questions heard throughout Book III.

While Psalm 89 as a whole truly encapsulates and summarizes much of the message of Book III, its final strophe (vv. 39-53) of lament reveals a remarkable concentration of vocabulary taken directly from previous psalms. The only difference is that former expressions of community lament are now used to decry the condition of the individual anointed Davidide of 89.

As has been shown above, 89.39 expresses divine rejection of the individual by a verb pair (מאס, התעבר) identical to that of 78.59 in reference to Israel. Then the two initial cola of 89.41 and 42 continue the lament about broken walls and passers-by who plunder, borrowing vocabulary identical to that of 80.13. The second colon of 89.42 then repeats what is found in the first colon of 79.4 regarding the reproach by neighbors. Each example in the previous psalms describes the nation, while in 89 they are all of the individual. The question of 89.47 wondering how long Yahweh's wrath would endure against this anointed one is practically word for word from 79.5, the latter being uttered by the nation. The consecutive 79.4a and 79.5 match closely 89.42b and 47. Psalm 79.12 continues lamenting the national reproach (mentioned already in 79.4), and 89.51-52 uses the same vocabulary and syntax (relative אשר clauses) to recall the same reproach against the

anointed one and his fellow servants. Even the rarer divine epithet
Adonay in 89.51 may be a reflexion of its use in 79.12. However, as
will be discussed later, this divine name also creates cohesiveness with
the following Psalm 90.

It appears then that the final strophe of Psalm 89 deliberately
reiterates lament expressions from 78–80, but chiefly from 79. Both
Psalms 79 and 80 are national laments, while the borrowing from 78
also involved the nation. As a result, the anointed Davidide, promised
so much in the first three strophes of 89, suffers the same indignities
experienced by the nation at large. Their suffering is expressed as his
own. At the same time it should be recalled that this same faithful individual mediated the divine answers back to the nation throughout Book
III (Psalms 75, 78, 85).

In the following Psalm 90 the community returns to the lament,
complaining of the shortness of life (90.9-10) due to its sins (90.8). The
mood is different for the faithful individual of Psalm 91, who experi-
ences exaltation, glorification, long life and the salvation of God
(90.14-16). As will be shown later, comparisons between the salvation
promised in 91.14-16 and the promises given to the Davidic descendant
in 89.22, 25, 27, 30, 34 confirm that the same righteous individual is
portrayed.

Various examples of inclusio create a frame around the bulk of 89.
Eternal praise opens and ends the psalm using parallel vocabulary:

> v. 2 –   יהוה עולם...אמונתך
> v. 53 –   יהוה לעולם אמן ואמן

Furthermore, the proper name Ethan, and its inseparable preposition
(לאיתן) within the superscription (which in the context of Book III
could be read 'perpetually'), also corresponds to the identical preposition plus semantically-parallel phrase 'forever' (לעולם) of the doxology.
The concept of eternality at both ends reflects the concern throughout
for the eternal (עולם) promise made to David (vv. 3, 5, 29, 37, 38).[16]

---

16. Most studies of individual psalms overlook the role of superscriptions and
doxologies. However, in his commentary, Hakham, *Sefer tehillim*, p. 158 (קנח),
observes correctly that the final doxology of v. 53 was designed intentionally in
contrast to the reproach (חרפו) of v. 52, and also corresponds to the opening v. 2.
This is achieved by the initial 'blessed' of the doxology contrasting with the preceding reproach of v. 52, while the final four members (יהוה לעולם אמן ואמן) parallel
v. 2 at the beginning (יהוה עולם...אמונתך).

Support for these parallels between title and doxology comes from Psalm 72, where inclusio was already observed between the 'son' of the doxology (בֶּן־יִשָׁי, v. 20) and the opening (לְבֶן־מֶלֶךְ, v. 1). The son of the king of v. 1 clearly corresponds to the name Solomon (שְׁלֹמֹה) given in the superscription, descendant of the father and son named in v. 20. Consequently, between vv. 1 and 20 is formed a short genealogy of Jesse, David and Solomon. Last but not least, the name שְׁלֹמֹה also alludes to the theme and atmosphere of peace (שָׁלוֹם) which is repeated across 72 (vv. 3, 7). Consequently, both 72 and 89 support what has been maintained throughout this study, that superscriptions (and doxologies) have been written with a careful eye to the content of the psalm and surrounding context.

As just noted, 89.53 corresponds to 89.2 in three of its elements, so that the psalm begins and ends with praise. The praise of v. 2 was a clear confession of faith in response to the affliction unto death and accompanying interrogatives of 88, and now the parallel v. 53 is a clear confession of faith in the face of affliction in strophe IV (vv. 39-52). Consequently, each member of this inclusio performs the same function in relation to the immediately previous text.

The blessing of v. 53 repeats the same term 'verily' (אָמֵן) twice, and this is not simply a prayer formula in the context of strophe IV or 89 as a whole. It is actually a statement of confidence in the final fulfillment of David's covenant, repeating the same root found in 'faithfulness' (אֱמוּנָתְךָ) in v. 50b. As stated above, this root dominates the psalm (vv. 2, 3, 25, 29, 34, 38). Moreover, the prepositional phrase לְעוֹלָם is also not simply a concluding prayer formula, but faith in the eternal validity of that same promise to David. It is used exclusively in describing the Davidic covenant, as vv. 2, 3, 5, 29, 38 demonstrate. Yahweh is to be faithfully blessed forever because his promise to David is faithful and eternal. So ends the lengthy poem which answers initially the questions of the previous 88, but returns to raise them again at the end. There is belief in the promises to David, but impatience with the delay of their fulfillment.

From the beginning of Psalm 89, reference to the Davidic covenant (v. 4, נִשְׁבַּעְתִּי לְדָוִד) matches the same (v. 50, נִשְׁבַּעְתָּ לְדָוִד) near the end. This reflects the major theme of the psalm as shown by references to the same promise in vv. 21, 36, 40. In v. 5 the throne and lineage of David are promised eternal existence, to which the response in v. 47 is,

'How long will Yahweh hide his face' (from the chosen line)? Matching prepositions point to a conceptual contrast:

עד־עולם – v. 5
עד־מה...לנצח – v. 47

Only the interrogative particle מה of v. 47 distinguishes between the
two constructions, since semantically parallel temporal nouns are present. On the surface it appears to be a bitterly ironic question,
wondering if God will wait forever to establish his eternal covenant.
However, if one continues reading in Ps. 90.2, 3, the same particle עד is
repeated in answer to these questions. Mere mortals ask how long (עד)
of a God who is not restricted by time, existing from eternity to eternity
(ומעולם עד עולם אתה אל, 90.2).

Yahweh's incomparability in v. 8 to those around him, and the
reproach suffered by his servant (speaking in v. 52b) from many nations,
reveal again the change in mood from one end of the psalm to the other:

רבה ונורא על־כל־סביביו – v. 8b
שׂאתי בחיקי כל־רבים עמים – v. 51b

If Yahweh exerts awesome divine power and his kingdom is over the
nations of the world (89.6-19), how is it that his own promised Davidic
regent is suffering rejection (89.39-52)? Contrast is evident again
between confident beginning and morose end of Psalm 89.

Complaints about the affliction suffered at the hands of many nations
recalls the international rebellion in Ps. 2.1-2 against the Lord and his
anointed. The following Ps. 3.2 continues along the same theme,
describing how enemies have multiplied (רבו...רבים), and in 3.7 they
are called multitudes of a nation (מרבבות עם). The similarities with the
description and context of 89.51 (רבים עמים) are quite clear. Psalm
89.51 laments the nonfulfillment of the Davidic covenant that promised
subjugation of the nations (89.23-28). Psalm 3 laments nonfulfillment
of the Davidic covenant as expressed in Psalm 2, which promised subjugation of the nations. His life (לנפשׁ) is in danger from these enemies,
according to Ps. 3.3, and the same is true in 89.49 (נפשׁו). The pattern of
promise and lament over its nonfulfillment is found between adjacent
Psalms 2 and 3 and within the single Psalm 89.

Further contrasts are evident between the two ends of Psalm 89.
Yahweh rules over waves 'when they rise up' (בשׂוא גליו, v. 10), but his
chosen one 'bears up in the chest' (שׂאתי בחיקי, v. 51) reproach from
many nations. His (Yahweh's) enemies (אויביך) are scattered in v. 11,

as it should be, but in v. 52 those enemies are reproaching him (אויביך).
Yahweh's enemies are also enemies of the Davidic servant (אויביו,
v. 43b), and they have gained the upper hand (ימין, v. 43a). This also
contradicts the explicit promise of v. 23 that no enemy (אויב) would rise
up against the anointed one, and that his right hand (ימין, v. 26) would
rule the world. As already mentioned, the oath to David recalled in v. 4
(נשבעתי לדוד) has not materialized by v. 50 (נשבעת לדוד).

Five strophes can be traced across Psalm 89, following the divisions
of *BHS*. Strophe I, the shortest, includes vv. 2-5, and strophe II the following vv. 6-19. The first praises Yahweh's eternal covenant with
David and the second the unparalleled divine power available to bring it
about. The Davidic covenant is recited in detail by the lengthy strophe
III from vv. 20-38. Complaints about its delayed fulfillment dominate
strophes IV (vv. 39-46) and V (vv. 47-53).

The opening verses reveal the pattern of praise (v. 2) followed by
reasons for it (כי, v. 3), and so also strophe II begins with praise (v. 6)
and reasons for it (כי, v. 7). Similarily, strophe II ends with praise (v.
17) and twice reasons for it (כי, vv. 18, 19). Strophe I (vv. 2 to 5) is
bound on either end by the same pair of temporal references:

$$\text{v. 2} - \text{עולם...לדר ודר}$$
$$\text{v. 5} - \text{עולם...לדר ודר}$$

A further example of עולם appears in v. 3, confirming the everlasting
nature of this covenant as the dominant theme of vv. 2-5. Further on in
vv. 29, 37-38 the noun עולם is repeated, and again in reference to the
covenant with David. By surrounding the explicit reference to this
covenant in v. 4 with three descriptions of its eternal nature (vv. 2, 3,
5), the speaker leaves no doubt as to the motivation of his words. Praise
is directed to Yahweh for the everlasting validity of the Davidic
covenant.[17] Furthermore, the faithfulness and fidelity introduced in this
opening v. 2 (חסד...אמונתך) are directly related in vv. 25, 34, 50 to the
pact sworn to David.

Since Psalm 89.2 is so similar to the words of the immediately preceding Psalm 88, the implication is that the speaker of 89.2 is the same
individual Davidide. His praise is not general thanksgiving for
Yahweh's faithfulness to any and all, but rather explicitly focuses on

17. Both vv. 4 (Davidic covenant) and 2-3 (faithfulness and fidelity) are brought
together in the one verse of Isa. 55.3 by parallel vocabulary: ואכרתה לכם ברית
עולם חסדי דוד נאמנים (v. 55.3cd).

the pact with David. Psalm 88 is asking for fulfillment of the Davidic covenant, and the following 89 provides an affirmative answer. He is assured rescue from the death of 88 by specific answers to the questions of vv. 12-13:

88.12-13 – חסדך אמונתך...היודע
89.2ab – חסדי...אודיע אמונתך בפי

The added reference to 'my mouth' (פי, 89.2b) is without parallel in the first colon (89.2a). Its presence emphasizes the affirmative answer to 88.11-13, where the speaker asks if God's deeds will be praised, recounted or known in the grave. The death experience of 88 will certainly not succeed in silencing him permanently.

Strophe I introduces the dominant topic of this whole psalm, that is, the eternal covenant made with David and his seed. Faithfulness (חסד), fidelity and truth (אמת, אמונה) are then repeated (vv. 2-3, 6, 9, 15, 25, 29, 34, 50) as the divine characteristics supporting that covenant. Establishment of the Davidic throne in v. 5 (cf. vv. 37-38) matches the established throne of Yahweh in v. 15, implying they are one and the same:

v. 5: Davidic throne – אכין...כסאך
v. 15: divine throne – מכון כסאך
vv. 37b-38a: Davidic throne – וכסאו...יכון

Two characteristics of the divine throne in v. 15 are righteousness (צדק) and justice (משפט). Both were prophesied in 72.1, 2 of the eschatological Davidic throne, and so canonically (within the Psalter) and rhetorically (within 89) there is an identity of Davidic and divine thrones.

The second strophe begins with the praise of 'holy ones' (קדשים) in v. 6, 8 and ends in v. 19 with reference to Yahweh as 'the holy one of Israel' (ולקדש ישראל). Now the congregation of vv. 6-9 partakes of Yahweh's holiness, as does the anointed Davidide of 89.21 (קדשי). Their ascension from the death of 88 through 'your righteousness' (v. 17) explains this attribution of virtue.

Not only do both the anointed king and the great congregation have status as holy ones, they also worship Yahweh for the same reason. Strophe I opens with the praise of the individual Davidide for Yahweh's covenant faithfulness and fidelity (חסד אמונתך, v. 2) and strophe II opens with thanks for the wondrous deed (פלאך). The individual of 89.2 is referring directly to his previous question in 88.12

concerning that faithfulness and fidelity (חסדי יהוה...אמונתך), while the company of 89.6 is responding affirmatively to the questions of 88.11, 13 concerning the wondrous deed (פלאך). In other words, common vocabulary demonstrates that the central question of 88.11 is answered by the individual in strophe I (89.2-5), and the two surrounding questions of 88.11, 13 are answered by the congregation in strophe II (89.6-19). However, the division between 88.11, 13 and 88.12 is not absolute between strophes I and II of 89, because both (89.2-3 and 89.6, 9) answer the question regarding 'faithfulness' (אמונתך) in the central question of 88.12b. Moreover, 89.6 repeats a term from each of the three successive questions in 88.11-13, 'they will give thanks', 'your covenant faithfulness' and 'your wondrous deed':

$$\text{ויודו} \quad - \quad (\text{cf. 88.11b, יודוך})$$
$$\text{אמונתך} \quad - \quad (\text{cf. 88.12b, אמונתך})$$
$$\text{פלאך} \quad - \quad (\text{cf. 88.11a, 13a, פלאך})$$

Nonetheless, strophe II is most resonant with 88.11 and 13, and strophe I with 88.12.

Thanksgiving for the wondrous deed of 89.6 (ויודו...פלאך) corresponds exactly to the single interrogative of 88.11 (פלא...יודוך). Surrounding the major part of strophe II (89.6-17) is reference to the wondrous deed (פלא, v. 6) and Yahweh's righteousness (צדקתך, v. 17). These are the exact terms found in the question of 88.13 (פלאך וצדקתך). As a result, strophe II of Psalm 89 is enveloped by the word pair taken directly from 88.13. Note as well that the resurrection from death envisioned in 88.11b (יקומו) also corresponds to the rising (ירומו, 89.17) in Psalm 89's second strophe. Furthermore, the question of 88.13 was of Yahweh's deed 'being known' (היודע) in death's domain, and this root also appears in the second strophe of 89 (יודע, v. 16). This is further evidence that strophe II has thus focused on 88.11, 13.

It becomes clear that a group of Sheol's former inhabitants now called 'holy ones', including the Davidic speaker, join in thankful praise for rescue from death's realm.[18] Proof that the wondrous work extolled in 89.6 is the resurrection from the dead comes from 88.11, where it (פלא) is defined as rising (יקומו) from the dead. Psalm 89 not only answers quite carefully the questions of 88, but at the same time explains the arrival in Zion of the joyful and loved company of peoples

---

18. Note that these same 'holy ones' in Ps. 16.3 are earth-dwellers and not necessarily celestial beings.

in 87. The happy 'people' (הָעָם, 89.16), also of the second strophe, is a generalized description that matches 'peoples' (עַמִּים) enrolled in Zion (87.6).

Two verse paragraphs constitute the second strophe, the first narrating Yahweh's incomparability in the heavenly realm (vv. 6-9) and the second his absolute dominion over the earth (vv. 10-19). Paragraph 1 is dominated by divine epithets including 'Yahweh' (four times, once as 'Yah', יָהּ), 'God' and 'God of hosts' (אֵל, אֱלֹהֵי צְבָאוֹת). In v. 7 he is incomparable among 'mighty ones' (בִּבְנֵי אֵלִים). Interrogatives introduced by the pronoun 'who?' (מִי, vv. 6, 9) are twice used to accentuate his uniqueness. They form an inclusio of sorts around the paragraph, as does the combination of יהוה...אֱמוּנָתְךָ in vv. 6 and 9. Paragraph 2 is dominated by direct address to Yahweh in the second person singular pronoun אַתָּה (vv. 10, 11, 12, 13, 18).

As noted above, it is clear that praise of God's fidelity (אֱמוּנָתְךָ) in v. 6 is for faithfulness to the Davidic covenant in vv. 2-5, where the same term is repeated twice. These latter verses of strophe I are responding to the death cry of 88.11-13 and thus assure deliverance from death. So the promise to establish David's throne forever in vv. 2-5 includes resurrection from the dead. As noted above, this is found by comparing 89.6 and 88.11, 13. God's 'wondrous work' (פֶּלֶא), praised in 89.6a, is nothing less than restoration from the death of 88.13 (פֶּלֶא) and 11 (פֶּלֶא). Therefore, the miraculous work of 89.6 assures the eternal establishment of David's throne (v. 5), through restoration from the dead (88.11) of its heir. The effusive praise to Yahweh's might in 89.6-9 is due to the incomparable ability to bring the dead back to life described in the previous vv. 2-5.

Psalm 89.6a declares that heaven will praise Yahweh's wondrous work. This is metonymy for the inhabitants of heaven who are called by their dwelling place (שָׁמַיִם). Immediately following in v. 6b they are named as 'holy ones' (קְדֹשִׁים). Since they give thanks for a miraculous wonder performed by Yahweh (וְיוֹדוּ, 6a), that being his fidelity (אֱמוּנָתְךָ, 6b), an explicit connection is made to the fidelity of 88.12b (אֱמוּנָתְךָ) and thanks of 88.11b (יוֹדוּךָ). Although one might identify these holy ones at first glance as being simply the retinue surrounding Yahweh in his heavenly court (סְבִיבָיו, vv. 8-9), the canonical Psalter identifies them as a company of resurrected dead from the previous Psalm 88.

In verse 7a the place identified as 'in the clouds' (בַשַּׁחַק) is equivalent to the 'heavens' of 6a. Again as in v. 6, it is followed by its inhabitants

in 7b (בבני אלים). These 'mighty ones' are the 'holy ones' of the surrounding vv. 6, 8,[19] and therefore also the former dead of 88.11-13.
Jeremiah 23.18 spoke of those with access to the 'counsel of Yahweh'
(בסוד יהוה; cf. בסוד קדשים here in Ps. 89.8) as prophets within Israel. If
the false prophets had stood in 'my counsel' (בסודי, Jer. 23.22), they
would have heard the true message for Israel. Clearly human beings
who have access to the divine counsel are in view.

Further support for this identification of the group described across
89.6-9 can be found in Psalm 82. The 'sons of the highest one' (בני
עליון) of 82.6 (cf. בני אלים of 89.6b) were identified canonically as
unscrupulous human judges within Israel. The same construction in Ps.
29.1 (בני אלים) refers to those who ascribe to Yahweh glory and
strength (עז). Undoubtedly, this refers to the worship coming from his
people after strength (עז) was bestowed upon them in the previous 28.7,
8, and reiterated in 29.11 (עז). Not coincidentally, the same power
(עז...תעז...עזמו) is praised in 89.11, 14, 18.

Strophe III (vv. 20-38) is an extended description of the Davidic
covenant and, appropriately, the final v. 19 of strophe II ends with
reference to 'our king' (מלכנו). Immediately following in strophe III is a
reminder of the promise made to raise up for David a king. Formal ties
between the final verses of strophe II and the content of strophe III also
exist to show how the former introduces the latter. In fact, both strophes
II (vv. 6-19) and III (vv. 20-38) are discussing one and the same kingdom. For example, 'our horn' (קרננו)[20] raised in vv. 17-18 (identified as
'our shield', מגננו,[21] and 'our king', מלכנו, in v. 19) is none other than
the horn of the promised Davidide in v. 25:

19. Note the parallel pattern between vv. 6-7: קדשים...מי, and vv. 8-9:
קדשים...מי.
20. In Ps. 132, likewise a comment on the Davidic covenant, a horn sprouts for
David in v. 17. Hakham, *Sefer tehillim*, p. 145 (קמה), rightly compares 1 Sam. 2.10
to this verse for its similar reference to raising the horn of the Lord's anointed
(וירם קרן משיחו). 1 Sam. 2.10 also speaks of strength given to the Lord's king
(ויתן עז למלכו). Psalm 89.18-19, with its parallel references to God's strength, the
raised horn and king, is clearly speaking of the same Davidic monarch. Furthermore,
the same term 'anointed one' is found in Ps. 89.21 (verb form) and 89.39. From this
comparison with 1 Sam. 2.10, it is clear that the lamedh of 89.19 is one of owner-
ship. Yahweh will raise our horn by his own good will (89.18b), because our shield
and our king belong to him (89.29).
21. The shield is identified in 84.10 as the anointed king.

89.17-18 – בשמך...תרים קרנו
89.25b – ובשמי תרום קרנו

Raising (תרים or *qere* תרום) of the horn is not just an ancient metaphor for empowerment, but here is used to affirm the raising of the Davidide from the death of 88. The same verb (ירומו) describes the raising of the jubilant nation in v. 17 through 'righteousness', a direct allusion to 88.13. As shown above, both the individual and congregation of holy ones in Psalm 89's first two strophes arise from the death of Psalm 88.

How and to whom the Davidic covenant was revealed is stated in v. 20. It was 'through a vision' (בחזון) to the 'pious ones' of Yahweh (חסידיך). The original promise to David was likewise called a vision in 1 Chron. 17.15 (החזון) and 2 Sam. 7.17 (החזיון). The original recipient of this vision was Nathan the prophet, but here in 89.20 a plurality of 'pious ones' is mentioned. This coincides with the same group in 85.9 (חסידיו), who were recipients of answers to the petitions expressed in the first half of the psalm and the previous 84. Included in the answer of 85.10-14 was a reiteration of promises given in the version of the Davidic covenant found in Psalm 72 (צדק ושלום), and a preview of that in 89 (חסד ואמת, 85.11-12; cf. 89.2, 3, 15, 25, 29, 34, 50). Alternatively, if the singular חסידך of other Hebrew manuscripts is accepted,[22] the reference would be to a single speaker such as the David of 86.2 (חסיד אני).

Both the strength and duration of God's dominion in strophe II is couched in terms repeated of the Davidic kingdom promised in strophe III. To Yahweh belong strength and power (זרוע עם גבורה, 89.14). The expected Davidide is a powerful one (גבור, 89.20), strengthened by God's own might (זרועי, 89.22).

Repetition of the root רום ('raise'), reiterated in descriptions of both divine and Davidic kingdoms, also implies their identity. By his favor, God would raise up (תרים, 89.18) Israel's horn, and so in 89.20 he raises (הרימותי) up a choice one from the people. In fact, the raising of a chosen one in v. 20 follows almost immediately the reference to the raised horn of v. 18, and so the latter identifies the former.[23] Yahweh's raised (תרום, 89.14) right hand of power raises (תרים, 89.18) Israel's Davidic horn.

---

22. See the critical apparatus of *BHS*.

23. This observation also supports the *kethib* of v. 18 (hiphil, תרים) against the *qere* (qal, תרום), since הרימותי of v. 20 is also hiphil.

The close parallel between vv. 18 and 25 points out another aspect of the relationship between deity and Davidide:

89.18 – וברצנך תרים קרננו
89.25 – תרום קרנו

According to the *kethib* (hiphil), it is by direct divine causation in v. 18 that Israel's horn is raised. This monarch depends wholly on Yahweh for his appearance and strength. In v. 20 Yahweh speaks in first person, using the causative form as well, in reference to the same act of raising up a king from within Israel. By contrast, v. 25 is a description of how that Davidic king's horn would be raised (qal, intransitive) through Yahweh's name. Two transitive verb forms with Yahweh as subject and one intransitive with the Davidide as subject underline the utter dependence of the latter on the former. That dependence is expressed directly by 89.22 (אף זרועי תאמצנו), with Yahweh stating that his own arm will strengthen him.

Between 89.14 and 25–26 are similar descriptions of the raised hand and right hand of both Davidide and Yahweh:

89.14 – ידך תרום ימינך
89.25b-26 – תרום קרנו ושׂמתי...ידו...ימינו

However, the active subject of raising in v. 14 is again Yahweh, while in vv. 25-26 the raising of horns and placing of hands of the chosen king is through direct divine action. The first raising (תרום, v. 14) is second person singular masculine, while the second (תרום, v. 25) is third person singular feminine (קרן is a feminine noun).

The evidence of Book III is of a figure that is often portrayed in terms indistinguishable from Yahweh, but at the same time is utterly dependent upon him. Prayers of the speaker in Psalm 88 being the same voice of 87 is a case in point, and now the same is repeated in 89.

Further evidence of the identity between divine and Davidic kingdoms can be given. In the example just illustrated, the right hand of this royal descendant is placed by Yahweh in authority on the sea (בים ידו, 89.26a), a position identical to the divine dominion over the sea in 89.10 (הים). Through Yahweh's strength, enemies are scattered (בזרוע...אויביך, 89.11), and that same strength pacifies the monarch's enemies (זרועי...אויב, 89.22b-23a). God's own throne is founded (מכון) in justice and righteousness (89.15). By use of the same verbal root (תכון), it is stated in 89.22 that Yahweh's hand supports him. In addition, the first strophe had asserted that God would establish (אכין)

David's seed and throne forever. Later in 89.38 it is stated by Yahweh that his (David's) throne would be established (יכון) forever. The throne (כסא) of God in 89.15 is identical to the throne of David (כסא, 89.5, 30, 37). These numerous similarities at the end of Book III, implying a close equivalency between the domain of Yahweh and that promised to David, are an appropriate setting for the immediately following Book IV. Assurances that Yahweh reigns in Pss. 93.1; 96.10; 97.1; 99.1 insure the persistence of David's kingdom as well.

As for the duration of David's kingdom, it is eternal like Yahweh's. There is no one 'in the clouds' (בשחק, 89.7) comparable to Yahweh, and the 'heavens' (שמים, 89.6) are where his fidelity is praised. This not only locates the kingdom of heaven, but describes it longevity. The 'eternity' (עולם) of 89.3 is parallel to 'heavens' (שמים) in a description of the oath to David. Later in 89.38, the phrase 'in the clouds' (בשחק) is also parallel to 'eternity' (עולם) and describing also the covenant with David. Note as well that David's throne will endure as the 'days of heaven' (כימי שמים) in 89.30.

Strophe IV begins with the strongly disjunctive waw in response to the extraordinary promises made to David of the previous strophe III (ואתה). This pronoun addresses directly the divine speaker of the previous 18 verses in a dialogue format and suggests that he is the same individual who will use the identical pronoun addressing God in v. 27 (אבי אתה). With good reason, this 'son of God' complains when the promises have not been fulfilled, and in fact the opposite conditions exist. The end of Psalm 89 returns the reader to the situation of Psalm 73 where the opposite conditions exist to those promised in 72.

From vv. 39 to 46 (verse paragraph one of strophe IV), the defeat and shame of the anointed Davidide is blamed on Yahweh. Indicative of its content is the casting to the earth of the crown in 40b (לארץ נזרו), and of the throne in 45b (כסאו לארץ). An inclusio of disaster for the royal symbols thus surrounds most of paragraph one. Following this accusation, paragraph two expresses a series of questions (three, vv. 47, 49, 50) and imperatives (two, vv. 48, 51-52), ending with a call for blessing on Yahweh (v. 53). Three interrogatives are matched by three requests.

Around the entire strophe IV is repeated the reference to God's anointed (משיחך, vv. 39, 52), another clear example of inclusio. The shame (חרפה) suffered in v. 42 near the beginning of strophe IV is reiterated twice in the latter verses, once in v. 51 (חרפת) and again in 52 (חרפו). Thus, the reproach suffered by the anointed servant (vv. 39, 40,

52) and his fellow servants (51) holds strophe IV together. The suffering of the Davidic servant of 88 continues in 89.39-53 in the face of promises such as those expressed in the previous vv. 20-38.

The singular עבדך of v. 40a and the plural עבדיך of v. 51a form another envelope, this time of servanthood around strophe IV. The servant identifies with his fellow servants in the reproach suffered. A similar device is used to unite strophe II, the plural 'holy ones' placed at the beginning (קדשׁים) and the singular at the end (קדשׁ, v. 19). The holy one of Israel (strophe II) shares the celestial abode and holiness with those resurrected ones around him. Likewise, the servant of Yahweh (strophe IV) submits to the same status, and shares the reproach of his fellows.

The common condition endured by both the individual righteous one and the community is evident by their similar laments. Close links between the questions of Psalm 74 spoken by the community and the individual in Psalms 88 and 89 confirm this:

למה...זנחת לנצח – 74.1
עד מה עד מתי...לנצח – 74.9-10
למה...תזנח – 88.15
זנחת – 89.39a,
עד־מה...לנצח – 89.47a

Interrogatives are present in every case except 89.39a, as the particles indicate, of which two are identical between 74.1 and 88.15 (למה) and between 74.9 and 89.47 (עד מה). Psalm 74.1b at one end of Book III is repeated at the other end, being divided up between 89.39a (זנחת) and 89.47a (לנצח). The latter two are the initial cola of paragraphs one (vv. 39-46) and two (vv. 47-53) in strophe IV. Consequently, Book III ends as it began, asking why and how long the rejection would endure. The complaint in 74.1 was communal or national, but individual in 89.47. At the same time, fulfillment of the covenant with the individual Davidide would satisfy the yearnings of the nation as well.

Just as the speaker in 88.11-13 wondered how the promises of lovingkindness and faithfulness to David could be fulfilled from the grave, so the interrogatives of 89.47-50 (strophe IV) reveal the same perspective. Between the final strophe of 89 and 88 are the praises and promises of strophes I–III in 89, which answered the lament of 88 on a positive note. Now the hard reality of the present makes itself felt again in vv. 39-46. Revival from the death of Psalm 88 is assured in 89, but the universal and eternal kingdom promised to David has not appeared.

Rescue from death and enemies may have fulfilled part of the Davidic covenant but much remains incomplete.

Undoubtedly, the final questions of 89 sum up then the theme of Book III as a whole. How long must Israel and the Davidic descendant wait for the fulfillment of the covenant made with him? A comparison between 89.50 and the beginning verses of the psalm illustrates the impatience of the speaker. Confidence in the eternal nature of the covenant at the outset is turned to impatience at the end. If the oath sworn to David is eternal, when would it begin?

vv. 2-4 – חסדי יהוה...אמונתך...חסד...אמונתך...נשבעתי לדוד
v. 50 – איה חסדיך...נשבעת לדוד באמונתך

This contrast between praise for the promise of vv. 2-4 and questioning in v. 50 could also be categorized as elements of inclusio around the totality of Psalm 89. The reference to a covenant declared previously in v. 4 is recalled explicitly by the adjective 'first' (הראשנים) in v. 50a. Similarily, the original pact mentioned here in v. 50a resonates semantically with the statement of v. 36a of a once-sworn oath (אחת נשבעתי). The contrast across Psalm 89 is further illustrated by the assurance in 89.5 that David's seed and throne would be established 'forever' (עד עולם), as opposed to the 'How long?' of 89.47 (עד מה).

The word pair 'faithfulness' and 'fidelity' (אמת/אמונה, חסד), found not only throughout Psalm 89, but also the preceding Pss. 88.12; 86.15; 85.11-12 is a deliberately chosen reference to the covenant as spoken by the prophet Nathan to David. The same noun (חסדי) and root (נאמן) open the successive 2 Sam. 7.15 and 16 at the end of the original oracle. What is either affirmed (vv. 2-38) or questioned (vv. 39-52) is 'faithfulness' and 'fidelity' to the Davidic covenant. Nathan had stated emphatically that God's faithfulness would 'not depart' (לא יסור, 2 Sam. 7.15) from David's son. It is precisely that point which Psalm 89 is questioning. In addition, the eternal (עד עולם) establishment (כון) of David's throne (כסא) repeated in 89.5, 15, 30, 37-38 is a direct reference to the promise of a throne eternally (עד עולם) established (נכון) (כסאך יהיה נכון) in 2 Sam. 7.17. Consequently, Psalm 89 is a discussion not only of the Davidic covenant as expressed in Psalm 72 but also of its original form in 2 Samuel 7.

The divine epithet 'Lord' (אדני) appears for the first time in the entire psalm within the second and final verse paragraph of strophe V (89.50, 51). Strophe V itself begins and ends with the Tetragrammaton (vv. 47, 52-53) and is the most common divine name of the psalm. There is no apparent reason for the sudden appearance of 'Adonay' here, and so one must look further afield. Immediately following in Psalm 90, the first word after the superscription is אדני, and it is repeated in the final v. 17 for a total of two instances, precisely the number found in 89. In the previous Psalms 87–88 it does not appear once (it is repeated across Psalm 86 numerous times), and so it provides a bridge across the divide between Books III and IV.

This study has focused on Book III of the Psalter, of which 89 is the final poem. However, the importance of 72 as a basis for much of the lamenting and questioning in Book III has been demonstrated time and again. Psalm 73 immediately began to question the promises of 72 in light of the present distress. Furthermore, from psalm to psalm throughout Book III it was seen that questions that appeared to be only rhetorical within individual psalms were given surprising answers in the subsequent psalm(s), just as demonstrated between 77 and 78 or here between 88 and 89. These patterns seen already would suggest that Psalm 90 could contain answers to the questions concluding 89, and this is indeed the case.

Psalm 90 is attributed to Moses speaking on behalf of the people in first person plural, as v. 1 demonstrates (לנו, 'for us'). It is a discourse on time and the ephemeral nature of humanity, two topics that are most important in Psalm 89, especially in 89.49. The answers to 89, a postexilic poem (cf. 89.39-52), are found in Psalm 90 ascribed to Moses. His words are seen by the canonical editor as prophetic answers to the later complaints of David's house.

As noted in comments on vv. 50-51, the same divine epithet אדני found twice in those verses is repeated at either end of 90 (vv. 1, 17). If 89.50 asks Adonay the whereabouts of the faithfulness promised to David, 90.1 confesses that Adonay has been with them throughout all generations. In other words, God has not forgotten them throughout the many years and even millenia (90.4) that may pass. If 89.51 asks Adonay to remember the reproach of his servants, 90.1 assures them that within the difficult circumstances they are not abandoned. Psalm 90.1 also addresses Adonay by the second person singular pronoun אתה, as if to reveal the other side of the anger and rejection by Yahweh addressed by the same pronoun in 89.39 (ואתה).

The opening verses of both Psalms 90 and 89 repeat the phrase 'generation to generation' (דר ודר, 90.1; 89.2, 5). In 89.2 the speaker has decided to praise Yahweh's faithfulness through all generations, and this is possible because as a Davidide his throne is to endure for all generations (89.5). In fact, rescue from the death of 88 as implied by 89.2-5 ensures eternal occupancy of the throne. This was brought into question by 89.39-52, but now reaffirmed by Psalm 90. Part of that questioning in the last strophe of Psalm 89 was how long the rejection would endure (v. 47). Moses' declaration in 90.1b (בדר ודר) is a direct answer, assuring the Davidide that even through difficult circumstances the divine presence had been constant. However, true to form, 90.13 will again ask how long before Yahweh would have mercy on his servants. As a result, the adjacent Psalms 89 and 90 both begin with assurances of perpetual presence (דר ודר, 89.5; 90.1b) and end with questions of a temporal nature (עד מה, 89.47; עד מתי, 90.13).

Psalm 89 praises the creative divine power in making the 'earth' and the 'world' in a direct address utilizing the second person singular pronoun. Psalm 90 stresses God's timelessness using the same pronoun and terminology:

$$89.12 - \text{ארץ תבל...אתה}$$
$$90.2 - \text{ארץ ותבל...אתה}$$

Yahweh's power in 89 is a guarantee of the covenant with David, and in 90 his eternal nature similarly assures its fulfillment. If the Davidic pact is eternally valid in 89.5 (עד־עולם),[24] it is because the God behind it is eternal, as stated in 90.2 (ומעולם עד־עולם).

God's perspective on time reaches across generations, which by his order are ever consigned 'to dust' (עד־דכא, 90.3). He survives any and all generational changes. In 89.11 he pulverized Rahab (דכאת) by his awesome power on one occasion. Again, 89 emphasizes Yahweh's power and 90 his timelessness.

Consignment to death is described by the indicative, 'you cause to return' (תשב) in 90.3a, and the imperative 'return!' (שובו) in 90.3b. In 89.44a, to Yahweh is attributed the action of turning back (תשיב) of the Davidide's sword, causing defeat in battle. However, the death of any individual or of any Davidide does not annul a promise from Yahweh, who endures through all generations. Mortals (בני־אדם, 90.3) go to their graves, and this only makes explicit a reference to their short duration (חלד) or emptiness (שוא) in 89.48b (בני־אדם). Immediately following is the logical question of 89.49, asking who that man may be who overcomes death, fulfilling the promises to David as expressed in 89.2-38.

24. Likewise in 89.2, 3, 29, 37, 38 (עולם).

The most explicit definition of time from the divine perspective occurs in 90.4, where it is said that one thousand years are like the passing of yesterday. In fact, a thousand years are to Adonay as a night watch (וֹאַשְׁמוּרָה, 90.4b) is to mortals. Consequently, the promise to guard (אֶשְׁמוֹר, 89.29a) forever the covenant made with David is not difficult for the one who promised it. Long centuries and numerous generations seem interminable to the house of David (89.47), but in Yahweh's perspective they are of short duration. One generation's appearance and disappearance is like the flowering and fading of grass from morning to evening (90.5, 6).

The interrogative of 89.47 asked how long Yahweh's fire-like wrath (חֲמָתֶךָ) would continue burning. Psalm 90.7 refers to the same anger (וּבַחֲמָתְךָ) as causing the demise of passing generations. Here both psalms affirm the reality and continued nature of divine wrath evident since the outset of Book III. The term for Yahweh's anger used in 90.7, 11 (אַפְּךָ) picks up that used repeatedly in Book III in either noun or verb form (74.1; 77.10, 17, 18; 78.21, 49, 50; 79.5; 85.4, 6). Psalm 90 does not signal a subsiding of wrath but rather another divine answer to the continued time question. Psalm 78 answered the same question given in the previous 77, stating that continued wrath was due to continued sin. Here in Psalm 90 the continued sin (v. 8) is still the reason for anger, with the added explanation of God's extra-temporal perspective. That wrath was also described in 89.39 by the verb הִתְעַבַּרְתָּ ('you have become furious'), and in 90.9, 11 by the noun of identical root עֶבְרָתֶךָ ('your fury'). In 89.39-46 the motive for Yahweh's wrath was never stated, but in 90.8 it is clear that their sins (עֲוֹנֹתֵינוּ) have brought it upon themselves. This statement is completely consonant with God's word to David's sons in 89.33 that their sins (עֲוֹנָם) would be punished. Moses' words in Psalm 90 become canonically the answer to laments over the desolation of the Davidic house in the latter part of 89. Sin (עָוֹן) in Ps. 78.38 and resulting divine wrath (יַתְעַבֵּר, 78.21, 59, 62) were similarily given as answers to questions in the previous Psalm 77. Moses' words in Psalm 90 are an answer to the complaints of 89, and narration of the rebellion in Moses' time serves as an answer to the complaints of 77.

Those sins admitted in 90.8 have been placed in the light of the divine presence (לִמְאוֹר פָּנֶיךָ, 90.8), serving as a contrast to the joyful nation that walks in the light of Yahweh's presence (בְאוֹר פָּנֶיךָ, 89.16). Faithfulness and truth proceed before the presence of Yahweh (פָּנֶיךָ,

89.15), and any nation that proceeds in the same light before him
(פָּנָיו, 89.16) is blessed and rejoices (89.16-17). This nation 'knows'
(יוֹדְעֵי, 89.16) the shout of joy, but the nation of 90.11 'knows' (יוֹדֵעַ)
only divine wrath and fury. A clear contrast emerges between the
downcast community speaking in Psalm 90 and the exultant nation of
89.6-19. Those of Psalm 89 have been raised from the grave of 88 (as
discussed above), while those of 90 are dominated by death. If the
individual Davidide laments in 89.39-52 the nonfulfillment of promises
in 89.2-38, the community of 90 laments the nonfulfillment of promises
in 89.6-19. Those in 89.11 and 14 rejoice in the power (עֹז) of God and
those of 90.11 sigh under the power (עֹז) of his anger.

Length of life is a theme of 90.9-15, and is counted in days (יָמֵינוּ) and
years. The individual in 89.46 is cut off prematurely in the days of (יְמֵי)
his youth. Neither this individual nor those in 90 appear to have
benefitted from the promise in 89.30 of an eternal throne lasting like the
days (כִּימֵי) of heaven. The seventy or eighty years of Psalm 90 are days
(יְמֵי, 90.10) full of toil and trouble, in contrast to those of 89.17 who
rejoice in God's name all the day (כָּל־הַיּוֹם). For this reason the speaker
in 90.14 asks for God's covenant faithfulness (חַסְדֶּךָ) that they might
rejoice all their days (בְּכָל־יָמֵינוּ). This is nothing less than a request for
the fulfillment of faithfulness to the Davidic covenant so fully discussed
in the previous Psalm 89. Constant joy as requested in 90.14-15 is precisely what was promised under the divine/Davidic kingdom in 89's
second strophe (vv. 16-17). Furthermore, the request for covenant faithfulness to David in 89.50 and 90.14 (חַסְדֶּיךָ/חַסְדֶּךָ) means these two
adjacent psalms conclude in like manner.

As noted above, both Psalms 89 and 90 include the question 'how
long?' near their conclusion (89.47; 90.13). Psalm 89.47 would like to
know 'how long' (עַד־מָה) Yahweh would hide his face, and 90.13
(עַד־מָתַי) 'how long' before he again showed mercy. The latter question
recognizes the reasons for wrath and the differing divine time perspective in the immediately preceding verses of Psalm 90. Given that God's
perspective on time is different, how long would it be before covenant
promises are enacted?

In Ps. 89.51 the speaker asked Adonay to remember his servants
(עֲבָדֶיךָ), a plural noun without parallel in Psalm 89. All other instances
of this noun are singular references (vv. 4, 21, 40). However, in the
immediately following Psalm 90 are requests are for the same servants

(עבדיך, 90.13, 16), and so 89.51 exhibits another bridge to Book IV.[25] The servants in 89.51 were fellows of the single individual of 89.40 (עבדך), as are those of 90.13 and 16. Their bodies were exposed to fowl of the air in 79.2, 10 because of their sins (עונת, 79.8), and those same sins are admitted again in 90.8 (עונתינו). This single servant suffers with them, but not for his transgressions. Psalm 91 will describe him again as the righteous individual seen across Book III who confesses Yahweh as 'my refuge' (יהוה מחסי, 91.2, 9), exactly as in 73.28 (יהוה מחסי).

Just as the first two strophes of 89 expressed the majority of explicit answers to the previous 88, so the final strophe IV (vv. 39-53) expresses questions that find a direct response in 90. Parallels with either of the surrounding psalms are found throughout 89, but the most explicit links occur in those strophes at its beginning and conclusion. The same was true of 73, where strophe I questioned most directly the promises of the preceding 72, while strophes I and II clearly anticipated the following 74. Questioning of 72's promises continued throughout Book III, and the repetition of those promises in 89.20-38 (strophe III), followed by pointed questions in vv. 39-53 (strophe IV), repeats the same pattern. Consequently, it becomes evident that Psalm 89 summarizes and recapitulates in itself the form and content of Book III.

Beyond Psalm 90 in Book IV is the refrain 'Yahweh reigns' (מלך יהוה) in Psalms 93–99. Psalm 89 anticipates well the divine kingdom of Book IV, whose throne is established in righteousness and justice, as the following parallel reveals:

צדק ומשפט מכון כסאך – 89.15
צדק ומשפט מכון כסאו – 97.2

The just and righteous foundation of this divine throne matches the eschatological throne of David's son in Ps. 72.1-4. However, it was seen within Psalm 89 itself that David's promised eternal throne was described in terms close or identical to that of Yahweh. The same is true when descriptions of David's throne in Psalm 89 are compared with 93.2:

עד עולם אכין...כסאך – 89.5
לעולם...וכסאו...יכון עולם – 89.37-38
נכון כסאך...מעולם – 93.2

As the previous comparison revealed (89.15 and 97.2), the same verbal root כון ('established') and noun כסא ('throne') are used in descriptions

---

25. See the discussion of the divine name אדני earlier in this Chapter.

of the divine throne. Therefore the divine/Davidic kingdom is considered a certainty in Book IV.

There is abundance evidence that Book IV at its outset describes an individual who fits exactly descriptions of the righteous Davidide in Book III. In 91.14 the individual described knows Yahweh's name (שמי), and it is in this name (בשמי, 89.25) that the promised son of David would raise his horn. If 89.25 promises 'his horn will be raised' (תרום קרנו), 92.11 repeats the words in the mouth of the Davidide himself (ותרם...קרני). Psalm 91.15 states that this individual will call on God and be answered (יקראני ואענהו), words that resemble closely those of the righteous speaker in 86.7 (אקראך כי תעני), 88.10 (קראתי) and 89.27 (הוא יקראני). In the same 91.15 Yahweh promises to be with this individual (עמו) in trouble, a promise given in 89.22, 25, 34 (עמו) to the son of David. When salvation (ישועתי) is promised to the faithful individual of 91.16, it fulfills a promise given to the ideal Davidide of 89.27 (ישועתי). Other examples such as the close resemblances between Ps. 102.2-3 and the prayer of the suffering individual in Psalms 88 and 86 could be cited. Therefore, Book IV asserts in a more confident tone than Book III the certainty of divine rule through the righteous and faithful Davidide.

Book IV begins the series of declarations that Yahweh rules beginning only in 93.1. The delay can be explained by the fact that the previous Psalms 91 and 92 describe the one faithful Davidide who receives an answer to the complaints of Psalms 89 and 90, before the promised kingdom is anounced. Further evidence exists to support this contention in addition to the examples just given. Part of the promise to David in 89.29 was eternal divine vigilance (אשמור לו) over the king, and so it is carried out in 91.11 (לשמרך) in the midst of dangers and attacks. Complaints about attacks of his enemies in 89.43 (צריו) are answered by a promise of divine presence in the distress (בצרה) of 91.15. Psalm 89.24 had already promised victory over his enemies (צריו), and so Psalm 91 is a demonstration of the fulfillment of the Davidic covenant. The trust confessed in 91.2 (אבטח בו) by this faithful one identifies him as the same faithful Davidide of 86.2 (הבוטח אליך) and 84.13 (בטח בך). In Ps. 92.11 he continues speaking and declares that Yahweh has raised his horn (ותרם...קרני), an exact fulfillment of the promise to the eschatological David of 89.25 (ובשמי תרום קרנו). He is anointed with oil (בשמן) here in the same 92.11, as was promised in 89.21 to David (בשמן). He confesses Yahweh as his 'rock' (צור)

in 92.16, to fulfill exactly what was prophesied of him in 89.27
(הוא יקראני...צור). The rejoicing through music of 92.2-4 includes
thankfulness for God's 'covenant faithfulness' and 'fidelity' (חסדך
ואמונתך, v. 3), precisely the motive for singing in 89.2 (חסדי...אמונתך).[26]
As noted many times, these two characteristics were definitive of the
Davidic covenant (cf. 89.34, 50) and so Psalm 92 is rejoicing
confidently in its appearance. The rejoicing is from morning to night
(בבקר...בלילות, 92.3), as if to reverse the laments in 88.2 (בלילה) and
14 (ובבקר) of the same individual. This evidence demonstrates that the
function of Ps. 89.1-19 as an answer to the laments of the previous 88 is
matched by Psalms 91–92 as an answer to the lament in 89 over nonfulfillment of the Davidic covenant.

The individual portrayed in Psalm 91 is a faithful one who is pro-
tected and delivered because of his trust in Yahweh. He is not only the
one to whom promises in the Davidic covenant of Psalm 89 are fulfilled, but also the one who in his person realizes ideally the community's requests of the immediately previous Psalm 90. The community had asked in 90.14 for the satisfaction of Yahweh's faithfulness in
the morning (שבענו בבקר חסדך). It is the individual of 91.16 who is
promised satiety by Yahweh (אשביעהו), and then in 92.3 anounces his
faithfulness in the morning (בבקר חסדך). Part of the request in 90.14
was to rejoice 'all our days' (בכל ימינו), instead of suffering the short
life spans of seventy or eighty years. Psalm 91.16 promises 'length of
days' (ארך ימים) to the righteous speaker, implying his freedom from
the judgment of Psalm 90. Since the Davidide was promised a throne
like the 'days of heaven' (כימי שמים) in 89.30, as opposed to the shortened 'days' (ימי) of 89.46, the reference of 91.16 implies freedom from
death. In fact, the questions of 89.49-50, asking what individual could
live forever and the whereabouts of the Davidic covenant, are both
answered in Psalms 91–92. As seen already, the juxtaposition of Psalms
88 and 89 already assured deliverance for the righteous Davidide from
the grave.

The community in 90.15 asks for relief from the years in which they

26. Note how the superscription of Ps. 92 includes the noun 'song' (שיר),
repeating the root used in the verb 'I will sing' (אשירה) of 89.2. The song of Ps. 92
is sung on the day of 'Shabbat', an apt description of the joy, peace and fruitfulness
of Ps. 92. The wicked of v. 8 are forever destroyed, the anointed king is established
in v. 11 and flourishes continually in vv. 13-15. In fact, this is the eschatological
'Shabbat' so desired throughout Book III.

have seen (ראינו) evil, and that Yahweh's work (פעלך) be shown (יראה) to his servants. The righteous one of 91.16 will be shown (ואראהו) Yahweh's salvation, and rejoices over his work (בפעלך) in 92.5. They recognize (90.1) the fact that Adonay has been their refuge (מעון) throughout all time. In 91.9 it is the faithful individual who has made God his refuge (מעונך). Twice the community of Psalm 90 requests that they be made to rejoice (ונשמחה, 90.14; שמחנו, 90.15), and in the afore-mentioned 92.5 it is the individual speaker whom Yahweh makes to rejoice (שמחתני). Again the righteous individual Davidide stands out from the nation, as seen already across Book III. He also speaks confidently in these two Psalms 91–92 of the promises made to David being fulfilled in his person. For this reason, the series of confident statements in Yahweh's rule begun in Ps. 93.1 should be interpreted in light of the immediately previous Psalms 90–91 and Book III.

Psalm 92.5, 6 state twice that the speaker has been made glad because of the works (מעשי) of Yahweh. Back in Ps. 86.8 those same works (כמעשיך) were mentioned in answer to the prayers of vv. 1-7, and defined in v. 9 as bringing about the universal and eschatological worship of Yahweh. Psalm 86.8-9 was a reaffirmation of the promised kingdom in Psalm 72, and now 86.8-9 is reaffirmed in 92.5-6. The kingdom of Psalms 72, 86 is now declared again in 92.5-6. Further-more, the gladdening of this individual in 92.5 (שמחתני) is a direct answer to 86.4 (שמח) from the midst of troubles. In 86.7 there is confidence that when he cried to Yahweh in a time of distress he was answered. Psalm 91.15 is a restatement of 86.7 from the divine point of view:

86.7 – ביום צרתי אקראך כי תענני
91.15 – יקראני ואענהו עמו אנכי בצרה

The transition between the first two strophes of Psalm 86 proceeds from calling out in time of troubles, and assurance of answers by the Davidic heir (86.1-7), to answers describing divine works that bring about a universal kingdom (86.8-13). That sequence is similar to the transition from answers in time of troubles for the Davidic heir (91.14-16) to rejoicing over the divine works to establish the universal kingdom (92.5-11). Such parallels demonstrate that the individual and eschato-logical kingdom of Psalms 91–92 is identical to the one seen in Book III.

The raised horn (ותרם...קרני) of the speaker in 92.11, and his desig-nation as the righteous one (צדיק) in v. 13, corresponds closely to the

description of the righteous one with raised horns in 75.11 (תרוממנה
קרנות צדיק). In both psalms the wicked (רשעים, 75.5, 9, 11; 92.8) are
assured destruction, a promise made to this same Davidide in 91.8
(רשעים). Psalm 75, as might be recalled, was an affirmative answer to
the laments of 73 (individual Davidide) and 74 (community), decrying
the long delay in implementation of the eschatological promises given
by Psalm 72. Psalm 92 likewise serves to answer the laments of 89
(individual Davidide) and 90 (community), over the delay of promises
given in 89.

Book III had opened with the righteous individual of Psalm 73
puzzling over the continued prosperity of the 'wicked' (רשעים, 73.3,
12). He pondered 'this' (זאת, 73.16), that is, the end of the wicked
(73.17b), finally 'understanding' (אבינה, 73.17) it. Later he admits, 'I
was brutish and ignorant' (ואני בער ולא אדע, 73.22a). Here in 92.8 the
'wicked' (רשעים) are also said to have prospered, albeit temporarily.
Whoever 'does not understand this' is also called 'brutish and ignorant'
(איש בער לא ידע...לא יבין את זאת) in 92.7. Close parallels are also
apparent between 73.27 and 92.10, each of which promises the destruction of God's enemies, who are those far from him:

> 73.27 – כי הנה רחקיך יאבדו
> 92.10 – כי הנה איביך יאבדו

In either case the individual calls God his rock (צור, 73.26; צורי, 92.16).
These striking similarities all go to show that the same speaker is heard
in both psalms. In 73 he is full of doubts before being assured that the
wicked will be destroyed, while in 92 is confident of their destruction
after temporary success. His description of those who doubt eventual
justice as brutish in 92.7 is so close to 73.22 that it appears to be a self-
confession. While the phraseology is quite close in these particular
citations, the difference in tone and attitude between 73 and 92 is striking. Psalm 73 expressed the complaints and doubts of a despondent
speaker that set the tone for the rest of Book III. The same righteous
Davidide in 92 expresses the confidence, faith and joy that permeates
the entire psalm and sets a different tone at the outset of Book IV.

Psalm 92.14 likens this Davidide to trees flourishing in the house
(בבית יהוה) and courts (בחצרות) of God. Indeed, this was his ardent
desire in Psalm 84. His soul sought the 'courts of Yahweh' (לחצרות יהוה
בחצריך..., 84.3, 11), also defined as the 'house of God' (ביתך...בבית
אלהי, 84.5, 11). Such longing has apparently been assured fulfillment
by Psalm 92. Moreover, the transplanting of palm and cedar trees in

92.14 (שְׁתוּלִים...כְּאֶרֶז...כְּתָמָר) recalls the simile of the blessed man in Ps. 1.3 (כְּעֵץ שָׁתוּל). In either case the fruitfulness of the tree is emphasized. It has already been shown that this righteous one in Psalm 92 is the Davidide from Book III, and now is identified as the flourishing one in Psalm 1. He is assured destruction (יֹאבְדוּ, 92.10) of the short-lived wicked, who are like grass (רְשָׁעִים כְּמוֹ עֵשֶׂב, 92.8). Psalm 91.8 also promised he would see the recompense of the wicked (רְשָׁעִים). Those same wicked are short-lived as chaff in the Psalter's introduction (רְשָׁעִים כִּי אִם כַּמֹּץ, 1.4), and will be destroyed (רְשָׁעִים תֹּאבֵד, 1.6). Thus, complaints about these wicked in Psalm 73 are now answered again, as they were in 75. The faithful individual of Book III is again reassured of the eschatological just judgment of the wicked here in Psalms 91–92. Since the righteous Davidide of Book III is now identified in Psalm 92 using tree similes, there is further support for identifying the Davidide of Psalm 2 with the righteous one of Psalm 1 who is also compared to a flourishing tree. The אִישׁ of Ps. 1.1 in the canonical scheme is none other than the royal son of Psalm 2, as I explained on p. 121 n. 10. See also following page.

Here, early in Book IV, the rule of Yahweh (יְהוָה מָלָךְ) is prefaced by fulfilled promises to the Davidic scion (Psalms 91–92), after portrayals in 89 that equate both divine and Davidic kingdoms. That enigma is stated quite explicitly in Ps. 110.1 (שֵׁב לִימִינִי), where the Davidide is sitting at Yahweh's right hand and ruling the nations. In fact, he is called 'my Lord' (אֲדֹנִי), meaning that not only is his kingdom identical to that of Yahweh but now again he takes on divine characteristics. The oath to David of 89.4, 36, 50 (נִשְׁבַּעְתִּי/נִשְׁבַּעְתָּ) is now being clarified in a remarkable way (נִשְׁבַּע יְהוָה) in 110.4. Book III and the opening psalms of Book IV imply this merging of Yahweh and his kingdom with that of the promised son of David and his kingdom, but the same was indicated earlier by Psalm 72, and even earlier in the Psalter's introduction.

Psalm 2 has already blurred the line between deity and anointed king, and so the same phenomenon in later psalms is not innovative. Rebellion against Yahweh is tantamount to rebellion against 'his anointed' (2.2), and 'their bonds' (plural suffix מוֹ-, 2.3), against which the rulers resist, is anaphoric to both Yahweh and his anointed. Therefore, 'his anger' in 2.5 (בְאַפּוֹ) can also find its referent in both Yahweh and the annointed, and matches the anger in 2.12 of the son (יֶאֱנַף...אַפּוֹ).[27]

---

27. The reading בַּר (Aramaic for 'son'), coheres well with the rhetorical characteristics of vv. 11-12; (בְּיִרְאָה...בִּרְעָדָה...בַּר...יְבַעֵר), where the beth-resh sequence

If one considers the canonical juxtaposition of Psalms 1 and 2, it becomes clear that contrasts between the wicked and righteous are continued in the latter. The blessed man of 1.2 meditates (יהגה) on the torah of Yahweh, but no information is given concerning the meditation of the wicked until 2.1 (יהגו). Their meditation is emptiness because it involves rebellion against God and his anointed as opposed to submissive attention to the Torah. We are told that the blessed man does *not* sit with scoffers (לא ישב, 1.1), but not where he *does* sit. That is revealed in 2.4, where we read of 'one who sits' (יושב) in heaven 'laughing', a direct response to the 'scoffing' of the wicked in 1.1. The wicked council of 1.1 is also explicated in 2.1-2 as a cabal of international rebellion. When Psalm 2 is read in isolation, the one in 2.4a who sits (יושב) in heaven is surely the deity, designated as Adonay by 2.4b. Nevertheless, when its obvious role as canonical comment to Psalm 1 is considered, the righteous and blessed man of the latter appears in Ps. 2.4 laughing in return from his heavenly seat at the scoffing of the wicked. In fact, he is enthroned in 2.6 in the heavenly Zion, which further commentary in Ps. 110.1-2 confirms. There Yahweh commands the Davidic king, who is given the epithet 'Adoni' (לאדני), to 'sit' (שב) at his right hand. In Ps. 2.4 he is already sitting (יושב) there, and the grammatical antecedent to the singular participle יושב could be either 'his anointed one' or 'Yahweh' of 2.2. It is 'Adonay' (אדני) who sits in the heaven of 2.4, and the command to sit in 110.1 is directed to the 'Adoni' ('my Lord') of the speaker (לאדני).[28] Consequently, the evidence here in Book III of divine characteristics attributed to the Davidic heir is consistent with evidence in the Psalter as a whole. It also explains how the following Book IV (Psalms 93–99) emphasizes divine kingship in response to the laments in Book III (and Psalm 90) over the fallen Davidic throne. The throne of Yahweh (93.2) is the same throne of David (89.5, 57-58).

---

is repeated fourfold. Note also how the consonants of 'in trembling' (ברעדה) are reorganized in the verb 'kindle' (יבער) to point out the effects of noncompliance. The three imperatival clauses from vv. 11 to 12a are increasingly shortened, whether one numbers syllables (7, 5, 3), or stress counts (3, 2, 1). This series ends climactically on the terse נשקו בר ('kiss the son'), which is consistent with the place and power given to this son (בן) in vv. 6-9, and the aforementioned merging of roles for the anointed one and Yahweh of v. 2. The use of Aramaic for 'son' is not incompatible with Hebrew poetry, being repeated three times in a single proverb (Prov. 31.2), in a context that includes the Hebrew form as well (בני, Prov. 31.5).

28. Without the Masoretic vowels the two epithets are indistiguishable.

In conclusion, Psalm 89 begins with surprisingly affirmative answer to the questions of 88 uttered from the grave. The Davidide and a company of people seen in Psalms 87 and 88 are alive and joyful in 89. After a long rehearsal of the Davidic covenant in 89, there is a renewed complaint about its delay, and so Book III ends as it began. Psalm 90 answers by explaining that God's perspective of time is different. This continues the pattern evident within Book III of answers to temporal questions in the following psalms. In consonance with Book III, Psalm 90 also includes a further temporal question by the community regarding implementation of the promised Davidic kingdom. An answer is given in Psalm 91 by a description of the faithful Davidide. The same individual is confidently rejoicing in Psalm 92 over implementation of his promised kingdom, and this serves as a fitting introduction to the confident series of statements beginning in 93.1.

The foregoing lengthy analysis of Book III's shape and message reveals several themes consistently reiterated. Repeatedly, questions of 'how long?' before the Davidic promises of Psalm 72 are fulfilled, and 'why?' God's anger continues, are asked. Various divine responses reveal that disobedience is the cause, while affirming the validity and certainty of a future restoration. Restoration means establishment of Psalm 72's conditions and a reigning Davidide. No timetable for the latter is ever revealed, and so continued desolation produces continued lament.

Pleas and complaints are directed to God not only by the community, but often by the voice of a single righteous one in the beginning Psalms 73, 75, 77, 78. In the last six psalms (84–89) his voice becomes much more prominent. He suffers along with the nation, while being distinguished from them by his righteous conduct. His suffering brings him into death's domain, but is rescued in keeping with the covenant made with David. Furthermore, by the end of Book III, he is promised a throne that is indistinguishable from that of Yahweh. This only repeats what is implied by Ps. 72.17-19 and the introductory Psalm 2.

This righteous and yet despondent individual first appears in Psalm 73, responding directly to the promise of a just and peaceful kingdom in 72. He complains that in fact the very opposite conditions of 72 were now prevailing, to the point that God's people have joined the wicked. This is followed in 74 by a lament of the community whose temple and city have been destroyed. By their own words in 74, the community identifies the wicked of 73 as Israel itself, and the judgment revealed to the speaker of 73 as that suffered by the nation. Psalm 74 includes questions of how long and why regarding the desolation and divine anger, before concluding with a call for the restoration of 72's kingdom.

Psalms 75 and 76 are divine responses to this call, declaring that a time of righteous judgment has been reserved and that peace will be established. Specifically, 75 promises in answer to 74 a time (unspecified) chosen for divine judgment, in which the wicked of 73 will be cut down. Psalm 76 details the final conflict to establish the universal peace and justice promised in 72. It is the God who dwells in Zion who will produce that kingdom, and it will be the worldwide capital to which all will bring tribute. The destroyed Zion in 74 is therefore promised restoration to a position more lofty than any seen heretofore.

Psalm 77 takes up the lament by the same pious individual again, asking how long God's anger will endure, to which 78 gives the divine answer. Continual sin of Israel in 78 explains the continual divine anger of 77. Remembrance of God's past deeds demonstrated by the speaker of 77 proves his obedience to the commands neglected by the nation in 78. Apparently, the individual speaker of 77 becomes the spokesman for God's response in 78, and his piety is parallel to the David portrayed in 78.65-72. His words of praise in 77.14 suggest that he dwells in the same Judah and Zion of 76.2-3, identical to the eternal Zion of 78.68-69. Such a royal identity and residence will be confirmed by the collocation of Psalms 86 and 87, while his faithful conduct in contrast to a wicked nation recalls Psalm 73.

Psalms 79 and 80 continue the dialogue as communal laments over the defeat of the nation, asking how long and why it persists, in similar fashion to Psalm 74. The speakers of 79 declare their faithfulness as opposed to the obstinate nation of 78. In fact, the lengthy statements of 79.8, 13 are directed specifically to the accusations and requirements laid out in 78. From a rhetorical point of view the latter verses resemble 78 more than 79 itself. The community of 79 pleads for forgiveness based on statements of divine mercy in 78, and then also declares its commitment to the commands spelled out in the same 78. Psalm 80 continues in the same vein as 79, repeating the double interrogative of 'how long?' and 'why?' (seen also in 74). A request for repetition of the exodus so fully narrated in 78 is given by Psalm 80, concluding with a request for the establishment of the chosen Davidide. The pattern of exodus account followed by a description of the chosen David in 80 repeats the same found in 78.

Another divine response comes in Psalm 81 with a call for Israel to remember through festival celebration, precisely what it had failed to do in 78. The speaker in the first half of 81 appears to be a member of the nation itself. Direct speech from Yahweh in the second half accuses the nation of disobedience. That disobedience is described as walking in their own counsels and paths, later characterized in the following 82 as walking in darkness. If they had obeyed Yahweh's voice, the enemies now oppressing them would have been quickly subdued.

Psalm 82 goes on to reveal that it is Israel's own leaders and judges who exalt the wicked. This confirms again that the wicked so lamented in 73 were none other than members of the chosen nation itself. The repeated query as to how long divine wrath would endure in previous psalms is now thrown back at the nation, asking how long their judges and princes would dispense injustice to the oppressed and poor.

Psalm 83 voices another lament of the nation, asking for vengeance on the Gentile nations, as was done to enemy princes in the book of Judges. Both 82 and 83 conclude with similar confident statements in the ultimate divine judgment of the nations of the earth. Psalm 84 will describe the righteous individual and nation who 'walk' in integrity, as opposed to the wicked 'walk' portrayed by Psalms 81–83. Psalms 84–86 portray the walk of the righteous, as opposed to the walk of the wicked in 82–83. The destination of the righteous is Zion, dwelling of God, promised in the previous Psalms 76, 78 and latter 87. The walk to Zion of 84.8 presages the walk of Psalms 84–86 ending in the Zion of 87. Furthermore, the speaker of 84.11 expresses the delight of habitation in Yahweh's courts, as opposed to the tents of the wicked. This can be identified as the tents of enemy Gentile nations in 83.7. Included in Ps. 84.9-13 is the prayer of the righteous speaker who pleads for divine intervention. Formal parallels reveal that his prayers and laments continue through Psalms 85, 86, 88 and 89.

His individual prayer is joined in the first half of 85 by the nation. Included are interrogatives, resembling closely those repeated so often previously, that ask how long God's wrath would endure. He awaits and becomes the voice of the divine answer again in the second half of 85, promising the establishment of 72's conditions. The qualities of peace, righteousness, kindness and truth are personified in that answer, and the following 86 reveals their embodiment in an ideal David.

Continued prayer in 86's first strophe by this righteous one is immediately answered in the middle strophe (vv. 8-13) by the promised establishment of the same worldwide kingdom portrayed in 72, along with personal deliverance from death. His death experience is further chronicled in 88, while details of that kingdom are given in 87. In the latter psalm, Gentile enemies named by Psalm 83 have become part of the peaceful citizenry of the eschatological Zion, having come into a close relationship with the Yahweh of Israel. That relationship was already implied by their worship of Adonay in 86. Therefore, the destroyed Zion of 74 has been re-established and war ended, even as 76 previously stated.

Psalm 88 is a descent down into the realm of death, far from the lofty and harmonious conditions of 87. The close relationship between Yahweh and his companions of Zion in 87 becomes that which is severed between David and his intimates in 88. Parallel vocabulary for 'loved one' and 'close acquaintances' confirms the link. At the same time, this Davidide prays to Yahweh from Sheol. So this Davidic figure again becomes closely identified with Yahweh (as seen at various points in Book III, such as Psalms 75 and 78).

Psalm 88 ends on a hopeless note, but 89 declares that the dead of 88, including the Davidic speaker and many others, will arise eventually and praise God for the eternal covenant with David. The threefold, and apparently rhetorical, interrogative of 88 uttered by the speaker consigned to death is answered explicitly in the affirmative by the first two strophes of Psalm 89 (vv. 2-19). The individual will sing and make known with his mouth forever God's faithfulness to the covenant, implying that the death of 88 will not silence him. The holy ones now risen to the heavens will also thank Yahweh for his faithfulness, fidelity and miraculous wonder through the Davidic covenant. That company of people can also be identified as those future inhabitants of Zion in 87.

The eternal kingdom promised in David's covenant as narrated in 89.20-38 is equated with the one ruled by Yahweh in the verses immediately preceding. If a Davidide is to rule over such a kingdom, an unending life is required. For this reason, the final strophe of Psalm 89 concludes Book III asking who such an immortal could be and when he would appear. Apparently, the individual portrayed in Psalm 86 and at the outset of 89, who will triumph over death, has not appeared to take the Davidic throne.

To these final questions of Book III asking 'how long?' and 'to whom?' the promises to David are to be kept, the opening Psalm 90 of Book IV responds. Centuries and even millenia may appear to mortals as interminable lengths of time, but not in God's perspective. For the eternal God (v. 2) a thousand years are like a human yesterday or even the few hours of a night watch, and so the promise to David has not been forgotten. Generations come and go under his oversight and his wrath consumes them in their sin (vv. 7-12), repeating the accusation against them in Book III. For this reason, they also still cry 'how long?' (עד־מתי, 90.13), as in Book III, before the faithfulness to David (90.14a) is brought to fruition.

Psalms 91–92 once again portray the righteous individual (seen throughout the previous Book III), in answer the lament of 90 and 89's final strophe. Indeed, verses such as 91.14-16 and 92.3, 5, 6, 11 portray the Davidide as satisfied and rejoicing over the performance of mighty divine deeds to destroy the wicked. He dwells as a flourishing plant in the house of the Lord, fulfilling his desire already expressed in Ps. 84.11.

The immediately following Psalm 93 begins the refrain 'Yahweh reigns' (יהוה מלך; also 96.10; 97.1; 98.6; 99.1). Yahweh's rule and throne is portrayed in terms closely parallel to both the divine and Davidic kingdoms of Psalm 89. Consequently, Yahweh's long-awaited kingdom, proclaimed triumphantly in Book IV, is the same as that promised to David's descendant in answer to the repeated laments of Book III.

Appendix

THE VOCABULARY OF BOOK III

The term *dis legomena* refers to twice-only occurrences of specific forms in a specified corpus of texts. Within Book III there are numerous examples of this phenomenon, supporting its integrity as a unit within the Psalter. As will be seen, not only are single lexical forms to be included under this rubric but also phrases, clauses and sentences.

The form איתן is found twice in the whole of the Psalter, once in 74.15 as an adjective and once in 89.1 as a personal name. Its meaning 'permanent'[1] is consistent with the temporal theme found throughout these two psalms and Book III as a whole.

Another example of *dis legomena* within the entire Hebrew Bible appears between 73.18 (למשואות) and 74.3 (למשאות). The speaker of 73.17-18 finally understood the fate of the wicked upon entering the 'holy places', declaring confidently that they had fallen into 'ruins'. The 'ruins' of the 'holy place' in 74.3 clarify how he came to this understanding. This concatenation also confirms that the wicked assured punishment in 73 were none other than the nation of Israel itself.

As noted in the discussion of Psalm 75, this psalm makes direct reference back to the wicked described in 73 by use of the word pair 'arrogant ones' and 'wicked ones' (הוללים...רשעים, 73.3 and 75.5).[2] Only in these two psalms does this combination occur in the entire Psalter, and in fact it is unique in the entire Hebrew Bible.

Concluding Psalm 74 is a lengthened imperatival clause (קומה אלהים, v. 22)[3] directed to God, asking vengeance for the shame perpetrated by Israel's enemies. In essence, it is a request to fulfill that which was promised in 72, and is repeated exactly in 82.8. This specific collocation is repeated nowhere else in the Hebrew Bible and expresses well the desire of the nation for vengeance on their enemies. Ironically, Ps. 82.8 is spoken as part of a denunciation of evil rulers within Israel itself. Therefore, those that should be judged are not only the foreign enemies seen previously in Ps. 74.22, but also the unjust Israelite rulers of Psalm 82.

Wicked Israel is 'poured out' (ימצו) abundant waters of the wicked in 73.10b. Their reward is ironically to drain (ימצו) to the dregs the wine of divine judgment in

---

1.   BDB, s.v. יתן, p. 450.
2.   The plural noun רשעים by itself is of course extremely common in the Psalter, beginning with Ps. 1.1. Here the combination with הוללים is unique.
3.   Note the similar but not identical form in Ps. 3.8: קומה יהוה.

75.9. Only in these two verses is the root מצה used across the entire Psalter.

Within the tricolon of 77.3 is found the verb מאנה ('refused'), describing the speaker's inability to be comforted. He appears to be at a standoff with Adonay, who does not deign to answer. The same root is found in the immediately succeeding 78.10 (מאנו), describing the refusal of Ephraim to walk according to God's counsel. Nowhere else in the entire Psalter is this verbal root again found. Clearly, the impasse between supplicant on behalf of the nation and deity described in 77.3 is explained by the refusal of that same nation (or one tribe at least) to obey in 78.10. At this point one may note again the contrast between the righteous individual who 'refuses' to be comforted and continually 'remembers' God (Ps. 77.3-4), and the nation who 'refused' to walk in his Torah and 'forgot' his deeds (Ps. 78.10-11):

מאנה...אזכרה – 77.3c-4a
מאנו...וישכחו – 78.10b-11a

Between the same two Psalms 77 and 78 are a pair of terms derived presumably from the same root עלל, that are repeated only here within all of Book III. In 77.12 the individual remembers the former 'deeds of Yah' (מעללי־יה), and meditates upon them (ובעלילותיך) in 77.13. Such remembrance is in keeping with the command-ment of 78.7 not to forget God's deeds (מעללי־אל), which instruction the Ephraimites promptly forgot in 78.11 (עלילותיו). Hence, both nouns create explicit ties between both psalms. Supporting evidence comes from the governing verbal predicates אזכיר ('I remember') and אשׂיחה ('I muse') of 77.12-13, both of which contrast semantically (while the latter also contrasts phonetically) with that of 78.7, 11 (שׁכחו). Again, the righteous individual speaker distinguishes himself from the disobedient nation.

The only three instances of שׁאר in the entire Psalter fall not coincidentally in 73.26 and 78.20, 27. While the individual speaker of Ps. 73.26 trusts faithfully in God even when his flesh (שׁארי) fails, the nation is showered with flesh (שׁאר) for food in 78.20, 27 and still doubts. The contrast of faith and doubt between these texts is confirmed by the accompanying references to the rock:

שׁארי...צור – 73.26
צור...שׁאר – 78.20

Israel ask sceptically in Psalm 78 whether God who brought forth water from a rock can also provide meat (flesh) for them. For the righteous one of Psalm 73, God is his rock in spite of failing flesh.

As a result of continual disobedience by the nation, Yahweh cannot contain his anger, and it overflows against his people. Three times that anger is described in 78 by the hithpael verb pattern (vv. 21, 59, 62) of the same root עבר. The same patterned root occurs only once more in the entire Psalter and, as expected, within the same Book III. In 89.39 Yahweh is angry (התעברת) with his own anointed king. Supporting evidence for the intentionality of this parallel is the identical accom-panying root 'reject' (מאס):

ויתעבר וימאס – 78.59
ותמאס התעברת – 89.39

Another expression for wrath is formed by the denominative root אנף ('be angry'), found in verb form only four times throughout the Psalter (2.12; 60.3; 79.5; 85.6). The two of Book III are identical second person masculine singular imperfects (תאנף), both differing slightly from the previous.[4] Both of these verses are part of a series of repeated interrogatives across Book III, wondering if God's wrath would endure forever. The noun form of this root (אף) is also found in several of these interrogatives (74.1; 77.10; 85.6) and many times in non-interrogative verses, especially Psalm 78. Given the mood of Book III, it is not surprising to find so many references to divine wrath.

Descriptions of that wrath include a pronominally suffixed noun, 'your shepherding' (מרעיתך), used only four times in the Psalter (74.1; 79.13; 95.7; 100.3). The two instances of Book III are identical in form, both pronominally suffixed with the second person masculine singular, and in a construct chain with the same noun, 'flock' (צאן):

74.1 – צאן מרעיתך

79.13 – וצאן מרעיתך

The latter verse from 79 is an odd tricolon that has no vocabulary common to the rest of the poem, and was shown to be a direct response to the previous 78.1-8.[5] It functions as much on the level of Book III as within 79 itself, answering 78 and resuming the lament begun in 74. The remaining two instances of the noun in question are found in Book IV and suffixed identically (מרעיתו, 100.3; 95.7). Likewise, they appear in the company of the same noun צאן. The distribution within Book IV is undoubtedly as deliberate as that of Book III.

Another denominative root עשן ('to smoke, to fume') also occurs four times within the Psalter in verbal form (74.1; 80.5; 104.32; 144.5), and again two of them are within Book III. The interrogative of 74.1 asks 'why' (למה) God's anger 'fumes' (יעשן) against his flock. In 80.5 another interrogative questions 'how long' (עד־מתי) he will 'fume' (עשנת) against his people's prayer. Within each of Psalms 74, 79 and 80 are a pair of interrogatives using the particles למה (74.1; 79.10; 80.13) and עד־מה/מתי (74.9-10; 79.5; 80.5).

The interrogative of 80.13 includes a clause unique to the Psalter, except for 89.41, accusing God of breaking open the protective wall around either Israel or the anointed Davidide:

80.13 – ...פרצת גדריה

89.41 – ...פרצת כל־גדרתיו

Within the same bicolon of 80.13 and in the closely parallel bicolon of 89.42 is found a reference to passers-by on the road, who plunder the unprotected nation and anointed king. This particular phrase is found twice only in the entire Hebrew Bible:

---

 4. The other two are Ps. 60.3 (אנפת), a qal second person masculine singular perfect, and 2.12 (יאנף), a qal third person masculine singular imperfect. All four examples predicate divine anger.

 5. Verse 8 is likewise a tricolon without obvious parallels in Ps. 79, while responding directly to Ps. 78.38-39, 59.

כל־עברי דרך – 80.13
כל־עברי דרך – 89.42

Brought together in these two psalms are the sufferings of the entire nation (80) and their anointed king (89).

As can be seen, *dis legomena* in Book III consist of various single lexical items and larger phrases as well. A more extended example occurs between the almost identical interrogatives of 79.5 and 89.47:

עד־מה יהוה האנף לנצח תבער כמו־אש קנאתך...חמתך – 79.5
עד־מה יהוה תסתר לנצח תבער כמו־אש חמתך – 89.47[6]

Again, the first query is put in the mouth of the nation and the second in that of the anointed Davidide. Both suffer the shame and reproach of their neighbors (79.4, 12; 89.42, 51-52). Undoubtedly, behind these numerous examples of twice-repeated terms, clauses and extended sentences is an editorial hand(s) creating a discrete unit out of the seventeen psalms compiled together in Book III.

---

6.   As noted previously, the two terms האנף and קנאתך of 79.5 are replaced by תסתר and חמתך in 89.47 in order to create explicit links to the immediately previous Ps. 88.8, 15.

BIBLIOGRAPHY

Allen, L.C., 'Psalm 73: An Analysis', *TynBul* 33 (1982), pp. 93-118.

—*Psalms 101–150* (WBC, 21; Waco, TX: Word Books, 1983).

—'The Value of Rhetorical Criticism in Psalm 69', *JBL* 105 (1986), pp. 577-98.

Auffret, P., 'Dieu juge: Etude structurelle du Psaume 82', *BN* 58 (1991), pp. 7-12.

—'La droite du très-haute: Etude structurelle du Psaume 77', *SJOT* 6 (1992), pp. 92-122.

—'Ecoute, mon peuple!: Etude structurelle du Psaume 81', *SJOT* 7 (1993), pp. 285-302.

—'Essai sur la structure littéraire du Psaume LXXIV', *VT* 33 (1983), pp. 129-48.

—'Essai sur la structure littéraire du Psaume LXXXVI', *VT* 29 (1979), pp. 385-402.

—'Essai sur la structure littéraire du Psaume 85', in *idem, La sagesse a bâti sa maison*, pp. 287-300.

—*Merveilles à nos yeux: Etude structurelle de vingt psaumes dont celui de 1Ch 16, 8-36* (Berlin: W. de Gruyter, 1995).

—'Les ombres se lèvent-elles pour te louer? Etude structurelle du Ps 88', *EstBíb* 45 (1987), pp. 23-38.

—'Qu'ils sachent que toi, ton nom est YHWH! Etude structurelle du Psaume 83', *ScEs* 45 (1993), pp. 41-59.

—'Qu'elles sont aimables, tes demeures! Etude structurelle du Psaume 84', *BZ* 38 (1994), pp. 29-33.

—*La sagesse a bâti sa maison: Etudes de structure littéraires dans l'Ancien Testament et spécialment dans les Psaumes* (Göttingen: Vandenhoeck & Ruprecht, 1982).

—*Voyez de vos yeux: Etude structurelle de vingt psaumes dont le Psaume 119* (VTSup, 48; Leiden: E.J. Brill, 1993).

Barth, C., 'Concatenatio im ersten Buch des Psalters', in B. Benzing, O. Böcher and G. Mayer (eds.), *Wort und Wortlichkeit: Studien zur Afrikanistik und Orientalistik* (Festschrift E.L. Rapp; Meisenheim am Glan: Hain, 1976), pp. 30-40.

Beaugrande, R. de, and W. Dressler, *Introduction to Text Linguistics* (New York: Longman, 1981).

Berlin, A., *The Dynamics of Biblical Parallelism* (Bloomington: Indiana University Press, 1985).

—'On the Interpretation of Psalm 133', in E.R. Follis (ed.), *Directions in Biblical Hebrew Poetry* (JSOTSup, 40; Sheffield: JSOT Press, 1987), pp. 141-47.

—'The Rhetoric of Psalm 145', in A. Kort and S. Morschauser (eds.), *Biblical and Related Studies Presented to Samuel Iwry* (Winona Lake, IN: Eisenbrauns, 1985), pp. 17-22.

Best, T.F. (ed.), *Hearing and Speaking the Word: Selections from the Works of James Muilenburg* (Chico, CA: Scholars Press, 1984).

Boadt, L., 'Intentional Alliteration in Second Isaiah', *CBQ* 45 (1983), pp. 353-63.

Booij, T., 'Psalm LXXXIV: A Prayer of the Anointed', *VT* 44 (1994), pp. 433-41.

—'Royal Words in Psalm LXXXIV 11', *VT* 36 (1986), pp. 117-21.

Brennan, J.P., 'Psalms 1–8: Some Hidden Harmonies', *BTB* 10.1 (1980), pp. 25-29.

—'Some Hidden Harmonies in the Fifth Book of Psalms', in R.F. McNamara (ed.), *Essays in Honor of Joseph P. Brennan* (Rochester, NY: St Bernard's Seminary, 1976).

Briggs, C.A., and E.G. Briggs, *A Critical and Exegetical Commentary on the Book of Psalms* (ICC, 38-39; 2 vols.; Edinburgh: T. & T. Clark, 1906).

Brueggemann, W., 'Response to James L. Mays, "The Question of Content"', in McCann (ed.), *The Shape and Shaping of the Psalter*, pp. 29-41.

Brueggemann, W., and P.D. Miller, 'Psalm 73 as a Canonical Marker', *JSOT* 72 (1996), pp. 45-56.

Campbell, A.F., 'Psalm 78: A Contribution to the Theology of Tenth-Century Israel', *CBQ* 41 (1979), pp. 51-79.

Caquot, A., 'Observations sur le Psaume 89', *Sem* 41-42 (1993), pp. 133-58.

Cassuto, U., 'The Sequence and Arrangement of the Biblical Sections', in *Biblical and Oriental Studies*. I. *Bible* (trans. I. Abrahams; Jerusalem: Magnes Press, 1973), pp. 1-6.

Childs, B.S., *Introduction to the Old Testament as Scripture* (Philadelphia: Fortress Press, 1979).

—'Reflections on the Modern Study of the Psalms', in F.M. Cross (ed.), *Magnalia Dei: The Mighty Acts of God. Essays in Memory of G. Ernest Wright* (Garden City, NY: Doubleday, 1976), pp. 377-88.

Clifford, R.J., 'In Zion and David a New Beginning: An Interpretation of Psalm 78', in B. Halpern and J.D. Levenson (eds.), *Traditions in Transformation: Turning Points in Biblical Faith* (Winona Lake, IN: Eisenbrauns, 1981), pp. 121-41.

—'Psalm 89: A Lament over the Davidic Ruler's Continued Failure', *HTR* 73 (1980), pp. 35-47.

Clines, D.J.A., D.M. Gunn and A.J. Hauser (eds.), *Art and Meaning: Rhetoric in Biblical Literature* (JSOTSup, 19; Sheffield: JSOT Press, 1982).

Costacurta, B., 'L'aggressione contro Dio: Studio del Salmo 83', *Bib* 64 (1984), pp. 518-41.

Craigie, P.C., *Psalms 1–50* (WBC, 19; Waco, TX: Word Books, 1983).

Creach, J.F.D., 'The Shape of Book Four of the Psalter and the Shape of Second Isaiah', *JSOT* 80 (1998), pp. 63-76.

—*Yahweh as Refuge and the Editing of the Hebrew Psalter* (JSOTSup, 217; Sheffield: Sheffield Academic Press, 1996).

Croft, S.J.L., *The Identity of the Individual in the Psalms* (JSOTSup, 44; Sheffield: JSOT Press, 1987).

Dahood, M., *Psalms II: 51–100* (AB, 17; Garden City, NY: Doubleday, 1968).

Delitzsch, F., *Commentary on the Old Testament*.V. *Psalms* (trans. F. Bolton; Grand Rapids: Eerdmans, repr. 1982).

Díez Merino, L. (ed.), *Targum de Salmos, edición príncipe del Ms.Villa-Amil n.5 de Alfonso de Zamora* (Madrid: Consejo Superior de Investigaciones Científicas, 1982).

Dumortier, J.-B., 'Un rituel d'intronisation, le Ps. LXXXIX, 2-38', *VT* 22 (1972), pp. 176-96.

Eaton, J.H., *Kingship and the Psalms* (Naperville, IL: Allenson, n.d.).

Ezra, I., *Miqraot gedolot* (New York: Shulsinger Bros., 1945).

Floyd, M.H., 'Psalm LXXXIX: A Prophetic Complaint about the Fulfillment of an Oracle', *VT* 42 (1992), pp. 442-57.

Freedman, D.N. (ed.), *The Anchor Bible Dictionary* (6 vols.; New York: Doubleday, 1992).

Gesenius, F.W., *Gesenius' Hebrew Grammar* (ed. E. Kautzsch; revised and trans. A.E. Cowley; Oxford: Clarendon Press, 1910).

González, A., *El libro de los Salmos: Introducción, versión y comentario* (Barcelona: Editorial Herder, 1966).

—*The Prayers of David (Psalms 51–72)* (JSOTSup, 102; Sheffield: JSOT Press, 1990).

Goulder, M.D., *The Psalms of the Sons of Korah* (JSOTSup, 20; Sheffield: JSOT Press, 1982).

Graber, P.L., 'A Textlinguistic Approach to Understanding Psalm 88', *Occasional Papers in Translation and Textlinguistics* 4 (1990), pp. 321-339.

Grossberg, D., 'The Disparate Elements of the Inclusio in Psalms', *HAR* 6 (1982), pp. 97-104.

Gunkel, H., *Die Psalmen* (Göttingen: Vandenhoeck & Ruprecht, 5th edn, 1968).

Hakham, A., *Sefer tehillim: Sefarim gimel–heh* (Jerusalem: Mossad Harev Kook, 1981).

Handy, L.K., 'Sounds, Words and Meanings in Psalm 82', *JSOT* 47 (1990), pp. 57-66.

Hieke, T., 'Psalm 80 and its Neighbors in the Psalter: The Context of the Psalter as a Background for Interpreting Psalms', *BN* 86 (1997), pp. 36-43.

Hossfeld, F.-L., and E. Zenger, *Die Psalmen I: Psalm 1–50* (Die Neue Echter Bibel, 29; Würzburg: Echter Verlag, 1993).

House, P.R. (ed.), *Form Criticism and Beyond: Essays in Old Testament Literary Criticism* (Winona Lake, IN: Eisenbrauns, 1992).

Howard, D.M., *The Structure of Psalms 93–100* (Winona Lake, IN: Eisenbrauns, 1997).

Jackson, J.J., and M. Kessler (eds.), *Rhetorical Criticism: Essays in Honor of James Muilenberg* (Pittsburgh: Pickwick Press, 1974).

Kessler, M., 'Inclusio in the Hebrew Bible', *Semitics* 6 (1978), pp. 44-49.

—'An Introduction to Rhetorical Criticism of the Bible: Prolegomena', *Semitics* 7 (1980), pp. 1-27.

Kikawada, I.M., 'Some Proposals for the Definition of Rhetorical Criticism', *Semitics* 5 (1977), pp. 67-91.

Korpel, M.C.A. and J.C. de Moor, 'Fundamentals of Ugaritic and Hebrew Poetry', *UF* 18 (1983), pp. 173-212.

Kraus, H.-J., *Psalms 60–150: A Commentary* (trans. H.C. Oswald; Minneapolis: Augsburg, 1989).

Kselman, J.S., 'Psalm 77 and the Book of Exodus', *JANESCU* 15 (1983), pp. 51-58.

Lohfink, N., 'Die Bedeutung der Endredaktion für das Verständnis des Psalters', in Wafs Kanko-Kai (ed.), *For not by bread alone shall a man live but by everything that comes out of the mouth of Yahweh shall a man live* (Festschrift K.H. Walkenhorst; Tokyo: Lithon, 1992), pp. 63-84.

—'Psalmengebet und Psalterredaktion', *Archiv für Liturgiewissenschaft* 34 (1992), pp. 1-22.

—'Der Psalter und die christliche Meditation: Die Bedeutung der Endredaktion für das Verständnis des Psalters', *BK* 47 (1992), pp. 195-200.

Lohfink, N., and E. Zenger (eds.), *Der Gott Israels und die Völker: Untersuchungen zum Jesajabuch und zu den Psalmen* (Stuttgart: Katholisches Bibelwerk, 1994).

Lowth, R., *De sacra poesi hebraeorum* (Oxford, 1733).

Mays, J.L., 'The Place of the Torah-Psalms in the Psalter', *JBL* 106 (1987), pp. 3-12.

McCann, J.C., 'Books I–III and the Editorial Purpose of the Hebrew Psalter', in McCann (ed.), *The Shape and Shaping of the Psalter*, pp. 93-107.

—'Psalm 73: An Interpretation Emphasizing Rhetorical and Canonical Criticism' (PhD dissertation; Durham, NC: Duke University, 1985).

—'Psalm 73: A Microcosm of Old Testament Theology', in K.G. Hoglund, E.F. Hutwiler, J.T. Glass and R.W. Lee (eds.), *The Listening Heart: Essays in Wisdom and the Psalms in Honor of Roland E. Murphy* (JSOTSup, 58; Sheffield: JSOT Press, 1987).

—'The Psalms as Instruction', *Int* 46 (1992), pp. 117-55.

McCann, J.C. (ed.), *The Shape and Shaping of the Psalter* (JSOTSup, 159; Sheffield: JSOT Press, 1993).

McCreesh, T.P., *Biblical Sound and Sense: Poetic Sound Patterns in Proverbs 10–29* (JSOTSup, 128; Sheffield: JSOT Press, 1991).

Meynet, R., 'L'enfant de l'amour (Ps 85)', *NRT* 112 (1990), pp. 843-58.

Miller, P.D., 'The Beginning of the Psalter', in McCann (ed.), *The Shape and Shaping of the Psalter*, pp. 83-92.

—'The End of the Psalter: A Response to Erich Zenger', *JSOT* 80 (1998), pp. 103-10.

Mitchell, D.C., *The Message of the Psalter: An Eschatological Programme in the Book of Psalms* (JSOTSup, 252; Sheffield: Sheffield Academic Press, 1997).

Mowinckel, S., *The Psalms in Israel's Worship* (trans. D.R. Ap-Thomas; Nashville: Abingdon Press, 1962).

Muilenburg, J., 'Form Criticism and Beyond', *JBL* 88 (1969), pp. 1-18.

Pardee, D., 'The Semantic Parallelism of Psalm 89', in W.B. Barrick and J.R. Spencer (eds.), *In the Shelter of Elyon: Essays on Ancient Palestinian Life and Literature in Honor of G.W. Ahlström* (JSOTSup, 31; Sheffield: JSOT Press, 1984), pp. 181-219.

Ploeg, J.P.M. van der, 'Psalm 74 and its Structure', in M.S.H.G. Heerma van Voss, Ph.H.J. Houwink ten Cate and N.A. van Uchelen (eds.), *Travels in the World of the Old Testament* (Assen: Van Gorcum, 1974), pp. 204-10.

Powell, M.A. (ed.), *The Bible and Modern Literary Criticism* (Westport, CT: Greenwood Press, 1992).

Preminger, A., and T.V.F. Brogan (eds.), *The New Princeton Encylopedia of Poetry and Poetics* (Princeton, NJ: Princeton University Press, 1993).

Prinsloo, W.S., 'Psalm 82: Once Again, Gods or Men?', *Bib* 76 (1995), pp. 219-28.

Rashi (Rabbi Shlomo b. Yitzhaqi), *Miqraot gedolot* (New York: Shulsinger Bros., 1945).

Reindl, J., 'Weisheitliche Bearbeitung von Psalmen: Ein Beitrag zum Verständnis der Sammlung des Psalters', in J.A. Emerton (ed.), *Congress Volume: Vienna 1980* (VTSup, 32; Leiden: E.J. Brill, 1980), pp. 333-56.

Sarna, N., 'Psalm 89: A Study in Inner Biblical Exegesis', in A. Altmann (ed.), *Biblical and Other Studies* (Cambridge, MA: Harvard University Press, 1963), pp. 29-46.

Schökel, L. Alonso., *A Manual of Hebrew Poetics* (Rome: Pontifical Biblical Institute Press, 1988).

—*Treinta Salmos: Poesía y oración* (Madrid: Institución San Jerónimo, 2nd edn, 1986).

Segert, S., 'Assonance and Rhyme in Hebrew Poetry', *Maarav* 8 (1992), pp. 171-79.

Seitz, C., *Word without End: The Old Testament as Abiding Theological Witness* (Grand Rapids: Eerdmans, 1998).

Seybold, K., *Introducing the Psalms* (trans. R.G. Dunphy; Edinburgh: T. & T. Clark, 1990).

Seybold, K., and E. Zenger, *Neue Wege der Psalmenforschung* (Herders biblische Studien, 1; Freiburg: Herder, 1995).

Sharrock, G.E., 'Psalm 74: A Literary-Structural Analysis', *AUSS* 21 (1983), pp. 211-23.

Sheppard, G.T., *Wisdom as a Hermeneutical Construct: A Study of Sapientializing of the Old Testament* (New York: W. de Gruyter, 1980).

Smith, M.S., 'The Structure of Psalm LXXXVII', *VT* 38 (1988), pp. 357-58.

Tate, M.E., *Psalms 51–100* (WBC, 20; Dallas: Word Books, 1990).

Trublet, J., and J.N. Aletti, *Approche poétique et théologique des Psaumes* (Paris: Cerf, 1983).

Tucker, W.D., 'Beyond the Lament: Instruction and Theology in Book I of the Psalter', *Proceedings of the Eastern Great Lakes and Midwestern Bible Society* 15 (1995), pp. 121-32.

Van Gemeren, W.A., *Psalms–Song of Songs* (The Expositor's Bible Commentary, 5; Grand Rapids: Zondervan, 1991).

Waltke, B.K., 'A Canonical Process Approach to the Psalms', in J.S. Feinberg and P.D. Feinberg (eds.), *Tradition and Testament: Essays in Honor of Charles Lee Feinberg* (Chicago: Moody Press, 1981), pp. 3-18.

Waltke, B.K., and M. O'Connor, *An Introduction to Biblical Hebrew Syntax* (Winona Lake, IN: Eisenbrauns, 1990).

Ward, J., 'The Literary Form and Liturgical Background of Psalm LXXXIX', *VT* 11 (1961), pp. 321-39.

Watson, D.F., and A.J. Hauser (eds.), *Rhetorical Criticism of the Bible: A Comprehensive Bibliography with Notes on History and Method* (Leiden: E.J. Brill, 1993).

Watson, W.G.E., *Classical Hebrew Poetry: A Guide to its Techniques* (JSOTSup, 26; Sheffield: JSOT Press, 1984).

Westermann, C., *Praise and Lament in the Psalms* (trans. K.R. Crim and R.N. Soulen; Atlanta: John Knox Press, 1981).

Williams, R.J., *Hebrew Syntax: An Outline* (Toronto: University of Toronto Press, 2nd edn, 1976).

Wilson, G.H., *The Editing of the Hebrew Psalter* (SBLDS, 76; Chico, CA: Scholars Press, 1985).

—'Evidence of Editorial Divisions in the Hebrew Psalter', *VT* 34 (1984), pp. 337-52.

—'Evidence of Editorial Divisions in the Hebrew Psalter', *VT* 34 (1984), pp. 338-52.

—'The Shape of the Book of Psalms', *Int* 46 (1992), pp. 129-42.

—'Shaping the Psalter: A Consideration of Editorial Linkage in the Books of Psalms', in McCann (ed.), *The Shape and Shaping of the Psalter*, pp. 72-82.

—'Understanding the Purposeful Arrangement of Psalms in the Psalter: Pitfalls and Promise', in McCann (ed.), *The Shape and Shaping of the Psalter*, pp. 42-51.

—'The Use of Royal Psalms at the "Seams" of the Hebrew Psalter', *JSOT* 35 (1986), pp. 85-94.

Youngblood, R., 'Divine Names in the Book of Psalms: Literary Structures and Number Patterns', *JANESCU* 19 (1989), pp. 171-81.

Zenger, E., 'The Composition and Theology of the Fifth Book of Psalms, Psalms 107-145', *JSOT* 80 (1998), pp. 77-102.

—'New Approaches to the Study of the Psalms', *Proceedings of the Irish Biblical Association* 17 (1994), pp. 37-54.

—'Das Weltenkönigtum des Gottes Israels (Ps 90-106)', in Lohfink and Zenger (eds.), *Der Gott Israels und die Völker*, pp. 151-78.

—'Zion als Mutter der Völker in Psalm 87', in Lohfink and Zenger (eds.), *Der Gott Israels und die Völker*, pp. 117-50.

—'Zur redaktionsgeschichtlichen Bedeutung der Korachpsalmen', in Seybold and Zenger (eds.), *Neue Wege der Psalmenforschung*, pp. 175-98.

INDEXES

INDEX OF REFERENCES

OLD TESTAMENT

Psalms (cont.)

Reference	Pages
73.3-12	16, 20, 23, 43, 105
73.3	15, 16, 19, 20, 22, 26, 39, 42, 43, 62, 103, 123, 132, 227, 236
73.4	20
73.5-10	20
73.5	20, 22
73.6	15, 16, 20, 23, 24, 30, 39, 104
73.7	18, 19, 20, 35, 151
73.8	15, 16, 43, 104
73.9	22, 23, 30
73.10-11	182
73.10	17, 19-23, 25, 28, 43, 44, 56, 102, 112, 236
73.11	19, 21-23, 28, 29, 35, 56
73.12	16, 19, 20, 22, 26, 39, 42, 43, 62, 103, 119, 123, 227
73.13-17	16, 17
73.13-15	21
73.13	17-19, 44, 56, 119, 142, 151, 191
73.15-17	21
73.15	20, 39, 182
73.16-17	23
73.16	22, 29, 227
73.17-28	61
73.17-18	236
73.17	19, 22, 29, 30, 70, 112, 227
73.18-28	16, 17, 25, 35, 182
73.18-20	21, 22, 24
73.18-19	28, 107
73.18	17, 19, 20, 22-25, 29, 30, 44, 103, 112, 236
73.19-28	17
73.19	17
73.20	23
73.21-26	18
73.21	18, 19, 56
73.22	22, 42, 44, 182, 204, 227
73.23	28, 30, 44, 182, 204
73.24	16
73.25	123
73.26	16, 18, 19, 24, 25, 30, 44, 56, 119, 122, 123, 142, 151, 182, 191, 236, 238
73.27-28	23, 25
73.27	20-28, 227
73.28	17-19, 23-26, 28, 39, 41, 42, 44, 61, 68, 80, 123, 142, 182, 191, 204, 223
74–75	38
74	10, 15-17, 21-23, 25, 27-30, 32, 34-38, 40, 41, 43, 45, 47-49, 51, 53-56, 61, 63, 66, 67, 70, 75, 76, 83, 85, 86, 88, 91, 95, 101, 104, 122, 145, 151, 153, 161, 162, 165, 166, 173, 177, 183, 190, 199, 217, 223, 227, 231, 232, 234, 236, 238
74.1-12	25
74.1-11	25, 28, 29, 31, 61, 74
74.1-8	160
74.1-3	32

Psalms (cont.)

Reference	Pages
	70, 72-75, 80, 84, 97
78.5-7	64
78.5	69, 70, 72, 73, 88, 97
78.6	66, 68-70, 72, 84
78.7-8	73
78.7	64, 66-68, 73, 237
78.8-64	79
78.8	58, 64-66, 69, 72-74, 239
78.9-64	85
78.9-11	72
78.9	65, 70, 72-74
78.10-11	237
78.10	64, 73, 74, 237
78.11-12	69
78.11	61, 62, 64, 66-68, 71, 73, 237
78.12-54	63
78.12	68, 91, 98
78.13	70, 71, 78, 81, 82
78.14-21	58
78.14	64, 71, 81, 82
78.15	71, 91
78.16	70, 71
78.17	55, 60, 65, 72-74, 83, 147
78.18	65, 69, 72, 74
78.19-20	67, 68
78.19	65, 68
78.20	67, 69-72, 236, 237
78.21	57, 66, 70, 81, 93, 187, 221, 237
78.22	70, 74, 82, 89, 188
78.23	71
78.24-25	91
78.26	69, 80, 91
78.27	80, 236, 238
78.29-30	91
78.29	80, 82
78.30	74
78.31	57, 66, 70, 81
78.32-39	73, 82
78.32	55, 65, 71-74, 83, 147, 191
78.34	64
78.35	61, 64, 67, 69, 82
78.36-37	64, 66, 72
78.36	61, 69, 188
78.37	65, 69, 72, 74, 187
78.38-39	82, 239
78.38	38, 57, 66, 67, 81-83, 85, 187, 221
78.39	64, 66, 82
78.40	65, 72-74, 147
78.41	74
78.42	61, 64, 66, 69, 72-74, 82, 189, 91, 141
78.43	80
78.44	92
78.45-53	92
78.45	92
78.49	57, 81, 92, 221
78.50	57, 80, 81, 221
78.51	91
78.52-55	92
78.52-53	71, 89
78.52	69, 71, 72, 84, 87, 89, 91
78.53	71, 92
78.54	67, 92
78.55	91
78.56	65, 72, 74, 88
78.57	74, 93
78.59	57, 82, 90, 187, 188, 205, 221, 237, 239
78.60	70, 74, 75, 188
78.61	69, 188
78.62	57, 69, 72, 187, 221, 237
78.65-72	65, 69, 70, 72, 76, 79, 84, 85, 92, 232
78.65	65, 72, 74, 75, 80, 84, 90, 188

INDEX OF AUTHORS